Environmental Construction Handbook

Environmental Construction Handbook

Anne Dye & Mike McEvoy

RIBA ⅏ **Publishing**

©Anne Dye and Mike McEvoy, 2008

Published by RIBA Publishing, 15 Bonhill Street, London EC2P 2EA

1st Edition published 2008

ISBN 978 1 85946 163 1
Stock code 55092

The right of Anne Dye and Mike McEvoy to be identified as the Authors of this Work have been asserted in accordance with the Copyright, Design and Patents Act 1988.

British Library Cataloguing in Publications Data
A catalogue record for this book is available from the British Library.

Publisher: Steven Cross

Commissioning Editor: Matthew Thompson

Project Editor: Melanie Thompson

Designed by Carnegie Book Production

Typeset by Carnegie Book Production

Printed and bound by MPG Books, Cornwall

Contents

Preface

When we were putting the finishing touches to this book, in late August 2007, the year had already set records for heat, followed by the 'wettest summer in living memory'. The press, of course, had had a field day: here at last, they said, was physical evidence – darkly seeping through front doors in Tewksbury and Sheffield – of anthropogenic climate change. Whether or not '07 is part of the overall pattern of climate change or largely a product of natural variation is yet to be seen but it did, nonetheless, bring climate change yet again to public attention.

Compelling scientific evidence along with the change in public and political opinion has led to an apparently exponential growth in the number of books published on the subjects of ecology, sustainability and 'green' architecture. When in 2002 we were starting to draft material for an educational CD-ROM about sustainability in schools and houses – funded by the EPSRC, aimed at older school children – we decided to build on the research for the CD, to include more building types and to expand it into a resource for building professionals and, to a lesser extent, for interested lay-people.

We found ourselves almost overwhelmed by the sheer volume of material that was at our disposal and it became increasingly clear that we were running to stand still. No sooner had we put our thoughts in order than another publication would arrive on our desks, or our regular trawls through Internet or library databases would land yet more research papers. It was disheartening: the book would be out-of-date before we had even finished the final chapter! And much of the material was contradictory: for instance, was thermal mass friend or foe? The arguments coming from the back-to-nature groups and the technophiles were equally passionate; they were increasingly able to back up their arguments with data of varying methodological rigour.

One afternoon we realised that we weren't talking to each other about the data we had unearthed so much as about how we ended up at a particular viewpoint, or how a design team had reconciled their design with their (or indeed the client's) sustainability agenda. We concluded that by adding 'how' and 'why' we had chosen the material included in the book it would become useful: it might show readers how they could move their own thinking forward. For these reasons some of the case studies we have included in the book are of slightly older buildings – which have proven their 'green' credentials over time – as well as newer ones.

Without the experiences of the designers, these studies could not have been written. We wish to pass on our heartfelt thanks for their time, the considerable attention they gave to the material they provided, as well as for the lengthy and enjoyable conversations we had with many of them – about aspects of sustainable design over and above those we were discussing in regards to the case study.

A number of students who have read for an MPhil in Environmental Design in Architecture at the University of Cambridge have generously contributed research undertaken during their time in Cambridge and for this rich source of material, and advice, we are extremely grateful. The contributors from both groups were: Arup; Lizzie Babister; Bennetts Associates; Chetwood Associates Architects; ECD Architects; Mark Gaterell; Alec Gillies (Hampshire County Council Architects' Department); Dean Hawkes (Greenberg and Hawkes); Jessica Hrivnak; Neath Port Talbot County Borough Council; David Thompson; Alan Tye Design; and Peter Williams.

It is our hope that the list of contributors, as well as the number of building types covered, will increase in any future edition of the Handbook. We would be glad to hear from readers who have suggestions for material that could usefully be included or new case studies.

Anne Dye and Mike McEvoy

October 2007

Introduction

Construction's contribution to climate change and resource depletion presents two of the greatest challenges facing building professionals today. Our original intention for this Handbook was to produce an edited summary of modern methods of construction which were consistent with sustainability principles. The existing material in the area seemed broadly to fall into a few categories: inspirational, lavishly illustrated books celebrating low-tech, almost vernacular, architecture using recycled and low-energy materials or high-tech computer-controlled low-energy buildings; how-to books, allowing an architect or competent homebuilder to recreate the low-tech buildings they had just drooled over in the inspirational books (often using methods of construction and materials that have fallen into disuse other than for craft or renovation purposes); technical books full of scientific data relating to both climate change and building performance; and government regulatory and guidance documents.

As our research for this book progressed the aim became modified somewhat: we wanted to show how we had approached the apparently bewildering array of advice and regulatory information. Because of the rate of change of this regulatory information this is, indeed, the most that any book of this type can achieve; UK Building Regulations, for example, are set to be updated every three years from now until 2016.

Change is not confined to legislation. In the case of factories, the decline in the UK's manufacturing base during the later part of the 20th Century meant that there was little impetus for new publications, although the construction of warehouse space continued apace. A recent resurgence in manufacturing (albeit from a low base) gives new relevance to the inclusion of this building type. Inevitably, however, these types of change mean that some of our sources pre-date the current millennium, but much of the reasoning in them remains relevant. Other building types, too, have found a life in new guises. Libraries, for example, are being transformed into 'learning resource centres', and we would hope to include them in a future edition of the book.

While this Handbook remains essentially a construction manual it differs from contemporary publications in two significant ways.

Firstly it departs from the familiar chapter headings of a construction manual, which are defined by building elements: the walls, floors and roofs. We felt that there were good reasons to revert to an historical taxonomy: ordering by building use. In the 19th Century this was more usual: indeed, the enthusiasm for classification at the *Ecole Polytechnique* was to result in J-N-L Durand's influential *Précis des Leçons Données à L'Ecole Polytechnique* (1802–09), a construction code for building types. The aesthetics of Modern Architecture, which adopted the visual qualities of ships, aircraft and factories as a universal formal language, largely invalidated Durand's system. This has made more contemporary examples of this taxonomy hard to find, with Pevsner's *A History of Building Types* being a rare – although peripheral – exception.

Both use and legislation has made the distinction between building types more marked; the variety of structural methods and forms of assembly that we have today has resulted in a far wider variation between building types than was the case in Victorian times. Despite this, it is sometimes helpful to be able to use a common language across the building types, and throughout this book we have employed an Ecopoints summary in order to look at the characteristic building types and construction methods in a comparative way.

Although we will be looking at various methodologies in greater detail later in the book it is worthwhile introducing Ecopoints here, because they are used throughout.

In order to reach an Ecopoint rating of a material, process or construction the Building Research Establishment (BRE) measures the item's overall environmental impact with respect to 13 indicators:

- climate change
- fossil fuel depletion
- ozone depletion
- freight transport
- human toxicity to air (the toxicity to humans if a substance is airborne)
- human toxicity to water (the toxicity to humans if a substance is waterborne)
- waste disposal
- water extraction (water use)
- acid deposition (acid rain)
- ecotoxicity (the toxicity to ecosystems)

- eutrophication (nutrients encouraging overgrowth of oxygen-consuming organisms to the detriment of other organisms)
- summer smog
- mineral extraction.

The data, however, only becomes meaningful when taken in context, so it is normalised and then weighted.

To normalise the data, the total impact on the UK by all its inhabitants is divided by the total population. This gives the impact of an average citizen, which is then scaled so that the impact of that citizen is equal to a total of 100 Ecopoints.

After this process the indicators, each with a different unit of measurement, have an implied equal importance. To correct this each indicator was considered by an expert panel (drawn from a range of industry stakeholders) and the measured units for each weighted to reflect the proportion of the total effect for which each indicator is responsible. The panel was generally in accord as to the relative importance, which (while somewhat surprising) increases confidence in Ecopoints as a meaningful tool and, by extension, in the other BRE Life Cycle Assessment tools, which include BREEAM and the *Green Guide to Specification*. (*BRE Digest 446* provides a full description of Ecopoints and their application.)

Throughout this book we have looked at the Ecopoints associated with particular construction types. To do this, we have used BRE's Envest tool: the amount of each material (and thus the Ecopoints associated with it) is calculated and modified in order to take into account maintenance of the material and its likely replacement interval.

The second departure from the contemporary norm is in the structure of the chapters. The Handbook is not just a construction guide; it is an *Environmental* Construction Handbook, with 'environment' here varying from global (which energy and resource use impacts upon) through to the local.

The context within which particular buildings types are found has a profound influence on their impact. It is, for example, impossible to discuss the construction of supermarkets without considering their location, which is characteristically at the edge of town, in the midst of a sea of car parking. On a smaller scale yet, the impact of the internal environment of a building upon human health is of particular contemporary concern.

For this reason a summary of factors relevant to the sustainability of the building type heads each chapter, in which we have tried to give as comprehensive and balanced a view as possible, although inevitably each has been shaped by our own opinions. These are followed by details of construction methods relevant to the building type and, finally, by case studies.

Given the time involved in any book project, some of the case studies which were in the design stage when we initially looked at them have by now appeared in print, whereas others have stalled and not yet found their way to the building site. All are, however, exemplary, while illustrating the wide range of approaches that characterise current British architecture.

Just as there is a variety of views regarding what constitutes 'sustainable' architecture so there is a range of ways of assessing the sustainability of buildings. The first chapter, therefore, reviews a variety of assessment methods which are currently available. In the same way that the number of publications in the area has been fast increasing, so too have these methods of assessment. The characteristic outcome of many of these is the 'star' diagram that illustrates the competing societal, ecological and energy-related vectors that influence any design solution. To arrive at objective measures, given the widely differing parameters involved, entails the application of expert knowledge. A BREEAM rating, for example, is based on weightings that have been incorporated by experts at the BRE, whence Ecopoints also originate.

An unfortunate by-product of the importance now afforded to sustainability is that consultants are also promoting the value of their own evaluation tools. Underlying these methods are databases that are deemed commercially sensitive, and which are understandably held as 'secret knowledge' by their originators. This has made our task in arriving at a recommendation for the relative merits of different methods less than easy. Despite this, we have tried to describe and compare those which are currently available in such a way that the reader can make an informed choice as to which would be appropriate for their own project, and how to choose between the other assessments which will evolve in the future.

While the design process is the outcome of subtle choices and decisions, it is also the result of meeting objective targets. In the future we can expect that formal evaluation methods will be applied to outline designs as a matter of course, in the way that SPeAR™ informed the design of Arup Fitzrovia.

The case studies in Chapter 1 make an interesting introduction, and concern building types that evade easy classification; both are examples of leading environmentally aware architecture that demanded inclusion.

Through the summary of methods of assessment the first chapter introduces a number of the ideas which will be addressed throughout the rest of the book. The first building type under consideration is 'houses'. As a type this is probably closer than any other to the affections of architects, given the infinite variety of possible solutions, and complexity of problems they entail, within a restricted format. The following chapters are concerned with housing (as a type distinct from the single, often one-off houses, in the preceding chapter) then offices (where the need to decrease energy use can call for considerable ingenuity), schools, supermarkets and factories.

We have thought of this book as being similar to a travel guide; you might be interested in reading the beginning of the book as background, and then dipping into the following chapters while journeying through the development of a design.

1   Methods of Assessing Buildings

It seems at first that there are nearly as many methods of assessing a building as there are ways of defining sustainability or ways of constructing the building in the first place. The number of assessment tools is growing fast, as architects and other building consultants each devise a system which best suits their needs. The one thing they all have in common is that they measure the performance for a number of **indicators**, such as the sustainability indicators issued by the government, against **benchmarks**.

With any assessment, the answer you get depends very much on how you ask the question. Any scientist will tell you that the results of an experiment can be meaningless – an artefact of the methodology used – if it is not devised properly. So too, eco-labelling can be merely 'greenwash', misleading or, at worst, factually inaccurate[1].

One eco-labelling scheme that has been successful is the EU energy label that must be displayed on all new domestic white goods and light bulbs. Part of the reason for the success of the EU scheme is that it compares relatively few variables for products that have the same basic purpose and then presents the results in a way that is easy to 'read'. Despite this, even though buildings vary enormously in size, function and construction, it can be possible to give them a single rating – as is done with BREEAM, EcoHomes, LEED – and for the result to be meaningful.

Assessments can vary from simple checklists, or rankings of construction materials, through to sophisticated models. However, more complicated need not necessarily be better. A number of factors determine which assessment or tool is the most appropriate for a project:

- indicators considered
- the inputs the methodology uses
- the outputs (the type of results)

- the creator of the methodology
- who the assessor is to be
- the scope of the assessment
- the building type it is intended for.

Appendices 1 and 2 provide a summary of these factors for a number of different building assessments.

Box 1.1 UK sustainability indicators

Following on from the 22 indicators of sustainability published in 2002[1] the government now has 20 UK framework indicators and a further 48 monitoring indicators[2]:

UK framework indicators

- Greenhouse gas emissions: Kyoto target and CO_2 emissions
- Resource use: Domestic Material Consumption and GDP (gross domestic product)
- Waste: arisings by (a) sector, (b) recycled or composted
- Bird populations: bird population indices (a) farmland birds, (b) woodland birds, (c) birds of coasts and estuaries, (d) wintering wetland birds – but (d) is not a framework indicator
- Fish stocks: fish stocks around the UK within sustainable limits
- Ecological impacts of air pollution: area of UK habitat sensitive to acidification and eutrophication with critical load exceedences
- River quality: rivers of good (a) biological, (b) chemical quality
- Economic output: gross domestic product
- Active community participation: informal and formal volunteering at least once a month
- Crime: crime survey and recorded crime for (a) vehicles, (b) domestic burglary, (c) violence
- Employment: people of working age in employment
- Workless households: population living in workless households (a) children, (b) working age
- Childhood poverty: children in relative low-income households (a) before housing costs, (b) after housing costs
- Pensioner poverty: pensioners in relative low-income households (a) before housing costs, (b) after housing costs
- Education: 19 year-olds with level 2 qualifications and above
- Health inequality: (a) infant mortality (by socio-economic group), (b) life expectancy (by area) for men and women
- Mobility: (a) number of trips per person by mode, (b) distance travelled per person per year by broad trip purpose
- Social justice: (social measures to be developed)

continued …

- Environmental equality: (environmental measures to be developed)
- Wellbeing: (wellbeing measures to be developed)

Monitoring indicators:
- CO_2 emissions by end user: industry, domestic, transport (excluding international aviation), other
- Aviation and shipping emissions: greenhouse gases from UK-based international aviation and shipping fuel bunkers
- Renewable electricity: renewable electricity generated as a percentage of total electricity
- Electricity generation: electricity generated, CO_2, NO_x and SO_2 emissions by electricity generators and GDP
- Household energy use: domestic CO_2 emissions and household final consumption expenditure
- Road transport: CO_2, NO_x, PM10[3] emissions and GDP
- Private vehicles: CO_2 emissions and car-km, and household final consumption expenditure
- Road freight: CO_2 emissions and tonne-km, tonnes and GDP
- Manufacturing sector: CO_2, NO_x, SO_2, PM10 emissions and GVA[4]
- Service sector: CO_2, NO_x emissions and GVA
- Public sector: CO_2, NO_x emissions and GVA
- Energy supply: UK primary energy supply and gross inland energy consumption
- Water resource use: total abstractions from non-tidal surface and ground water sources and GDP
- Domestic water consumption: domestic water consumption per head
- Household waste: (a) arisings, (b) recycled or composted
- Biodiversity conservation: (a) priority species status, (b) priority habitat status
- Agricultural sector: fertiliser input, farmland bird population, and ammonia and methane emissions and output
- Land use: area used for agriculture, woodland, water or river, urban (contextual indicator)
- Land recycling: (a) new dwellings built on previously developed land or through conversions, (b) all new development on previously developed land
- Dwelling density: average density of new housing
- Emissions of air pollutants: SO_2, NO_x, NH_3[5], PM10 emissions and GDP
- Productivity: UK output per worker
- Investment: (a) total investment, (b) social investment relative to GDP
- Fear of crime: (a) car theft, (b) burglary, (c) physical attack
- Economically inactive: people of working age who are economically inactive
- Young adults: 16–19-year-olds not in employment, education or training
- Pension provision: working age people contributing to a non-state pension in at least three years out of the last four
- Healthy life expectancy: healthy life expectancy (a) men (b) women
- Mortality rates: death rates from (a) circulatory disease, (b) cancer, below 75 years and for areas with the worst health and deprivation indicators, (c) suicides

continued ...

- Smoking: prevalence of smoking (a) all adults, (b) 'routine and manual' socio-economic groups
- Childhood obesity: prevalence of obesity in 2- to 10-year-olds
- Diet: people consuming five or more portions of fruit and vegetables per day and in low income households
- Getting to school: how children get to school
- Accessibility: access to key services
- Road accidents: number of people and children killed or seriously injured
- Air quality and health: (a) annual levels of particles and ozone, (b) days when air pollution is moderate or higher
- Housing conditions: (a) social sector homes below the decent homes standard, (b) vulnerable households in the private sector in homes below the decent homes standard
- Households living in fuel poverty: (a) pensioners, (b) households with children, (c) disabled/long-term sick
- Homelessness: (a) rough sleepers, (b) households in temporary accommodation: (i) total, (ii) households with children
- Satisfaction in local area: households satisfied with the quality of the places in which they live (a) overall, (b) in deprived areas, (c) non-decent homes
- UK international assistance: net official development assistance (a) % of gross national income (comparison with selected countries), (b) per capita (comparison with selected countries)

Contextual monitoring indicators:

- Demography: total population and population of working age
- Households and dwellings: households, single-person households and dwelling stock

Monitoring indicators under development:

- Water stress: *(to be developed to monitor the impacts of water shortages)*
- Farming and environmental stewardship: *(to be developed to monitor progress in new stewardship schemes)*
- Flooding: *(to be developed to monitor sustainable approaches to ongoing flood management)*
- Sustainable development education: *(to be developed to monitor the impact of formal learning on knowledge and awareness of sustainable development)*
- Local environment quality: *(to be developed using information from the Local Environment Quality Survey of England)*

1. DEFRA, *Foundations for our Future – DEFRA's Sustainable Development Strategy*, DEFRA, London, 2002. p14.
2. From *The UK Government Sustainable Development Strategy*, Cm. 6467, DEFRA, London and www.sustainable-development.gov.uk, March 2005, pp168-176. Crown copyright.
3. A measure of particulates that can be carried into the lungs.
4. Gross Value Added. A measure of economic output.
5. Ammonia.

1 Inputs

The government's framework indicators above (Box 1.1) will no doubt be edited as our understanding of sustainable development advances, but at the present time it appears fairly comprehensive. So we will move on to consider the inputs needed for the assessment. The amount of information that is available about a project will depend largely on the design stage.

1.1 Early design stages

Early in the design process, assessments are more akin to tools to optimise the design of the building, to aid in the selection of sustainable materials and to minimise the use of energy or water.

Early design tools may be self-consistent but meaningless for the absolute judgement of the resulting building. For example, the LT Method (see Appendix 1) is useful for evaluating the relative performance of a number of design solutions for a proposed building, with differing floor plans, orientations and façade penetration. It is not intended to provide an accurate prediction of the actual energy use in operation.

1.2 Late design stage, or completed building

Assessments conducted on late designs, or completed buildings position the building within the lexicon of building practice. In general, they require much more detailed information in order to complete the assessment, even if the result of the assessment is a single rating, such as EcoHomes or the Australian Nationwide House Energy Rating Scheme (NatHERS) considered later in this chapter.

In order to give designers guidelines as to how to meet the requirements of the assessment a cut-down version of the assessment, or a checklist, may be issued as a design tool, as in the case of the NatHERS and the French ESCALE assessment.

2 Outputs

Whether the results from an assessment are going to be useful depends very much on who is going to use the results: building professionals, large client organisations, home owners or building managers.

For example, the 'My Home' online home energy check[2] from the Energy Saving Trust could help a homeowner who wants to improve the energy efficiency of their home but who doesn't know where to start. However, it would be completely inappropriate for a housing association which, from April 2003, has been required to use the BRE EcoHomes assessment and achieve at least a 'pass' (if it builds grant-funded social housing).[3] (The Housing Corporation increased the requirement to a 'very good' rating in 2006.[4])

3 Creator

3.1 Location

A number of assessment methods have been tailored by their creators in relation to the conditions found in specific countries or regions. Climates and economic conditions vary considerably around the globe and can have huge effects on a building's performance – one reason for the different emissions targets for different countries under the Kyoto protocol.

3.2 Environmental agenda

Just as there is disagreement among the international community about how best to tackle global environmental problems, so there is a variety of opinions about how to improve the sustainability of buildings, ranging from enthusiasm that borders on green-fundamentalism through to near apathy, and even antipathy. Protecting the environment has often been opposed on the grounds of possible harm to the economy, although this needn't be the case – see Box 1.2.

Box 1.2 The triple bottom line in action – from one to five stars

Sustainable development is often thought of as development which has a positive impact on all three 'bottom lines': economic, environmental and social. While it is a common concept (see, for example, www.forumforthefuture.org.uk, www.tbli.org or www.sustainability.com), many remain sceptical about whether it can be put into practice. When Australia's State of Victoria proposed more stringent building codes for housing, they were concerned that the changes would be unpopular and so made the case for legislative change in economic and social terms too.

Background

Australia has one of the higher per capita rates of CO_2 emissions: it is ranked 16th in the world, with the average Australian emitting just under twice the CO_2 of an average Briton.[1]

continued ...

Victoria was the first Australian state to introduce, in 1991, minimum standards for the insulation of dwellings, decreasing energy use by slightly over a third[2]. This represented an increase in the rating from 1 to around 2.2 'stars'. (The Star (House Energy Rating) system is described in greater detail in Appendix 1). If the State was to meet its Kyoto commitment – the treaty requires a slowing of the increase in CO_2 emissions to only 8% on 1990 levels by 2008/2012[3] – a decrease in domestic energy use was urgently needed, since energy use in the sector was growing by 1.24% per annum.

After consultation, the State brought in a requirement that, from 1 July 2005, for single dwellings or apartments, compliance with the new residential energy standard will require a building to be five-star energy rated. In addition, water saving features and a rain water tank or solar hot water system will be required.[4]

A five-star dwelling is estimated to use around half the energy of a typical existing building in Victoria, though it will be somewhat less energy efficient than new buildings in Europe or North America.

To meet the new standards the design of a new home would need to have increased insulation (both in walls and improved glazing), improved airtightness and a change in the distribution of glazing. For winter, north-facing glazing increases useful solar gain, while shading decreases the need for summer cooling. The use of thermal mass is considered too, with buildings with low-mass timber floors being required to have better insulation and smaller windows.

Environmental benefits

Increasing the energy efficiency of Victoria's homes has two main environmental benefits: a decrease in the total amount of energy used and a decrease in the peak amount of energy used. The State estimates that peak demand on the power grid, caused by comfort cooling, could be reduced by up to 45%. This should decrease the risk of power shortages in summer and save money that would otherwise have to be invested in additional power stations.

The main advantage is the reduction in the total energy demand. Growth in domestic energy consumption would be slowed from 1.24% pa to 0.46% pa. Analysis modelled the effect of the changed regulations over a 20-year period, at the end of which the energy savings would total some AU$124 million per annum (£51 million[5]). This is an annual saving of around 760,000 tonnes of CO_2 equivalent (CO_2-e) and a total abatement over the entire 20-year period of 7.6 million tonnes CO_2-e.

Economic benefits

Analysis suggests that the changed regulation would provide an economic stimulus, with an increase in GDP of AU$500–570 million NPV (net present value) which is around £206–235 million. Also, 900–1100 new jobs could be expected to be created.

continued ...

Social benefits

As well as the social benefit of job creation, there are other advantages to the changes. The estimate that a five-star home would be up to 5°C warmer in winter and 10°C cooler in summer (compared to a two-star dwelling) was lauded in Victoria's Minister for Planning's introduction to the consultation document on the proposed changes to the Building Code. The effect of fuel poverty on vulnerable groups is predicted to be reduced: another political benefit.

For owner-occupiers too, a five-star home is predicted to be more affordable. Heating and cooling equipment can be smaller, and therefore less expensive, and the increased capital cost of a dwelling could be offset against lower energy bills.

1. The USA is ranked 10th, the UK 36th. The highest per capita emissions are from the US Virgin Islands at around 550% of USA emissions. See Marland, G., Boden, T. and Andres, B., *Ranking of the world's countries by 2000 per capita fossil-fuel CO$_2$ emission rates*, http://cdiac.esd.ornl.gov, Carbon Dioxide Information Analysis Centre, 2000.
2. State of Victoria, *Regulatory Information Bulletin – Energy Efficiency Standards for New Residential Buildings*, www.buildingcommission.com.au, Sustainable Energy Authority Victoria, 2002.
3. *United Nations Framework Convention on Climate Change – A Guide to the Climate Change Convention and its Kyoto Protocol*, UN Climate Change Secretariat, Bonn and http://unfccc.int, 2002.
4. www.buildingcommission.com.au
5. Exchange rates as in *The Times*, 18 May 2005, £1: AU$2.43

Superimposed on this there is a 'technical' vs 'vernacular' standoff. Some are 'wild about technology...'[5] while others advocate living a more 'natural' lifestyle, building mainly with reclaimed materials such as tin cans and vehicle tyres[6] with minimally controlled building services.

Though these differing viewpoints of sustainable construction aren't automatically at odds with the Brundtland definition of sustainable development,[7] they are somewhat at odds with each other. This is important where weightings are applied to the relative relevance of data in an assessment.

4 Assessor

Early design stage tools or assessments are usually used by the building's designers. Some tools which have the advantage of being easy to use, have in-built data and assumptions that are hidden to the architect or engineer. The immediacy of the results may consequently be undermined by their simplification.

For completed designs and buildings, assessments often need to be completed by an accredited assessor, who may or may not be part of the design team. This is partly a quality assurance step – particularly necessary when the assessment is required for regulatory purposes, as in the case of the SAP which may be used to show Building Regulations compliance – and partly to protect the intellectual property of the creators of the assessment.

Box 1.3 The effect of weightings on assessment results

The effect of weightings on an analysis can be seen in this example. Consider a super-insulated house constructed of natural materials (e.g. stone, sheep's wool insulation and timber window frames). A wood-burning stove, fuelled by locally coppiced wood, which is controlled manually, heats the house. In an assessment, it might score, say, 9/10 for the insulation, 8/10 for the choice of materials and 2/10 for the relatively crude controls.

The house's three scores could be simply averaged, to give an overall score of 63%, or the three components of the assessments could have weighting applied. Here the 'tech' weighting scheme rewards technical features of the building whereas the 'vernacular' weighting preferentially rewards more 'natural' or 'traditional' building forms. As can be seen from Table 1.1, these weighting schemes can have a considerable effect on the building's overall score.

Table 1.1 The effect of weightings on assessment results

	No weighting	'Tech' weighting	'Vernacular' weighting
Insulation	9/10	0.3	0.5
Controls	2/10	0.5	0.2
Materials	8/10	0.2	0.3
Overall weighted score (%)	**63**	**53**	**73**

For example, the BRE's *Green Guide*[1] uses a weighting system[2] agreed upon by representatives of interested groups, from central government to materials manufacturers and environmental activists. Out of the 13 indicators considered, the effect on climate change is given the greatest importance, with a weighting of 38%.

Weightings can also be variable, as in the GBC Tool discussed at the end of this chapter. This can be appropriate where a methodology is being used in a number of different climate zones or economic areas. Obviously the limitation here is that only assessments which use the same weightings are directly comparable.

1. Anderson, J., Shiers, D.E. and Sinclair, M. *The Green Guide to Specification*, Watford, 3rd Edition, BRE, 2002.
2. Dickie, I. and Howard, N. *Assessing environmental impacts of construction – Industry consensus, BREEAM and UK Ecopoints*, BRE Digest 446, Watford and www.brebookshop.com, BRE, May 2000.

5 Scope

The assessment may deal only with building components or systems (in which case it is likely to be used mostly in early design stages), with whole buildings or sometimes with whole developments and urban environments. Arup's SPeAR™ tool is one assessment that can deal with these.

Box 1.4 Arup's SPeAR™ appraisal tool

by Laurie Richards, Associate Director, Environmental Group, Ove Arup and Partners, and Lucy Dakin, formerly Senior Environmental Scientist, Ove Arup and Partners, (currently Sustainable Projects Officer at Bristol City Council).

SPeAR™ (Sustainable Project Appraisal Routine) has been developed by Arup as a tool to enable organisations to assess, demonstrate and improve the sustainability of their projects, or corporate performance.

It is based on an analysis of performance in respect of the four key aspects of sustainability – economic, social, natural resources and environmental issues – as defined in the UK government's sustainability strategies.[1]

A key aspect of SPeAR™ is the composite output diagram, see Figure 1.1, which summarises, in a clear and visually striking format, the wide range of issues that need to be considered. This clarity of communication of complex issues is a key strength of the tool, considerably aiding the decision-making process. The four quadrants of the SPeAR™ diagram correspond to the four key aspects of sustainability.

The SPeAR™ diagram is designed to show negative, as well as positive, effects. Examples of negative effects could include the emission of pollutants, the loss of ecological features, high energy usage or loss of employment opportunities. In comparison, positive effects could include the use of renewable energy, provision of ecological enhancement measures, or adoption of public transport in place of the private car.

In order to display both negative and positive results, a median line on the diagram (cream/light yellow) designates good practice, (see Figure 1.2). Positive (sustainable) performance (usually shown in green

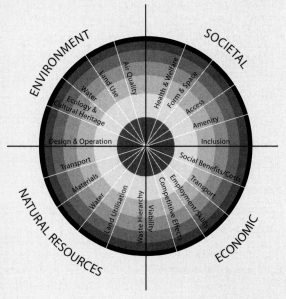

Fig. 1.1 The SPeAR™ diagram
Copyright: Arup

continued …

tones) is represented from the median line towards the centre of the diagram. Negative (unsustainable) performance (usually shown in red tones) is represented towards the circumference of the diagram.

Fig. 1.2 The SPeAR™ scale
Copyright: Arup

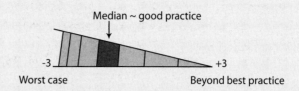

Median ~ good practice

-3 ... +3
Worst case ... Beyond best practice

The aim of a sustainable design project, therefore, should be to obtain a balanced diagram with positive results (green tones) distributed across all four quadrants.

Spreadsheets are used to complete the assessment. Each quadrant of the SPeAR™ diagram is divided into a series of sectors, or topics, see Figure 1.1. For example, 'environment' includes air quality, land use, water, ecology and cultural heritage, design and operation, and transport topics. The spreadsheets include a series of indicators for each topic, see Figure 1.3. These include both a set of 'core' indicators as well as project specific indicators. The fact that the indicators used in each appraisal are tailored to a specific project makes it a flexible and highly adaptable tool.

Natural Resources: Water	Optimum measures	Worst case	3	2	1	0	-1	-2	-3	Degree of certainty (%)	Average score for subject
Consumption	Extensive use of rainwater and black/grey/green water systems. Metered water supply	No awareness of the need to reduce water consumption rates	☐	☐	☒	☐	☐	☐	☐		
Potable Water	Minimise percentage of water needs met by 'bottled water' as opposed to tap purifier	All potable water brought in	☐	☐	☐	☐	☐	☐	☐		
Harvesting	Exploitation of opportunities for harvesting water	No harvesting of water	☐	☐	☐	☐	☐	☐	☐		
Appliances	Install water meters, dual flush WCs and spray taps	No consideration given to low-water-use appliances	☐	☐	☐	☐	☒	☐	☐		
											0

Fig. 1.3 The SPeAR™ indicators for the 'Water' sector of 'Natural Resources'. Copyright: Arup

The user works through the spreadsheets, usually in a workshop context with appropriate specialists and design team representatives, and the software then completes the output diagram automatically. See the Arup Fitzrovia case study in Chapter 4, for examples.

Sustainability appraisals can highlight areas where a project/design/development performs poorly in terms of sustainability principles. These highlighted areas can then be investigated in more detail, and their performance improved by adopting best practice or using new technology.

1. Department of the Environment, Transport and the Regions, *A Better Quality of Life*, TSO and www.sustainable-development.gov.uk and The Stationery Office, London, 1999, ISBN 0-10-143452-9.

5.1 Building components

It is well known that some materials are more desirable in environmental terms than others. Various methods of comparison have been proposed to circumnavigate the shark-infested waters of manufacturers' information. The two main types of assessment are measurements of embodied energy and life-cycle analysis (LCA). There are also a number of websites and books offering advice on

---

Box 1.5 The Forest Stewardship Council

The Forest Stewardship Council (FSC) is an NGO (and a charity in the UK) founded in 1993 which works in 28 countries worldwide. It certifies forests that are managed according to its ten principles and ensures that timber products from the forests are tracked through to the end user.

FSC's ten principles cover issues regarding:

- compliance with local laws, international treaties and FSC principles
- tenure and use, rights and responsibilities
- legal and 'customary' rights of indigenous peoples
- community relations and workers' rights
- benefits (environmental, economic and social) from the forest
- environmental impact (on issues such as biological diversity, water resources, soil health, ecosystem health and landscape value)
- management plans for the forest
- monitoring of forest health, etc.
- maintenance of high conservation value forests
- management of plantations (especially with a view to reducing negative impacts on natural forests).[1]

There are other wood certification schemes around the world (examples of others are discussed in a Friends of the Earth briefing paper[2]), but in the UK it is the FSC that predominates and earns support from NGOs such as Friends of the Earth and Greenpeace.

Specifying FSC certified products can earn points for building certification schemes. For example, specifying FSC certified timber for 75% of the timber in housing gives full credits in the appropriate section of the EcoHomes assessment.[3] The FSC website, www.fsc-uk.info, has an online product search for private and trade customers, and also a database of internationally certified forests and products.

1. *FSC Principles and Criteria For Forest Stewardship*. FSC, www.fsc-uk.info, 2000.
2. Counsell, S., *Briefing – Timber: Eco-labelling and Certification*. Friends of the Earth, London, 1995, www.foe.co.uk
3. www.fsc-uk.info

materials selection, and which either do not neatly fall into either the embodied energy or LCA camp, or offer a stripped down version of these methodologies (FSC at www.fsc.org, for example).

Embodied energy

Embodied energy is simply the amount of energy that has been consumed in the manufacture, transportation to site and, sometimes, use and disposal of a material. It may be quoted as 'cradle to gate' or 'cradle to grave'.

Data about embodied energy can be given as a per mass figure or in terms of structural elements, as in the case of the BRE's *Green Guide* (discussed later in this chapter). Data for structural elements, can be more informative as it takes into account different structural and other properties. The ratings given in the *Green Guide* are a useful starting point for the discussions of construction methods in later chapters.

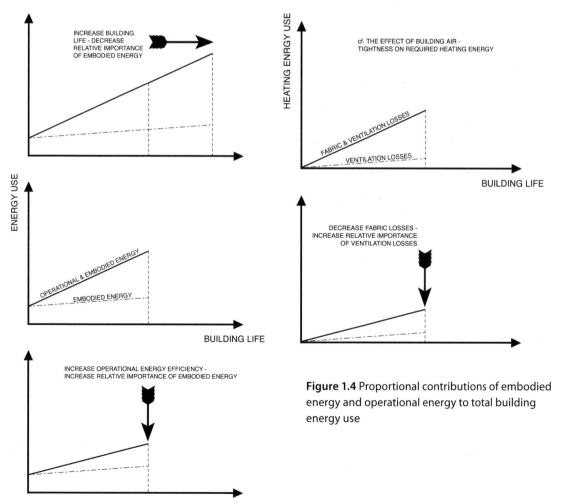

Figure 1.4 Proportional contributions of embodied energy and operational energy to total building energy use

The embodied energy of a building is generally low in comparison to its energy consumption over its life time. So why consider it at all? This is best understood by considering the parallel situation, where designers are paying increased attention to the airtightness of buildings. As the insulation value of building fabric increases, so the proportion of energy lost from the building through ventilation losses increases. Likewise, as the energy used during operation of a building decreases, so the embodied energy becomes a greater proportion of the total energy used by the building over its life.

It may therefore be worthwhile to use some high-embodied-energy materials in a long-life building if they deliver significant savings in running energy and to use low-embodied-energy, short-lived, easily recyclable or reusable materials and components in buildings with short design lives, see Figure 1.4.

It is a fair assumption that materials with a high embodied energy are likely to be manufactured by a process that has negative environmental consequences other than purely energy use, for example in the case of ore-smelting which may result in heavy metal pollution. However, this doesn't always hold true (blowing foam insulation using gases containing ozone depleting substances (ODS) – thankfully a practice on its way to extinction – is a good example). Life cycle analysis can be used to quantify these other environmental impacts.

Life cycle analysis

A life cycle analysis (LCA) for a construction material rates its impacts from extraction or growth of materials through to its disposal. The methodology for an LCA could be extremely simple, a matter of ensuring consistent units throughout, for example. More rigorous methodologies would also ensure consistent data collection and, if more than one data set is being used, apply weightings to different data sets, as shown in Figure 1.5.

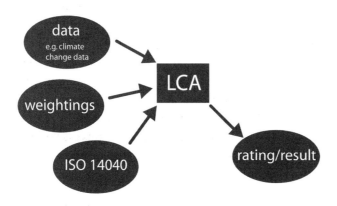

Figure 1.5 LCA analysis

The international standards for LCAs are the ISO14040 series[8] though results from different ISO compliant LCAs may not be comparable. As the BRE points out, there is "no single 'right' answer for applying LCA".[9]

6 Building type

If a building's performance is to be ranked against benchmarks then obviously a building-type-specific assessment needs to be used. Finding a suitable assessment method can be problematic for less common building types, or for buildings that are for mixed use, although the BRE can undertake bespoke BREEAM assessments.

7 Building assessments

A summary of the features of a selection of UK assessment methods is given in Appendix 1.

There are a number of assessments that have been developed overseas. A good starting point for obtaining information about them is the UN's Sustainable Building and Construction Forum[10] or the IEA's Energy Conservation in Buildings and Community Systems Programme – Annex 31[11], but a summary of the assessments mentioned in this chapter is given in Appendix 2.

8 Case studies

The Cambridge case study below is the first in the book for several reasons:

- It has the ideal combination of both client and design team for whom the environmental performance of the building is a prime concern.
- It does not fall neatly into any of the categories of building type that are to follow. This is in part deliberate, though it also allows the discussion of an interesting example which we would have had difficulty finding a home for elsewhere! The building is to accommodate a range of uses, and the design solutions in the case study introduce concepts which are common to a range of different building types which we will return to throughout the book – for example, how to plan the appropriate use of thermal mass. This is also the reason that this case study will be somewhat longer than most in the book.

- This is a project in the process of conception. While no truly sustainable building can be built without being informed by successes and failures of the past – and indeed we will consider existing buildings of various ages later on – the design approach used on this embryonic building is emblematic of the way forward. Design cannot be 'good' unless it is also 'sustainable'.

Oxstalls Campus at the University of Gloucester, the second case study in this chapter, has been included by way of contrast. Although it also serves an educational purpose, and is the work of a leading practitioner of environmental architecture, it is a completed project. It illustrates that embracing sustainability as an opportunity, rather than being a tedious constraint, can promote design quality.

8.1 Cambridge University Botanic Garden

This section has been written in collaboration with Philip Armitage at Max Fordham LLP.

Design Team
Architects: Edward Cullinan
Service engineers: Max Fordham LLP
Structural engineers: Buro Happold
Construction cost consultants: Gardiner and Theobald
Design: 2002
Cost: est. £16.5 million

Background

The Cambridge University Botanic Garden, founded in 1762, has been at its present site since 1846. It accommodates an important collection of living plants, an extensive herbarium[12] containing specimens collected by Charles Darwin, among others, and a specialist library, known as the Cory Library. The buildings in which the herbarium and library are housed are separated from each other and do not currently provide conditions suitable for their delicate collections. The University proposes a new, purpose-built home for them which will also contain teaching and lecture spaces.

The Botanic Garden has more than purely academic functions: it is a place of great beauty and heritage value, attracting both tourists and local residents. Like so many other historic cultural attractions the Garden's visitor facilities are both limited and rather outdated. Hence, the new library and herbarium are to be part of a much larger Education and Interpretation Centre, with interactive exhibitions, a shop, cafe and offices for the Garden's staff.

Not surprisingly, the natural environment and its ecosystems are of great importance to the Garden and its staff. The brief for the new building asked for the design to reflect this ethos by being at the cutting edge of 'green' architecture and engineering, in part because the building can be used as a tool for raising public awareness of the issues involved in its construction.

Planning, form and construction

The site for the new building is on University-owned land (currently occupied by a bowling club) to the south-west of the Garden.

Access to the Garden is to be rationalised: the three existing entries to the Garden are somewhat difficult to locate. There is also a fourth entrance – the original entrance to the Garden – on Trumpington Road.

The new building will provide a higher profile main entrance to the Garden, as well as being an emblem of the Botanic Garden's environmental aspirations.

The brief and design rationale

Accommodation within the new building is to include:

- a 'Plant Lab': an information, orientation and exhibition space with access to reference material, databases and experimental equipment
- accommodation for the 9000 volumes and 2000 periodicals of the Cory library, incorporating a public reading room for the first time

---

Box 1.6 Project goals for the Cambridge University Botanic Garden

- Design a building and landscape which presents a 'public face' to Cambridge and thereby strengthens links between the local community and the University.
- Design with accessibility in mind for all types of people: young and old, students and families, the able and the less able.
- Design a building that people will love and take care of for a long time; for its beauty, practicality and ability to accommodate changes in use and technology.
- Express the importance of trees, as the most fundamental plant to our survival, as our client says... 'plants are the basis for all life on earth.' Timber has proved itself to have 'green' credentials which are hard for other materials to compete with. Timber for the project must come from sustainable sources.

continued...

- Create a landscape which harmonises with the historic garden, supports biodiversity and does not require excessive water and energy to maintain.
- Reduce the demand for energy by:
  - linking the building to public transport, cycle and walkways
  - placing the building to maximise its solar potential
  - shaping the building to facilitate natural ventilation, solar shading and daylighting
  - choosing and detailing materials which improve the thermal performance
  - choosing materials to have low embodied energy where possible.
- Create a building which will be 'carbon neutral' at 20 years of age by using renewable energy sources such as PVs and biomass fuel.
- Reduce water consumption, collect rainwater locally for building use, and recycle and treat grey water locally.
- Use salvaged materials where possible – take advantage of web sites for sourcing.
- Specify materials which are neither toxic to the environment in their production nor toxic to contractors or building users in their use.
- Source products locally where possible, thereby supporting local economies and avoiding transport pollution.
- Detail to protect vulnerable materials through overlapping and 'breathing' configurations.
- Detail to reduce material wastage [i.e. to standard sheet or component sizes] and to prefabricate where possible to reduce site wastage
- Set up an on-site, monitored recycling system
- Detail for future dismantling/recycling, not demolition; use screws and bolts instead of glue and nails.
- Design easy access systems for maintenance of building fabric and services thereby reducing material damage and replacement/costs [sic].
- Design within financial parameters while also analysing life cycles, energy savings and CO_2 emissions.
- Choose a procurement route which promotes quality of product while ensuring value for money.

Source: Edward Cullinan Architects et al., Cambridge Botanic Garden Stage C report.

- accommodation for the University Herbarium
- formal teaching facilities
- a 120-seat auditorium
- two classrooms for both schools and adult education programmes.

This list does not fully convey the complexity of the task that the designers have been set; in fact, it is a very different list – the list of the project goals – which makes the complexity of the task explicit.

Design

Sustainability has been a principal concern during the design of the building. An exhibition about the building and its 'green' credentials will be housed in the new building to raise awareness about sustainable construction; this is in part why the sustainability has been made explicit in places, such as in the use of timber for the main structure and the proposed photovoltaic (PV) cladding. These aims have knock-on effects, such as requiring the long axis of the building to run east–west, to maximise the southerly façade.

However, it also suffuses every other decision from the choice of materials, or the depth of the building, which is dictated by the maximum depth for natural ventilation and by daylighting considerations.

Other key concerns are the minimisation of waste on site and reducing the impact of construction on the surrounding environment, the people who live locally, and those working on site. This can be achieved by decisions such as using components prefabricated off site so as to minimise time on site, as does avoiding the wide-scale use of concrete and by substituting elements traditionally cast in-situ with precast elements. In fact, decisions such as designing for change of use minimises the impact on local people by reducing the likelihood of the building being demolished in the near future if the Garden's needs change.

These have all been very quantifiable design aims; less so are the aims to design in response to the Garden itself, and to create, in the words of the architects, "a beautiful, expressive and evocative building".

An integrated, efficient structure

The lamella structure of the roof is a form of construction that originated during the early years of the 20th century. It is a two-way spanning structure, with the members orientated at an angle to the edge of the structure: it can be seen as a grid of diamonds rather than a grid of squares.

The roof is to be of two shells of constant curvature joined at the apex to form a distinctive three-pin arch. Once the fittings at the nodes between the 400 mm grid elements are tight, the structure resists deformation. These nodes can be either pinned or moment (rigid) connections, both of which can be accommodated by a fitting such as the 'Shearlock' fitting developed by Cowley Structural Timberwork, though at the moment pinned joints are envisaged.

A lamella roof is an inherently efficient structural form, and this theme is carried through to the rest of the building with stressed skin floors, which can span further for a given loading and structural depth than conventional floors.

Source: Edward Cullinan Architects

Figure 1.6: Botanic Garden – south elevation and cross-section through the entrance hall

Box 1.7 Laminated veneer lumber (LVL) and formaldehyde adhesives

Laminated veneered lumber is made from thin veneers of timber, glued together in large sheets. The standard size is 21 m long, 900 mm deep and 27 mm to 90 mm thick, although thicker sections can be fabricated by gluing a number of sheets together.

The mechanical properties and longevity of LVL are better than those of solid timber. It is sealed in a controlled environment at optimum moisture content, so the risk of the laminated members warping/deforming is greatly reduced.

The adhesive used is generally urea-formaldehyde or resorcinol-phenol-formaldehyde. Formaldehyde, a volatile organic compound (VOC), is implicated in sick building syndrome. It is very toxic, thought to be allergenic, is mutagenic (damages DNA, so it can cause cancer, and the damage can be inherited), damages mucous membranes, eyes, skin and respiratory tract and probably damages the kidneys too.[1]

In terms of LVL the risk is minimised in two ways. First, the amount of adhesive in the thin glue lines between the laminates is small, and tightly controlled, and second the LVL is manufactured in closely controlled conditions, so that there is practically no unpolymerised (free) formaldehyde within the material.

1. Safety data for formaldehyde, 37% solution, University of Oxford, http://ptcl.chem.ox.ac.uk/MSDS/FO/formaldehyde.html, 2002.

Both lamella and floor elements can be prefabricated under controlled conditions off site. This means that build quality can be assured as well as minimising both time on site and, therefore, disturbance to local people.

The lightweight structure minimises the need for extensive foundations, and the proposed piled foundations reduce the need for excavations still further.

Though the designers have tried to avoid the use of concrete where possible, the ground beams are to be precast reinforced masonry beams. Where blinding is required under the ground floor, it is proposed that limecrete is used.

Materials

Inevitably, of course, the design of any building calls for pragmatism as we have seen in the use of precast ground beams and will look at in the use of cement fibre boards to provide thermal mass, and also as we shall see in our discussion of the environmental servicing strategy for the building. Nonetheless, the choice of materials is of great importance to the success of any 'sustainable' building. A final choice regarding materials would be inappropriate at stage C, but broad criteria have been laid down.

Box 1.8 Materials selection criteria

- Use natural, local (within a 30-mile radius), renewable or reclaimed materials with a low embodied energy.
- Use timber wherever possible, e.g. as the primary structure, cladding, internal linings, furniture etc.[1]
- Design to save materials using standard modules, and for ease of maintenance, replacement and recycling.
- Avoid, wherever possible, the use of concrete and gypsum-based products.
- Use natural finishes, and avoid coatings and materials which contain harmful substances or preservatives.
- Reuse materials 'found' on site, e.g. hardcore from the demolished Bowls Club building, timber from felled trees.
- Create a super-insulated building using environmentally friendly insulation such as sheep's wool.

Source: edited extract from Edward Cullinan Architects et al., Cambridge Botanic Garden Stage C report.

1. Stone in the Cambridge area is generally unsuitable for building: clunch from the surrounding areas is very soft. In older buildings in the town which use it, a cladding of a more weather-resistant (and grander) material has generally been used.

This can then inform design choices such as, for example, in the case of the selection of a timber structure. The actions arising from the broad criteria are:

- to research supplies of reclaimed and FSC certified timber in the local area
- to take advice from manufacturers about prefabrication
- to investigate bolt assembly to decrease time on site, and for ease of reuse
- to investigate timber treatments, for fire protection and preservation, that are both effective and as non-toxic as possible.[13]

This in turn leads to design decisions such as making internal partitions, ceilings and acoustic panels from timber, treated with beeswax or linseed oil, on timber stud.

Likewise, it means that the insulation materials such as sheep's wool (preferably from local sources), blown cellulose, shredded newspaper and cork (for floor underlay and acoustic absorption) will be considered in preference to, for example, phenolic foam.

Even the choice of furniture is to be influenced by the guiding principles. The use of noxious glues and finishes is to be avoided, and wood felled on site is earmarked for possible bespoke furniture.

Services

The designers worked on the building so that all of its parts work together, for example its PVs would be both a weatherproof layer and a power source as well as having a very definite aesthetic. However, it is still worthwhile to look at the environmental systems separately, as follows.

Box 1.9 Other areas of investigation

- Roofing materials – areas with no PV cells are to be clad in timber shingles or thatch. Underlay is to be bitumen and mineral/vegetable fibre sheets.
- Rainwater goods – metal downpipes and flashings will make for ease of replacement and recycling.
- Flooring – recycled slate or stone are to be used in areas with high foot traffic and need for thermal mass. Offices will have carpeting for acoustic deadening. This is to be of sheep's wool with as few treatments as possible.
- Finishes – low-VOC and low-toxin paints and varnishes are to be used.

Thermal performance

The requirement for thermal energy in the building has been minimised as far as possible through increasing the performance of the envelope, something that is still important even when energy is to be supplied from renewable sources. Wind turbines were in the news at the time that this case study was written because it appears that they create a warmer nocturnal microclimate beneath them[14]: a timely reminder that even renewables are not entirely benign.

Insulation – Double-glazing or high-performance triple-glazing (frameless to maximise daylight) are proposed.

Thermal mass – Spaces, such as the office, classrooms and exhibition areas will benefit from having some thermal mass to even-out temperature fluctuations. A stereotypical thermally massive building would be one with thick masonry walls and possibly stone floors: the thermal mass being part of the structural system of the building.

However, stone floors are intended for areas with high foot traffic, so in areas such as the offices (which will have carpets that decouple the thermal mass from the occupied space) a more inventive approach is needed. Cement fibreboard panels, 75 mm thick, will provide all the thermal mass needed over a diurnal cycle to give reasonable summertime temperatures. In addition, because the thermal mass is decoupled from the structure of the building, the amount of thermal tempering could conceivably be changed if the building's use changes.

Ventilation

Unwanted air infiltration can add considerably to heating loads, and undo the benefits of thick insulation. Careful detailing and quality control strategies on site can decrease unwanted air infiltration that would add considerably to heating loads. The [now compulsory] pressure testing of completed buildings will assess the success of these strategies.

Controllable ventilation is needed, however. The strategy for ventilation in the building has been to exploit both wind and the stack effect, and this has affected the development of the cross section of the building, as shown in Figure 1.7, with apex rooflights designed to encourage stack effect ventilation irrespective of wind direction.

The manually operated windows and user-controlled, electrically actuated, rooflights will give the building's occupants adaptive opportunities to control both air quality and comfort.

Mechanical ventilation – costly in energy, materials, maintenance and space – has been avoided except in kitchen and sanitary areas.

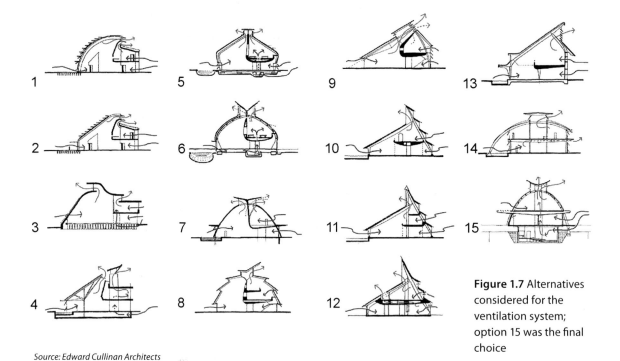

Figure 1.7 Alternatives considered for the ventilation system; option 15 was the final choice

Light

- Windows and rooflights for the building have been planned to minimise the need for artificial lighting and to minimise unwanted solar gain while allowing occupants to experience the beauty of the surrounding gardens.

- Most occupied spaces are located on the north side of the building to avoid direct solar gain while providing views out over the main garden.

- North-facing openings have been sized to achieve a 5% areas-weighted daylight factor. For example, the classrooms will have an average illuminance of 250 lux on an overcast day. It is estimated that artificial lighting can be avoided for 80% of the working day.

- South-facing openings in the roof have been minimised to control solar gain and to increase the area over which PV cells can be installed.

- South facing glazing on the ground floor incorporates a brise soleil to exclude high angle summer sun but to admit warmth from the sun in winter while allowing views out into the entrance garden, and first floor offices are to be equipped to reduce glare on computer screens where appropriate.

- The ground floor exhibition space and cafe will be naturally daylit via windows to the north and south – which will allow views through the building to the garden beyond – and by a north light in the roof.

- Glazed partitions are to be used within the interior to allow inner areas to benefit from natural light.

- The internal surfaces of the building are to be of pale wood, possibly using veneered ply, to reflect light.

Water

The aim in the design of the new building is not only to minimise water use, where possible, but also to use the three sources of water on the site (mains water, rainwater and groundwater) in the most efficient way.

Mains water will supply all of the new building's needs for drinking, washing and food preparation. This frees up water obtained on site for uses where the quality of the water need not to be so high; very little water treatment will be needed in the new building. Demand is to be minimised by the use of low-water-use appliances.

Rainwater collected on site is estimated to meet 80% of the demand for WC and urinal flushing (WC and urinals account for one-third of the building's total demand).

Water for WCs does not need to be potable quality, and the only treatment is to filter the rain water before it reaches the 60,000 litre storage tank. The tank is underground, which keeps the temperature of the water low (10–20°C) and will retard the reproduction of bacteria. From the main store, water will be pumped to a smaller high-level tank (this will also have a backup connection to the mains water supply) from where it will reach WCs by gravity flow.

Groundwater currently supplies irrigation water for the main garden, and the existing pipework system is to be extended to supply the planted areas around the new building.

A wastewater connection is likely to be needed for foul water only, as the combination of permeable paving and soakaways are to absorb rainwater run-off.

The use of reed beds to treat grey- and blackwater was investigated, but the reed bed would need to be 1–2 m² per person, and with the large number of visitors expected, this would not be possible. However, a demonstration project to treat waste from the offices has been considered.

Energy supply

One of the design aims for the building was for it to be carbon neutral after 20 years. This means that energy for the building will need to come from non-fossil fuel (i.e. renewable) sources.

As can be seen from Table 1.2, there is plenty of energy coming onto the site but, as always, harnessing it is not an entirely simple proposition.

Table 1.2 Approximate energy sources and requirements on site

	kWh pa	(kWh/m² pa)
Total energy incident on site	**8,843,750**	-
Solar energy incident on site (horizontal plane)	7,718,750	-
Solar energy incident on building only	1,539,000	-
Wind energy crossing site at 10m height	1,125,000	-
Total building energy requirement, of which:	189,700	**(70)**
electrical load	81,300	(30)
space heating load	67,750	(25)
hot water load	40,650	(15)

Assumed CO_2 conversion factors: electricity 0.47 $kgCO_2$/kWh; natural gas 0.2 $kgCO_2$/kWh; oil 0.29 $kgCO_2$/kWh.

Source: Edward Cullinan Architects, Cambridge Botanical Garden Stage C report

Electrical load – One way to decrease the CO_2 emissions resulting from the electrical requirements of the building would be to buy electricity through a 'green tariff' scheme from the National Grid. However, generation on site is preferred as this would not only reduce transmission energy losses but would be a very visible statement of the building's green aspirations. Though the use of a wind turbine was investigated, the favoured solution was to install PVs on the roof of the building.

In Cambridge, maximum solar radiation can be collected by a surface facing due south at an incline of 32° from horizontal. The roof of the proposed building is 10° east of due south, but this only results in a 5% reduction in PV output over a wide range of roof slopes. The building is also being designed to minimise overshadowing by nearby mature trees.

One of the major problems with weather-dependent on-site generation is load matching. Though it should be possible to supply the annual electrical demand of the building from PVs, the building will also have a grid connection; excess energy will be exported during periods when generated supply exceeds demand.

PV installations are currently very costly so, though there is the possibility of grant funding from the government's large scale demonstration programme, the building is being designed to allow installation either during initial construction or in the future.

Heating and hot water – It is proposed that a biomass fuel should be used in the new building to help towards the aim of creating a carbon neutral building – see Box 1.11.

A woodchip-fired boiler would meet the building's base heating load. Combustion emissions are below that required by the *Clean Air Act* and, although there can be some water vapour pluming in winter, flues do not emit visible smoke. Modular high-efficiency, low NO_x, natural gas boilers will provide extra heat at peak periods. Heat would then be supplied to the building with standard low-pressure hot water circuits.

Box 1.12 Building-integrated photovoltaics

Photovoltaics can be incorporated into a building in a number of ways, but one of the most economic is to get them to do double duty as building components as well.

For example, building-integrated photovoltaics (BIPV) can be used in the form of tiles/shingles (such as the ones developed by XCO2 and Solar Century) or can form solar shading as was used in the Feilden Clegg Bradley designed canopy at the (former) Earth Centre in Doncaster.

Table 1.3 Efficiencies for PVs and photosynthesis

	efficiency (%)	cost (£/W)
Monocrystalline silicon	13	4.5
Polycrystalline silicon	11.5	3.5
Kaneka thin film	7	2.91
Thin film shingle or pan	6	3.5
Theoretical PV maximum*	**30**	-
Tree†	0.5–1.5	-
Maximum theoretical photo-synthetic efficiency§	**13**	-

Source: All from Edward Cullinan Architects, Cambridge Botanical Garden Stage C report apart from:

* from Thomas, R. (ed), *Photovoltaics and Architecture*, Spon, London, 2001, p7.

† from Bowen, H. J. M., *Introduction to Botany*, Newnes, London, 1965, p. 119. quoted in Thomas, R. (ed), *Photovoltaics and Architecture*, London, Spon, 2001, p7.

§ Hall, D. O., 'Biomass energy', *Energy Policy*, Vol 19, No 8, 1991, pp. 711–737 quoted in Ormerod, W., Riemer, P. & Smith, A., *Carbon Dioxide Utilisation*, International Energy Authority Greenhouse Gas R&D Programme, www.ieagreen.org.uk, 1995.

The initial purchase cost of a woodchip-fired boiler is higher than that of an oil or gas boiler, but operational costs are expected to be lower.

Unfortunately, sufficient fuel cannot be produced on the Botanic Garden site – space heating alone would require two hectares ($20,000m^2$) – so local sources are being investigated in order keep the amount of energy used in the fuel's transport to a minimum.

8.2 Oxstalls Campus, University of Gloucestershire, Gloucester

Design team
Architects: Feilden Clegg Bradley

Background
The new faculty of Sports Science for the University of Gloucestershire, which was commissioned in October 2000 and completed September 2002, was designed with the intention of setting new standards in sustainability for higher education buildings. Following research funded by the EUBART programme (European Bio-climatic Architecture with Integrated Renewables and Real-Time User Feedback), various innovations have been introduced to enable the scheme to exceed current best practice. In addition, the main faculty building was one of 18 projects to get a share of the UK DTI's £14million large scale photovoltaics demonstration grant. Feilden Clegg Bradley (who subsequently designed the Sports Science faculty, the high-tech 'Learning Centre' and residential accommodation for 200 students) initially undertook the masterplan for the campus.

Planning, form and construction
Site: built on a 15-acre brownfield site on the edge of Gloucester's city centre, the educational hub of the campus is formed by a Learning Centre and the Sports Science faculty (which includes the University's Administration Department); these two buildings are linked by a glazed 'bridge' that crosses a pool at the centre of the site, which reflects daylight between the buildings. Together, the educational buildings give a strong definition to the external space occupied by the main approach and parking that is defined on its opposite edge by the student housing, a series of four-storey linked 'villas'.

Figure 1.8 Glazed bridge crossing pool

Source: Feilden & Clegg (photo: Mandy Reynolds)

The brief: the Learning Centre provides space for 300 computer workstations and study areas, a series of teaching rooms and a lecture theatre for 200 people.

The Sports Science building contains a variety of laboratories and teaching spaces for the study of physiology, biomechanics and sports psychology, along with office accommodation for staff. The key resource of the building is the sports hall, providing a facility for teaching, training and competitive events.

Design

The central external space, for both drop-off car parking and pedestrian circulation, runs north–south and, as a result, has maximum exposure to sunlight. This zone extends northwards to form a *tapis vert* of all-weather sports surface, a public footpath forming the division. The east side of the central area is bounded by student accommodation and the Students' Union.

On the other side of the central space are the educational facilities, the multi-level Learning Centre being designed as if it were a gatepost to the campus. A grand staircase within a timber-lined vertical hall provides its vertical circulation; the galleried floors for computer use are lit from the north. A double-height glazed colonnade links the visitor to the building across a rectangular body of water which extends from the central space, out to the tree-lined edge of the site.

The open-plan study area is distributed across three levels, united by the top-lit atrium that contains the vertical circulation. On the southern side of the atrium a suite of teaching rooms, offices and a lecture theatre for 200 people are organised along corridors that look back into the atrium.

The café is attached to the visually recessive Sports Science and Administration building, and faces across the water to the glazed wall of the Learning Centre. The café faces the sunlight reflected from the pool of water.

Materials

The student accommodation comprises simple cubic terraced groups clad in two-tone render and oak boards that will, with time, turn silver. The palette of render, oak boards and glazing is disposed across expanses of elevation, relating well to the clear larger-scale mass of the buildings.

Recycling

In terms of sustainability, the architects wanted (in their design evaluation) to give weight to the reuse of existing buildings, in order to conserve their embodied energy. In the end, however, they reluctantly decided on the demolition of all buildings on the site, recycling as much material as possible and, in the process, creating crushed and ground brickwork and concrete that would provide hardcore for the new buildings.

Thermal performance

The residential and Student Union buildings were constructed to a high standard of thermal insulation, in excess of the requirements of the Building Regulations at the time. To moderate the internal environment of the library and teaching spaces, the building has a Termodeck™ system that utilises the thermal mass of concrete floor planks to provide cooling in summer and reduce heating loads

Figure 1.9 Sport hall
roof with PV cells

Source: Feilden & Clegg (photo: Mandy Reynolds)

in winter. In winter, warmer air is drawn through the floor slabs, raising their temperature and radiating the heat to the occupied spaces.

The air is then discharged into the raised access floor and emitted through the floor diffusers, as if it were a displacement ventilation system. Stale air rises in the atrium to a roof-level plant room, and heat from this air is transferred to the incoming fresh air stream by a thermal wheel.

A buffer zone and entrance space for both new buildings is heated minimally to avoid condensation. The heat is supplied from the exhaust air from the Termodeck™ floor in the Learning Centre. During summer nights, cool outside air is used to pre-cool the floor slab, thus decreasing the risk of summertime overheating and therefore the need for air-conditioning in the Learning Centre.

Light

To minimise lighting loads, the library areas are well illuminated by diffuse daylight from the north-facing windows, while carefully designed shading to the windows eliminates most direct sunlight from the internal spaces.

The 'waveform' roof over the sports hall and the adjoining laboratories admits north light that reduces artificial lighting loads and ensures an even distribution of daylight in the spaces below.

Occupant and light-level sensors are incorporated into luminaires to reduce the energy consumption of unoccupied areas, switching and dimming the lamps in response to the availability of natural light. The lamps used throughout are efficient T5 fluorescents. Artificial lighting is used in conjunction with a sophisticated building management system (BMS) for individual and central control over the lighting system.

The control system will also provide user feedback on comfort criteria by linking the networked workstations in the Learning Resources Centre to the BMS control system. This is part of an experimental programme being conducted in conjunction with universities in Kassel (Germany) and Visby (Sweden) to assess the value of providing improved access to energy data and control systems in shared workspaces.

Energy supply

The 'waveform' roof over the sports hall also provides 30° south-facing roof slopes that are clad with PV cells. The PV installation was designed to yield an annual electricity output of approximately 65% of the energy consumption of the Sports Science building, or approximately 25% of the electrical requirements of the two new buildings. This final phase of the building's construction

Figure 1.10 Café terrace facing the Learning Centre

Source: Feilden & Clegg (photo: Mandy Reynolds)

included connection to the building energy management system, enabling the performance of each sub-array to be closely monitored, and providing valuable research data.

Sustainability was prioritised for the design of the new buildings: the Learning Centre was designed to an overall energy consumption target of 110 kW-hours per m^2 per year.

Landscape
The context of the project is entirely suburban. The parkland setting, including the canalised Wotton Brook and a large number of mature trees, has been preserved and incorporated into the landscape of the reconstructed college.

Transport
As is true for any major higher education campus, planning for transportation has been a key issue. The University's policies on sustainability have led it to ban the use of students' cars on its campuses in Cheltenham, and to establish a dedicated bus service linking its sites. These routes have now been extended to Gloucester. The concerns expressed by the occupants of the housing adjacent to the campus led, in this instance, to the provision of slightly more car parking spaces on site than the design team and the local authority planning officers initially recommended. Considerable effort has been put into the provision of facilities for cyclists, dedicated cycle parking areas being located next to all the main building entrances. In the future, it is to be hoped that more extensive cycleway development throughout the existing network of footpaths and green spaces adjacent to the site will further encourage this mode of transport.

9 Notes

1.   Greer, J. and Bruno, K., *Greenwash: The Reality Behind Corporate Environmentalism*, Apex, Third World Network, 1996, Penang and New York, 1996. Cited in Williamson, T., Radford, A. and Bennetts, H., *Understanding Sustainable Architecture*, Spon, London, 2003. p. 10.
2.   www.est.org.uk/myhome
3.   RIBA Practice Bulletin No. 189 (13 February 2003)
4.   ODPM, *Sustainable Communities: Homes for All*, The Stationery Office, London, 2005. p. 69.
5.   Rogers, R., *Cities for a small planet*, Faber and Faber, London, 1997, p. 23.
6.   www.earthships.org
7.   The Brundtland Commission's definition of sustainable development has been followed by others such as the government's 'ensuring a better quality of life for everyone, now and for generations to come'. See GB Office of Science and

Technology, *A better quality of life: A strategy for sustainable development for the United Kingdom*, The Stationery Office, London, 1999. para 1.1.

8. ISO 14040:1997 deals with LCA principles and framework, 14041:1998 with goal and scope definition and inventory analysis, 14042:2000 with life-cycle impact assessment and 14043:2000 with life-cycle interpretation. More information on the International Organisation for Standardisation (ISO) website, www.iso.org.

9. Howard, N., Edwards, S. and Anderson. J., *BRE methodology for environmental profiles of construction materials, components and buildings*, BR370, BRE, Watford and http://cig.bre.co.uk/envprofiles, 1999. p. 4.

10. www.unep.or.jp/ietc/sbc

11. www.annex31.com and www.ecbcs.org

12. A systematically classified collection of dried plants.

13. Edward Cullinan Architects, Cambridge Botanic Garden Stage C report, p28.

14. Ravilious, K., 'Weather hots up under wind farms', New Scientist, www.newscientist.com, 4 November 2004.

10 Further reading

1. IEA, *Types of Tools – Annex 3. Energy-related Environmental Impact of Buildings*, International Energy Agency, www.annex31.com, 2001.

2. Anick, D., Boonstra, C. and Mak, J., *Handbook of Sustainable Building: An Environmental Preference Method for selection of Materials for Use in Construction and Refurbishment*, James and James, London, 1998.
    For each building application a maximum of four choices of material are presented, falling into categories from 'preference 1' (recommended) through to 'not recommended'.

3. Berge, B., *The Ecology of Building Materials*, Architectural Press, Oxford, 2001. Not so much a guide to specification as a whistle stop tour of history, politics, economics, chemistry and manufacture of materials. It gives a personal view of the effect of materials on the environment. Ratings are given from one to three, one being the least destructive to the environment.

4. Panek, A. and Suchecka, M., 'Environmentally Friendly Buildings and Assessment Methods', *ECBCS News*, Issue 35, www.ecbcs.org, October 2002, pp. 9–10.

5. Porkka, J., Huovila, P., Al Bizri, S. and Gray, C., *Decision Support Tools for Performance Based Building*, Performance Based Building Thematic Network, www.pebbu.nl, 2004. This gives a compehensive overview of 'decision support tools' and makes an assessment as to which are more 'promising'.

2   Houses

We begin by considering the design of individual new houses, and the case studies concluding this chapter are two notable examples of contrasting approaches to the design of houses where environmental concerns have been to the fore. But firstly we begin by establishing the environmental context.

Buildings account for around half of the UK's total energy consumption: the domestic sector – housing – accounts for the lion's share of this. In terms of 'final energy'[1], domestic consumption accounts for 28%[2] of the total, just behind transport, which consumes a little over a third of the total.

However, through modern housing design there is great potential to reduce the domestic sector's overall energy consumption, and therefore the national CO_2 production. For example, houses constructed to the 2002 revision of the Building Regulations are likely to have fabric heat losses that are over 30%[3] lower than those built to the 1995 revision. These in turn having 50%[4] of the space heating requirements of pre-20th century housing.

UK housing is one of the more enduring parts of our building stock, with many properties lasting over 100 years[5]. Not only does this mean that there are a large number of older buildings where energy savings may be made (either through refurbishment or replacement) but that new housing could similarly have a long life during which time energy saving measures will be of benefit.

We can see that, just by tackling thermal efficiency alone, there is the potential for significant and on-going energy savings. This would be a worthwhile aim purely in terms of the promise of a decrease in the national production of CO_2. However, the benefits go beyond the purely environmental.

For instance, fuel poverty, defined as the situation where a household needs to spend more than 10% of its income on heating, affects over four million people in the UK[6]. Cold homes, and mould growth due to the consequential condensation contribute to poor health and premature deaths among vulnerable groups such as the very young, the elderly and the sick. It is estimated that this contributes to, on average, 40,000 additional deaths[7] each winter and puts considerable strain on the NHS. Furthermore, there is also a clear link between poor quality housing and social poverty, with correlations to high crime, unemployment statistics and related costs. Thermal efficiency is clearly not the only indicator of sustainable housing.

Box 2.1 Refurbishment vs rebuild

Some argue that, even taking into account the embodied energy that is tied up in existing buildings, the difficulty of making substantial improvement to them mitigates in favour of phased replacement with new housing as an appropriate way to lower energy use and CO_2 emissions.[1] There are, however, many reasons why this may not be either practical or desirable.

Many historic buildings are less than energy efficient, but of great cultural and historical importance. Likewise, there are many houses where relatively simple interventions can reduce energy use. The cost to society of poor, energy inefficient housing, is greater than that of the CO_2 emissions alone. Fuel poverty is, for example, a significant problem in the UK. If issues such as these are taken into account, the balance may shift in favour of refurbishment in many cases.

1. XCO2 – Conisbee. *Insulation for Sustainability – A Guide.* XCO2, London and www.xco2.com, XCO2, 2002.

1. Indicators of sustainable housing

Low energy use is not the only indicator that a house is 'environmentally friendly' or sustainable. For example, the BRE EcoHomes assessment looks at seven different areas:

- *Energy*: operational energy and CO_2
- *Transport*: location issues related to transport
- *Pollution*: air and water pollution (excluding CO_2)
- *Materials*: environmental implications of materials selection, recyclable materials
- *Water*: consumption issues
- *Ecology and land use*: ecological value of the site, greenfield and brownfield issues
- *Health and well-being*: internal and external issues relating to health and comfort.[8]

Rather than consider each category to be of equal importance, the final assessment gives weightings to each area. The weightings were agreed upon by a panel of interest groups, from government policy makers through construction professionals to environmental lobby groups. We will look briefly at each of these categories and the issues related to them before considering methods of construction.

1.1 Energy

There is great potential for reducing the amount of energy used to heat homes (and thus the amount of anthropogenic CO_2 emitted into the atmosphere) by increasing insulation standards. In fact, the single most effective measure for reducing the UK's dependence on fossil fuel, in relation to housing, is to reduce the total amount of space heating required in winter

A building's heating requirements can be split into two. The heat losses through the walls roof and floor of the building are considered together as fabric losses, while the losses incurred as ventilation air leaves a building are, unsurprisingly, referred to as ventilation losses – and include both losses through planned ventilation and infiltration through the building fabric.

Fabric losses

The 2002 amendment to the Building Regulations (Part L) made the U-values for the elemental method of demonstrating compliance much more onerous than those from the 1995 amendment. However, in addition to the elemental and target U-value methods of demonstrating compliance, there is the Carbon Index method – defined in the 2001 SAP – which is intended to allow for greater flexibility in design while still minimising energy use, and this was incorporated into the 2006 revision to Part L.

Box 2.2 Operational energy vs embodied energy

The proportion of overall lifetime energy use that is due to operational energy consumption relative to embodied energy grows with increased building life.

Housing is one of the longer-lived building types, when compared with offices for example; the lifespan of a house in the UK is likely to be over 100 years. For such a long-lived building type, it can be argued that the use of higher embodied energy components is worthwhile if their use can decrease the amount of energy used within the building over its lifespan. For example, as seen in Fig 2.1, even in the worst case of a super-insulated dwelling having twice the embodied energy as one of standard construction, if the building uses 10% less operational energy, the total energy used is less than for the standard house if the lifetime is greater than 60 years. This drops to 50 years if the operational energy is 20% less, and to less than 20 years if 30% less energy is used.

continued …

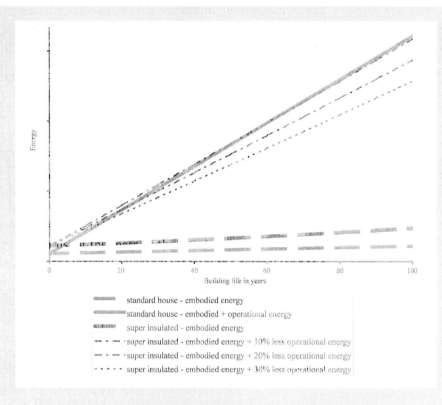

Figure 2.1
Embodied energy and total energy use for a standard house and a super-insulated one.*

Y-axis: Energy

X-axis: Building life in years (0, 20, 40, 60, 80, 100)

Legend:
- standard house - embodied energy
- standard house - embodied + operational energy
- super insulated - embodied energy
- super insulated - embodied energy + 10% less operational energy
- super insulated - embodied energy + 20% less operational energy
- super insulated - embodied energy + 30% less operational energy

Note:
* The standard house is assumed to have 10% embodied energy at 50 years. The super-insulated house is assumed to have twice the embodied energy as the standard house. A 1% growth in embodied energy is assumed for replacement of fabric in both cases. Edwards, B. and Turrent, D. (eds), *Sustainable Housing – Principles and Practice*. Spon, London, 2000. p. 24.

Having arrived at a construction strategy to accommodate the thickness of insulation required, it is often cost-effective to increase the amount of insulation beyond the minimum requirements represented by the Regulations. This is now accepted practice among many housing associations. Inexorably, insulation values are heading towards Scandinavian levels, beyond which further increases in the amount of insulation may become less valuable in terms of energy saved as we will discuss in Chapter 3.

In the past, domestic heating systems in houses have generally been sized either by rule of thumb, or by steady-state heat-loss calculations based on the worst design day in the location (a very cold, clear, winter night) plus a factor for heating from cold, where choice of method depends on the size and complexity of the system. This has the potential to result in a somewhat oversized heating system.

Table 2.1 U-values for domestic construction (elemental method)

Element:	1995* SAP 60 or less	1995* SAP over 60	2002†
Pitched roof with insulation between the rafters	0.2	0.25	0.2
Pitched roof with insulation integral	0.2	0.25	0.25
Pitched roof with insulation between joists	0.2	0.25	0.16
Flat roof	0.2	0.25	0.25
Walls, including basement walls	0.45	0.45	0.35
Floors, including ground floors and basement floors:			
(i) exposed	0.35	0.45	0.25
(ii) semi-exposed	0.6	0.6	0.25
Windows, doors and rooflights (area-weighted average), glazing in metal frames	3	3.3	2.2
Windows, doors and rooflights (area-weighted average), glazing in wood or PVC frames	3	3.3	2.0

Sources

* Department of the Environment, *The Building Regulations – Approved Document L*. London and www.odpm.gov.uk: HMSO, 1995. p. 8.

† ODPM, *The Building Regulations – Approved Document L1*. London and www.odpm.gov.uk: TSO, 2002. p. 12.

Heat gains such as solar gain and heat from the occupants may, in a well-insulated building, be of the same order of magnitude as the heat loss of the building. Taking these gains into account, as well as the potential thermal mass of the building (with its potential to temper diurnal temperature fluctuations) will inevitably lead to the installation of a heating system with a lower output. Indeed, where a house has been designed to maximise and control solar gains an *admittance procedure* calculation may indicate that a traditional heating system may be omitted altogether. While this makes the additional insulation attractive from the point of view of both the environment and construction costs, it can have major drawbacks. For example, it would be very difficult to warm a cold house from empty on just casual gains after an unoccupied period.

Solar utilisation

The most readily available form of renewable energy is solar energy. In northern Europe, 'direct gain' passive solar methods are favoured, where solar energy is admitted to a room through windows and rooflights orientated towards the sun. Because the solar irradiation varies throughout the day, positioning thermal mass within the space, in the path of the sun, evens out some of the temperature fluctuation through the day. The heat from the sun can then be stored relatively effectively until later in the day so that the requirement for artificial heat can be lessened.

The problem is to balance the admission of solar energy in relation to winter heat loss. Summer overheating in houses is most easily avoided by ventilation, reducing the size of the windows (as long as this does not significantly restrict ventilation) or by providing external shading, which would preferably be adjustable. As buildings become more heavily insulated, direct gain becomes less useful because it can lead to overheating, even in winter. Methods of utilising solar energy are therefore open to ingenuity.

The value of solar gain varies not only throughout the course of the day, but also from season to season. In the middle of winter, nearly all solar energy retained indoors will be useful. However, the greatest heat losses are in the evening and morning when sunshine is not available, although exposed thermal mass may be used to store energy for later in the day. As a consequence, other methods of capturing solar energy become of interest.

Box 2.3 Direct, indirect and isolated solar gain

Direct solar gain is where solar energy enters into the space being considered, where – depending on the details of the design of the space – it can warm the occupants directly, increase the air temperature or be stored in the thermal mass of the room for re-release later in the day.

Indirect solar gain is where the radiation is intercepted by an element that absorbs the solar gain before it enters the room and where it is stored for later in the day when the sun has set.

Isolated solar gain is where the solar gain is captured by a separate space such as a conservatory/sunspace.

Examples of technologies are:

- Trombe walls, where a thermally massive wall (usually painted black to absorb solar energy better), with ventilation gaps top and bottom, is placed between glazing and a room

continued . . .

- Mass walls – unventilated trombe walls
- Remote storage walls – trombe walls with insulation on the room side of the thermal mass
- Water walls – trombe walls where the thermal mass is in the form of water[1]
- Sunspaces.

These may also be used in conjunction with TIMs – transparent (or translucent) insulation materials – to improve the insulation value of the glazing element. The British Fenestration Rating Council defines a TIM as having a thermal transmittance of less than 1 W/m²K.[2] [3] However, as U-values for window glazing units creep downwards[4] the division will become increasingly redundant. The more novel materials used in TIM include silica aerogels, honeycomb capillaries and transparent foams which may be used in conjunction with a noble gas (such as argon) or partial evacuation – all with the aim of cutting down heat loss through convection in the space between glazing panes.

Blinds are fitted in the space between wall and glazing to decrease unwanted solar gain in summer.

Sunspaces act as a thermal buffer in winter but, owing to the solar heating of their internal surfaces, they can supply preheated background ventilation to rooms in winter. To gain the most benefit, the sunspace has to be separated from the internal spaces by doors that are kept shut in the winter. It has been found, however, that the vast majority of conservatories tend to be used as occupied rooms and are heated, even if they were not originally designed to be; in this case, the sunspace can act as a thermal drain on the building.

1. See Goulding, J.R., Lewis, J.O. and Steemers, T.C. (eds), *Energy in Architecture – The European Passive Solar Handbook*, Batsford, London, 1992. Chapter 5 gives an in-depth discussion of passive solar heating, plus equations for design use.
2. The units are the same as for U-values but the two are not equivalent because transmittance takes account of surface effects.
3. www.bfrc.org
4. For example, Pilkington make double-glazed insulating glazing with a mid-pane U-value of 1.2. PDF: *Pilkington Solar Control Glass Range,* Pilkington, www.pilkington.com, Jan 2005. p. 4.

Another way of significantly reducing a dwelling's fabric losses is to reduce its surface area: to build semi-detached, terraces or apartments in preference to detached homes. We will look into this further in the next chapter.

Ventilation losses

When insulation values are increased, the ventilation losses become proportionally more important. In older UK housing, background ventilation in winter is provided by air leakage through cracks in the structure and chimney stacks. In fact, lighting a fire could set up such strong convection currents that enough air could be drawn into the building to provide a comfortable cooling breeze in summer – although with uncomfortable draughts in winter.

Ventilation has to perform different functions at different times of the year. In winter, enough fresh air is required to dispel indoor pollutants but without undue energy loss. Apart from the variable quantity of air provided, the amount of air that is admitted through infiltration is strongly dependent on changes in wind direction. In this case, a well-sealed construction in conjunction with engineered trickle ventilation – the 'build tight; ventilate right' method – has become an accepted solution to providing ventilation while limiting heat loss and draughts.

In summer, higher air velocities are required to increase thermal comfort, and these are usually provided by opening windows, doors or louvres. This works as long as the air outside is cooler than the air within the building or if warmer air can be cooled by evaporation (for example, by being drawn through a garden or past a courtyard fountain), without uncomfortably increasing the humidity. In the UK, there are a few summer days when external air temperatures are so warm as to pose a problem for passive systems. Under these circumstances, it is best to keep windows closed, draw the blinds or curtains and to use some form of air movement generator, ceiling fans being quite effective for this purpose.

Box 2.4 The fuel issue

The amount of heat required in a home is not the only variable that affects the amount of CO_2 produced. The efficiency of the heating system also has a bearing, as does the fuel which supplies it. Systems with boilers are more desirable than those with electrical heating, which has significant inefficiencies in terms of the generation and transmission of the electricity.

In terms of fossil fuels, natural gas is preferable to LPG and oil, despite having lower attainable boiler efficiencies than oil – see later in the chapter. However, because natural gas has smaller molecules compared to oil – and thus lower ratio of carbon to hydrogen – it has a lower ratio of CO_2 to water in its combustion products and thus a lesser amount of CO_2 is evolved for a given heat output (and boiler efficiency). The amounts of CO_2 evolved are 54 $kgCO_2$/GJ for mains gas, 69 $kgCO_2$/GJ for LPG and 75 $kgCO_2$/GJ for oil, i.e. nearly 40% more CO_2 is emitted by oil than by gas.[1]

1. Anderson, B.R. *Review of Part L of the Building Regulations: U-values, Heating Efficiency, SAP and Index methods*, Oscar Faber, DETR and BRE, www.odpm.gov.uk, 1999. Sections 3.1.2 and 3.1.3.

Electrical demands

Heating is obviously not the only demand for energy in a house; there is hot water to be provided as well as electricity for lighting and household appliances.

Water heating is a significant domestic energy requirement. Solar hot water generation is now a very viable alternative to fossil-fuel-fired boilers or electric immersion heaters (which are extremely inefficient in terms of primary energy and should be avoided wherever possible).

In most homes, there is sufficient daylight during most of the day, so little artificial light should be needed apart from, perhaps, some task lighting. This is, of course, dependent on a relatively shallow floor plan and ample, suitably placed, windows. Light walls, ceilings and furnishings are to be preferred from a daylighting point of view – though they may not necessarily be aesthetically desirable. Choosing lamps with a greater efficiency than the traditional tungsten filament is essential if energy use is to be decreased.

There has been an enormous increase in the number of electrical goods used in recent years. It used to be that a living room would have two or four socket outlets; now we have a double, or even a quadruple, gang on every wall! And then there are all of the television and FM aerials, phone sockets, cable TV outlets and broadband connections that connect us to the outside world.

It is difficult to know what a designer can do to ensure that the multitude of appliances are used responsibly, other than locating the socket where it can be reached easily, and ensuring that they are of the switched type. Whether mobile phone chargers are unplugged when not in use and whether TV sets are not left on standby is up to the occupant. However, the provision of an outside area with a clothes line gives the opportunity to dry clothes without resorting to the use of a drier, and is awarded points in the EcoHomes assessment.

It has been suggested that significant savings in electricity use will be made by improvements in the efficiency of household appliances. In the short term, however, since the number of appliances per household is steadily rising, and given the increasing number of households of smaller size, each with their own appliances, the demand for electricity is unlikely to fall.

1.2 Transport

It is often quoted that a family car can produce around the same amount of CO_2 per annum as a house for a family of four[9]. The location of housing has a considerable impact on how far a building's occupants need to travel, what form of transport they use, the 'food miles' embodied in their groceries and so forth.

In terms of a single house, there is little that can be done to encourage use of more sustainable forms of transport, other than to provide covered bike parking, as the location of the house is often out of the designer's control. It is in relation to housing that there is the possibility of affecting change, such as was undertaken at the BedZED development, discussed in Chapter 3.

1.3 Materials

Transport and energy use are not the only culprits when it comes to pollution. In addition, there are the environmental impacts due to the quantity of materials used in construction, which account for over half of the total materials use in the UK.[10] In turn, aggregates account for half of the 420 million tonnes (about seven tonnes per person) of materials used annually for construction.[11]

Timber is a favourable material for use in house construction in terms of its embodied energy characteristics, and also because it captures and entrains CO_2 throughout its period of growth (although mature trees produce and absorb CO_2 at about the same rate). Timber should, however, only be obtained from carefully managed woodland with a mixture of young and mature trees, since the older ones are important for the water cycle of the forest and its ecosystem. A mixture of species is also important, as it maintains ecological diversity, although a drawback is that a smaller percentage of the trees will be suitable for logging.

In an equatorial rain forest only a small percentage of the tree population is suitable for logging. These ecosystems are particularly fragile, so care obviously needs to be taken if tropical hardwoods are to be specified. The Forest Stewardship Council (FSC) is a good source of information on sustainable timber (see Box 1.5), as is the International Tropical Timber Organisation (ITTO) for tropical timber, and in the UK, the UK Woodland Assurance Scheme (UKWAS).[12]

Because timber is imported from so many different sources, it remains difficult to assess the precise levels of environmental impact. The best aim should be to use timber from well-managed and regulated forests, and to reuse timber if possible. And it is best not to specify simply 'timber from sustainable forests' but to look into the environmental policy of the supplier.

1.4 Water

A major impact of housing construction and use is in relation to water economy. Consumption in the UK continues to rise with each person in a household using around 150–154 litres per day.[13] Although new sources of supply have been introduced, and new infrastructure has been constructed to move water from areas with excess supply to those in deficit, both high capital cost and energy expenditure is involved, as well as environmental impacts. For this reason, an aim for future housing is to reduce water consumption.

Water used for showers and baths and washing machines also impacts on the energy consumption of a home.

1.5 Health and well-being

A current area of concern is the poor indoor air quality (IAQ) found in new houses. Trying to seal buildings to limit heat loss may also seal-in toxins that are detrimental to human health.

These toxins can be innate to the construction, for example the off-gassing of organic compounds such as the formaldehyde used in many contemporary sheet materials (see Box 1.7), or they can result from activity within the building. Non-smokers, for example, are exposed to serious health risks from the passive inhalation of slowly clearing tobacco smoke. All of this can lead to potentially dangerous levels of airborne pollution. In the absence of an adequate level of winter ventilation, the concentration of particulates in the air can exceed safe levels. In some parts of the country, the concentration of radon gas within buildings may also pose problems, but in the humid climate of the UK the main problem encountered is that posed by condensation.

Care is needed to ensure that measures intended to decrease energy use do not exacerbate these problems, as was seen in the mould breeding ground of 1960s' high-rise housing. Condensation can be the result of poor ventilation, poor detailing, inadequate heating, poor maintenance and inadequate insulation. The resulting mould growth adversely affects many people. In addition, humidity and inadequate ventilation are also implicated in the propagation of dust mites that are associated with the increasing incidence of asthma in the population.

Condensation

Condensation in buildings can lead both to health problems and to structural problems within buildings. If it occurs on the inner surface of a wall, moulds can breed, causing respiratory problems, an issue particularly associated with poorly insulated, poorly ventilated buildings. If, however, it occurs within the fabric of the building, problems such as the corrosion of metal components, the rotting of wooden ones and the saturation (and thus decreased performance) of insulation may result.

The amount of air required for respiration is usually much less than that required to dilute pollutants and to reduce the humidity of the air in a room: a person requires 0.03 l/s of air to supply their oxygen requirements, 1.3–5.6 l/s to dilute the CO_2 they produce and more than 8 l/s to dilute pollutants.[1]

In the UK, with our mild and wet winters, it is particularly important to maintain enough ventilation to reduce humidity to check the growth of mould and to maintain comfort. For example, a larger air change rate is required to remove water vapour in typical UK winter conditions (~5°C external temperature) than in Sweden where the external temperature is lower (–10°C) and air, when warmed to room temperature, has a lower relative humidity.[2]

1. Yet more ventilation will be required if smoking is permitted. Thomas, R. (ed). *Environmental design – An introduction for architects and engineers (second edition)*. Spon, London (1999). pp. 22–3.
2. Anderson, B.R., *Review of Part L of the Building Regulations: U-values, Heating Efficiency, SAP and Index methods.* Oscar Faber, DETR and BRE, www.odpm.gov.uk, 1999. Para 2.10.3

Condensation occurs when the temperature of a material drops below the dewpoint temperature of the air in contact with it. In buildings, two factors are needed for condensation to form: there needs to be relatively humid air and it needs to be in contact with a cold surface.

There are two basic ways to remedy the problem:

1) Reduce the humidity of the air within the building by:

- reducing the amount of water vapour released in the building
- dehumidifying the air
- heating the air in the building[14] (which will reduce the relative humidity and warm the construction).

2) Prevent humid air from meeting a cold surface by:

- the use of a vapour control layer so that water vapour, which will be driven by the difference in vapour pressures inside and outside the building, cannot move through the construction
- ensuring that the temperature of the construction does not reach the air's dewpoint temperature by insulating the building and locating the insulation appropriately.

Condensation only becomes a problem when it persists for a long period of time. Bathrooms and kitchens, if they are well ventilated, are unlikely to suffer any serious damage.

2. Construction issues

The indicators of sustainability (discussed in Chapter 1) can be applied to all types of housing. From a historical point of view, however, it makes sense to discuss single houses first.

In the 1970s the autonomous house (one that existed in a symbiotic relationship with its local surroundings and made no demands on local mains services) was the exemplar of current thinking in the field of environmentally responsible housing. In recent times, this approach has been re-evaluated, and attention has shifted to the rather broader issues that are involved in the design of sustainable communities. We will move on to consider these in the next chapter.

Box 2.6 The autonomous house

The autonomous house – one that, by being in a symbiotic relationship with its surroundings, made no demands on local mains services – was an idea which guided the development of sustainable housing from the 1970s. Examples include the Autarkic House project undertaken by the Martin Centre at Cambridge University, the construction of Robert and Brenda Vale's Autonomous House at Southwell, Nottinghamshire, and Sue Roaf's 1995 Oxford solar house.

The Vale's house is perhaps the most complete statement of the concept. The main body of the building is very heavily insulated. The roof structure required to accommodate the insulation has led to the adoption of an innovative form of construction. Inclined plyweb beams have been used to create rafters of a depth corresponding to the thickness of insulation. The superinsulated envelope allows the house to function throughout the year with the minimum of energy inputs. Rather than relying on solar energy for space heating, a conservatory on the south side of the house acts as a supplementary living area. Plant in the basement which is the full area of the floors above, includes tanks for collection of rainwater (which are actually reused bulk orange juice containers) and a sewage treatment system that enables the house to work independently of the mains.[1]

1. Vale, B. and Vale R., *The New Autonomous House*. Thames and Hudson, London, 2002.

2.1 Insulation – location and accommodation

We have already seen that increasing insulation is one of the methods that can have the greatest impact on domestic energy use.

Increasing the thickness of insulation results in thicker walls which, since houses (particularly detached ones) have a relatively large surface area to volume ratio, has implications for the site area occupied and the extent of the foundations, as well as on the viability of conventional construction methods.

In terms of construction, there are two main issues to be considered. The first is the question of thermal performance: minimising heat loss and the avoidance of both interstitial condensation and cold bridging. The second is structural: how to accommodate the insulation within the wall or roof without causing structural weaknesses.

Location

The preferable arrangement is to locate the insulation on the outside of the construction. In flat roofs, this has led to the now familiar 'upside-down' roof; for pitched roofs, various systems are marketed where profiled insulation panels are fixed at the *outside* of the rafters.

Walls having external insulation with a render of weathercoat is one way of addressing the problem, although there is some anecdotal evidence of this being unpopular with planners. This removes the option of brick being the outer visible material, but it has the additional advantage that thermal mass within the building can be employed to help temper the internal temperature. (Thermal mass is discussed in detail in Chapter 3.) Vapour control layers, correctly employed, are essential for managing condensation risk.

It is unlikely that condensation can always be avoided, so thought should be given to ensuring there is an escape route for moisture.

To locate the insulation at the centre of the construction is a good compromise since the structural temperature across the thickness of the wall can be held above the dewpoint temperature of the air. There are, however, attendant construction problems: the thickness of insulation needed in contemporary construction is a challenge to the usual methods of making walls and roofs in houses. The width of cavity required in masonry walls makes it difficult to achieve an adequate connection between the two leafs of the wall without using special wall ties, such as those developed for use at the BedZED development. Similarly, roof rafters are usually of insufficient depth, while placing the insulation at ceiling level creates a considerable temperature differential between the roof structure and the rest of the building in wintertime. New components such as plyweb beams are being used to create the necessary depth while not greatly increasing the weight of the structure.

Alternatives are to locate the insulation at the inside of the construction, although the condensation risk is then greatly increased, and exacerbated by the inevitable cold bridges where the structural connections to the floors and roof breach the insulation.

Insulation materials

Insulation materials have a low thermal conductivity and trap air (or other gases) in pockets or between fibres. They can cut down on the passage of heat in three ways:

- conduction: since both the solid material and the trapped gas are poor conductors of heat
- convection: because the numerous small bodies of air cannot set up convection currents in the same way that an unfilled cavity would
- (to a lesser degree) radiation.[15]

Insulation materials have a very low density (as a consequence of the large amounts of gas within them) particularly in relation to other materials that may be used on site, such as brick and steel. Usually, a good general rule of thumb to estimate the relative environmental impact of different materials is that the less dense material will have a much lower impact than the denser one. Because many foamed insulation materials use gases other than air as the blowing agent (which may have serious environmental implications), and because of the large volume of insulation needed, the type of insulation should be chosen with care.

Box 2.7 Blowing agents, ozone depletion and climate change

A particular issue is the use of CFCs as a blowing agent, a practice that, because of the extremely damaging environmental characteristics of CFCs, required them to be phased out under the Montreal Protocol. Their substitute – HCFCs – also increase the thermal capabilities of closed cell foam but they also are a greenhouse gas and responsible for ozone depletion. The alternatives, pentane and CO_2 have less than a third of the impact.

HCFC-blown foam insulation, even though it has rather less than half of the climate change impact of CFC, and slightly more than half the ozone depletion capability, is excluded from the BRE's system of rating because its use is so enormously damaging to the environment.

Embodied energy from processing

Insulation materials that use little energy during processing, such as low-density mineral wool, expanded polystyrene (EPS), corkboard and recycled cellulose, can be advantageous. More heavily processed materials such as polyurethane can have an improved environmental profile as a result of their decreased conductivity: polyurethane is a better insulator than polystyrene, which is less dense.

There is, of course, a large range of insulation materials whether natural products (which can require a minimum of processing), or entirely man-made

Table 2.2 Environmental characteristics of common insulation materials

		BRE overall rating†
Expanded polystyrene (EPS)	Little potential for recycling.	A
Glass wool with density 160 kg/m³ or less		A
Mineral wool with density 150kg/m³ or less	Some recycled material used in manufacture.	A
Recycled cellulose insulation	Made from recycled materials (for example, newspaper), but unlikely to be recycled itself.	A
Corkboard insulation with density 120 kg/m³	Has potential to be recycled, but rarely is. Also the amount of transport it needs is considerable (imported material).	B
Foamed glass	Extensive transport requirements. Excellent recyclability, but little recycled material used in its manufacture.	B
Glass wool with density over 160 kg/m³		B
Mineral wool with density over 150 kg/m³		B
Polyurethane (PU) (HCFC free)	Ozone depleting, toxic to humans and wildlife.	B
Extruded polystyrene (XPS) (HCFC free) with density less than 40 kg/m³	Poor performance in terms of fossil fuel depletion and climate change.	C

Notes: The BRE functional unit is 1 m² of material to give an equivalent performance to a 50mm thickness of expanded polystyrene (EPS).

† BRE ratings: A = within the top third across a range of environmental impacts, B = within the middle third, C = within the bottom third

Source: Anderson, J. and Howard, N., *The Green Guide to Housing Specification – An environmental profiling system for building materials and components used in housing*, Watford, BRE (2000). pp. 30–31.

foams and fibres. The Buildings Research Establishment (BRE) assessed a number of common insulation materials used in the construction of housing, giving them an overall rating based on their (weighted) performance regarding climate change, fossil fuel and ozone depletion, freight transport, human- and eco-toxicity, waste disposal, water use, acid deposition (causing acid rain), eutrophication (release of nutrients to water which may cause problems such as algal blooms), summer smog production and mineral extraction. These can be seen in the Table 2.2.

3. Generic construction methods

3.1 Typical UK house construction

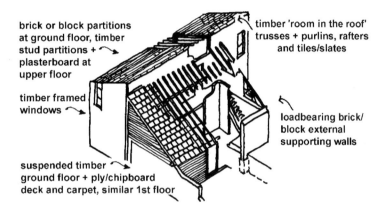

brick or block partitions at ground floor, timber stud partitions + plasterboard at upper floor

timber framed windows

suspended timber ground floor + ply/chipboard deck and carpet, similar 1st floor

timber 'room in the roof' trusses + purlins, rafters and tiles/slates

loadbearing brick/block external supporting walls

Figure 2.2 Typical UK house construction

• *Loadbearing brick and block …*

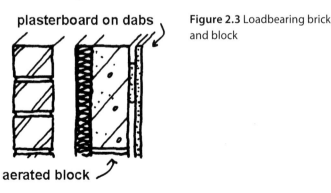

plasterboard on dabs

aerated block

Figure 2.3 Loadbearing brick and block

Bricks are capable of a long life and can be readily recycled, if they are used in conjunction with lime mortar. In spite of this, the environmental performance of brickwork is less than other masonry materials because of the energy used in firing, even when manufactured using a mechanised continuous kilning process.

The mass of the walling materials means that they do not rate as favourably as low-mass framed structures, although the difference is less marked when considering aerated blocks which have the advantages of being both light-weight and having good insulation properties. Consequently, both brick cavity construction (with cavity insulation and an aerated block inner leaf) and framed construction achieve a BRE 'A' rating.[16]

- + *clay tile pitched roof ...*

Figure 2.4 Clay tile pitched roof

clay tiles on battens

Although trussed rafters use 30% less timber than 'room-in-the-roof' construction[17], the actual structure has little environmental impact compared with the materials covering it. Both methods can achieve an 'A' rating.[18]

Traditional roofing materials do better in terms of their overall performance than contemporary synthetic roofing slates. Reclaimed tiles are more brittle than new, so there are more breakages during installation and they may need replacing more often. One of their advantages over new is that the embodied energy (which can be attributed to the new building) is much lower and they can be transported over considerable distances without losing this advantage. It is, however, always better to source recycled tiles locally if at all possible.

The insulation material chosen does not affect the overall rating of the roof structure significantly because of its (relatively) low mass – although, as we have noted, materials which use ozone-depleting blowing agents should be rigorously avoided.

• + suspended timber floor …

t & g floorboards

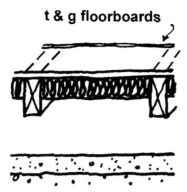

Figure 2.5 Tongue-and-groove boarding

The timber structure performs well because of its low mass, renewability and because its processing is not particularly energy intensive or polluting.

The decking material has little mass relative to the structure, and so has relatively little environmental impact. Despite this it is worth noting that:

- tongue-and-groove boarding requires relatively little processing, which is advantageous
- plywood is often made from tropical hardwoods so it is necessary to establish that the material is from a well-managed source
- many sheet materials off-gas formaldehyde
- insulation for the ground floor should not use ozone depleting gases.

(Floor coverings are not discussed here as they are usually laid by house-owners; nonetheless, since they are relatively frequently replaced, their impact can be considerable, particularly if they are synthetic fibres, i.e. made from fossil fuels. Wool, cork and timber are thus preferable, as is natural or recycled underlay.)

Where suspended ground floors are laid over concrete, the concrete impacts poorly on the overall rating, especially in terms of mineral extraction. Recycled aggregate mitigates this effect as long as transportation distances are not too great. Ideally, aggregate would be recycled from the site – and crushed on the site.

• *+ timber windows and doors …*

Again, timber is a renewable resource with relatively little energy used in its processing. Its embodied energy is therefore low. It must be sourced from sustainably managed woodland, in which case locally grown hardwood can achieve an 'A' rating,[19] unlike many other materials used in window manufacture. PVC[20] is frowned upon for its poor sustainability profile.

The major problem with timber windows is durability, although working timber windows are in existence that date back centuries. Paint finishes have greatly improved in recent years, particularly with the introduction of microporous paints. Stained finishes need to be renewed comparatively often, but need little in the way of surface preparation.

3.2 An alternative

• *Loadbearing stone cavity walls + slate pitched roof …*

stonework outer leaf

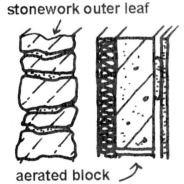

aerated block

Figure 2.6 Stone and block cavity wall

Stone and slate require limited processing and so have some advantage over brick and blockwork.

Although slate is a traditional roofing material in the UK, slates are now frequently sourced from Spain and South America. This should be avoided as both slate and stone are heavy to transport. If used, they should preferably be sourced locally.

- *+ solid concrete ground floor …*

The mass of concrete required, along with the large amount of mineral extraction, explains the 'C' rating of this flooring.[23] However, the use of recycled aggregate (provided it is sourced relatively locally) can improve things somewhat.

The mass of the concrete, which is undesirable in terms of transport energy, can improve the internal environment in the completed homes. Compared to traditional masonry construction, where thermal mass is exposed, stud walling has relatively little thermal mass. Where the house is in near continuous occupancy, a concrete floor can provide valuable thermal mass, as long as it is not covered by carpet.

- *+ timber joisted upper floor with chipboard or orientated strand board (OSB) decking*

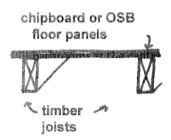

chipboard or OSB floor panels

timber joists

Figure 2.7 Timber joisted floor with chipboard or OSB floor panels

Chipboard and OSB are made from waste materials but require a relative large amount of energy in their processing. They also suffer from the off-gassing of organic chemicals, such as harmful formaldehyde. Consequently, the environmental rating falls, in comparison to solid wood boarding, scoring only a 'B'.[24]

Table 2.3 Ecopoints evaluation of generic constructions for houses, using BRE's Envest tool

	Generic house type: 12m × 8m (ground and upper floors each 96 sq m); no. storeys: 2; storey height: 2.8 m; % cellular: 80%; location: S.E. England; soil type: firm clay	Ecopoints	%
Ground floor	200 × 50 mm timber joists 600 mm c/c + 80 mm rockwool insulation + 19 mm t&g floorboards	12	1.5
Upper floor	200 × 50 mm timber joists 600 mm c/c + t&g floorboards	8	1.0
External walls	Block	157	19.3
	Brick	123	15.3
	Rockwool	8	1.0
	Sub-total	288	35.4
Internal partitions	50% (ground floor) 100 mm block	53	6.5
	50% (upper floor) 75 × 50 mm timber stud + 12.5 mm plasterboard	15	1.9
	Sub-total	68	8.4
Windows	Softwood double-glazed	40	4.9
Roof	Pitched timber with gables + purlins 1.4 m c/c, 0.75 kN/m² loading	7	0.9
	Clay tiles + 150 mm rockwool insulation	32	3.9
Floors	10% 3.2 mm lino	2	0.3
	90% wool carpet	37	4.6
	Sub-total	39	4.8
Wall finishes	95% plaster + 2 coat emulsion paint	65	8.0
	5% 6.5 mm ceramic tiles	17	2.1
	Sub-total	82	10.0
Ceiling	Plasterboard, skim and emulsion	23	2.8
Sub-structure	300 × 150 mm strip foundations	142	17.5
Total embodied including material replacements over 60 year lifespan		813	
Total embodied per sq m of floor area		4.23	

Source: based on Anderson, J., Shiers, D.E., Sinclair, M., *Green Guide to Specification*, (3rd Edition), BRE, Watford, 2002.

Commentary: Houses are a relatively low impact building type in terms of their basic construction form due to the extensive use of timber for floors and roofs. The most heavyweight components, forming the substructure and external walls, account for the largest proportion of the total. A more accurate appraisal would, however, have to take into account the extent of kitchen and bathrooms fittings and servicing that are subject to relatively high rates of replacement.

3.3 Other technologies – Earth-sheltered houses

In conventional houses the thermal mass within the structure acts to somewhat even out the diurnal air temperature fluctuation. The thermal mass of the ground is immense. Rather than damping only short-term temperature changes it will tend to act to damp temperature fluctuations in the monthly to seasonal range, with the length of the period damped increasing as the depth increases.

In 2004, the annual mean temperature in the UK was 9.5°C, ranging from an average of 4.4°C in winter to 14.9 °C in summer[27] – all temperatures that are a little too cold for most people! Although an unheated, entirely earth-sheltered building will be warmer than this (owing to casual gains) it is likely to still be very cool and to suffer from condensation problems.

There are, however, some advantages to the type. Heat losses due to wind passing over the surface of the earth-sheltered part of the building are nil, as are losses from unwanted ventilation.

Insulation can solve the problem of heat loss to earth. One approach is to mound soil over the roof and place a layer of insulation and sheet waterproofing over the mound, and then to mound additional soil on top to complete the construction. In this way, a considerable thickness of dry soil can be effectively combined with the mass of the structure to ensure a constant level of thermal performance.

The thermal mass available to the interior is then only that between the rooms and the insulation, in which case it is likely that the thermal mass advantage will be lost (depending on how much mass is between the room and insulation). And as discussed in Chapter 3, the energy advantages of thermally massive buildings (though exploiting solar gains) are highly dependent on orientation and glazing ratio, and it may be difficult to achieve the optimum balance between these factors in an earth-sheltered dwelling.

In addition, there are construction considerations which make earth-sheltered structures problematic. Access to below-ground buildings is difficult; as is obtaining natural light and ventilation. The pressure of soil and water at the outside of the structure makes a reinforced concrete structure almost inevitable, although timber retaining walls are used in Scandinavia. For these reasons, examples of fully earth-sheltered structures remain rare in the UK, though in warmer climates earth-sheltered dwellings can be quite successful, providing a cool and shady haven.

Other alternative technologies include rammed earth and straw bale construction. The Centre for Alternative Technology (www.cat.org.uk) is a good source of information for these, as well as on other aspects of 'green' lifestyles.

4. Issues regarding typical servicing strategies

4.1 Lighting

Daylighting

New houses, designed to passive solar guidelines, have windows concentrated on the southerly elevation, with windows of limited size on the north elevation. This leads to poor daylight levels in rooms on the north side and to the use of artificial light during the day. This is particularly a problem in frequently used rooms such as kitchens and living rooms. The effect can be partially overcome by locating little-used rooms (such as bathrooms) towards the north.

It is also sensible to aim to locate windows on more than one wall of a room because having light from more than one direction can alleviate problems with glare.

Artificial lighting

The GLS lamps that are most widely used in houses, although generally popular because of their colour temperature, are inefficient.

In the past, fluorescent lamps were often disliked on account of lamp flicker, gear hum, poor colour rendering and the blue/green colour temperature, which was unflattering to skin tones. These problems have been largely solved by newer lamps. For example, a 58W/827 lamp provides a warmish light (colour temperature 2700K) with good colour rendering (the colour rendering index is RA 80–89) and can be dimmed with a hum-free high-frequency (HF) ballast.[28] It also has an impressive life: around 20,000 hours, compared to the 1000 hours of a GLS lamp.[29]

To show compliance with Building Regulations a proportion of the lighting circuits inside a new dwelling – $1/3$ to $1/2$ depending on the number of rooms – should accept only lamps with an efficiency greater that 40 lumens per circuit-watt.[30] Of course, in a truly sustainable home (a best practice or advanced standard home) the proportion of energy efficient lamps will be much higher.[31]

4.2 Ventilation

Natural ventilation

Unwanted infiltration can account for up to 25% of the total heat loss from the average UK home.[32]

Many air leakage paths are associated with the junctions between timber and other components, for example where windows join walls, and around the edges of window sashes and doors. These problems are exacerbated by our damp climate since timber components expand, shrink and move with changes in humidity. Infiltration rates in older homes are often around 2 ach, but this may be reduced to 0.3–0.6 ach by draught-proofing windows and doors.[33]

The suspended timber floors common in many older properties are, in terms of their environmental impact, a relatively good form of construction. However, they are responsible for a high proportion of infiltration, particularly where square-edge timber is used, when there are unsealed gaps at the junction with skirting boards and when floor joists pass through the inner leaf of walls. Coverings such as carpet can partially ease the problem.

Similarly, gaps in ceilings, around loft hatches and light fittings etc., are potential infiltration routes.

While uncontrolled infiltration is best avoided, some ventilation is needed in winter. Trickle vents at high level above windows are the most usual way of providing winter background ventilation. They help both to reduce condensation and to reduce the extent to which windows are opened in winter, thereby cutting down heat wastage.

Passive stack ventilation (PSV) may be used as an alternative to extract fans in kitchens and bathrooms. The ductwork needs to extend to, or beyond, the highest point of the roof. The system draws air out from the warm and wet rooms of the house (in much the same way that heat disappears up a chimney) and so effectively encourage loss of heat. However, it can be fitted with heat exchangers, as was undertaken at the BedZED development, or it can be used in conjunction with supply air windows to form a dwell-vent whole-house ventilation system.[34]

Artificial ventilation

Extract fans and fan-driven cooker hoods are the most commonly used domestic mechanical ventilation. Fully ducted mechanical ventilation and heat recovery (MVHR) systems, which are a standard component in Scandinavian housing, are becoming more common in the UK – the Red House case study at the end of this chapter is one such home.

MVHR systems rely on a constantly operating fan and, though they may be variable in speed, their energy consumption can be a concern to a house's occupants. That there is permanent ventilation may be seen as beneficial in terms of air quality, but only if ducting is kept scrupulously free of dirt, allergens and pathogens.

4.3 Space heating

In the majority of contemporary homes the central heating is a low-pressure hot-water system combining a boiler with radiators or, less frequently, under-floor heating. Some homes have electric storage heaters, but these should generally be avoided as they have the high built-in inefficiencies of the electrical generation and distribution system. Hot-air heating is not frequently seen in the UK, although it enjoys some popularity in the US.

In a well-insulated house a boiler will most often operate at low loads for much of the year, and only when warming the house from cold (during very cold weather), or when there is a demand for hot water, is it likely to operate at full capacity. The provision of thermostatic radiator valves also reduces the load on a boiler since they permit the amount of heat provided to be reduced if there are other heat inputs (solar, occupants etc.) in individual rooms.

Boilers tend to operate less efficiently at low outputs, so over-sizing a boiler should be avoided.

Boiler technology has advanced greatly in recent years. Oil-fired condensing boilers can reach up to 97% seasonal efficiency, natural gas boilers 91.3% and LPG boilers 93.3%.[35] Compare this to, for example, a boiler last manufactured in 1988 – a Baxi-Potterton Marathon 14.7 kW boiler – which had a seasonal efficiency of 65%.[36]

5 Case studies

The case studies in this chapter represent two different approaches to the design of sustainable one-off detached houses. Although the Red House is a new construction and the Hawkes House is old enough to have been recently extended as the occupants' needs changed, they have their green aspirations in common, as well as providing exemplary insights into the reinterpretation of the English detached house.

Though both are heavily insulated they do show considerable differences, through their differing sites, ages, client requirements and designer's view of the sustainability debate. The Hawkes House, with its careful orientation (it has good solar access and is designed to take advantage of it) and spatial elaboration has the Arts and Crafts Movement as its spiritual predecessor, whereas the Red House looks to Scandinavia to inform its design. The Red House is on a shaded site and lowers its energy consumption through good airtightness and highly controlled services. They both, however, form essays on living with sustainability.

5.1 The Red House, Great West Plantation, Tring

This case study was written in conjunction with Alan Tye who is "...glad to share this package of information with friends who are also on the 'Way'".

Architects: Alan Tye Design (ATD)
Client: Kevin and Jacqui Tye
Garden design: Peter Aldington OBE RIBA
Building contractors: Gavin Brothers. Mike Gavin, 60 Oliver Road, Hemel Hempstead, Herts HP3 9PY
Garden contractors: Seasons. David Hollick, 2 Hopedale Road, London SE7 7JJ

Planning, form and construction

Site

The site was previously occupied by a log cabin, and the new house had (for planning reasons) to fit within a prescribed volume, making the orientation predetermined. The site is a shaded, wooded area, so the potential for passive solar design was low.

The brief and design rationale

The designers of the house, Alan Tye and his son (who is also the client), are much concerned with the making of healthy indoor environments both in this project and in others. The intention was to build a modest, economic, healthy and easy-to-maintain house, tailored to the client's needs. It was also to have good security, ideally be sustainable by way of low energy consumption, to be low-allergen and to have exemplary air quality.

The fundamental priority of ATD is health, as Alan Tye explains: "There is little value in sustainable or ecological design if, as has happened in the past, it is unhealthy."

Design

The design was intentionally kept as simple as possible, using proven technologies.

The house consists of two storeys plus a basement. This increases the floor area over that of the demolished building, while still meeting planning requirements. The house incorporates both living and working spaces.

A steeply pitched roof and special trusses allowed the first floor to be built into the roof, making for an efficient use of available space. Although the staircase is fixed in position, the layout of the rooms around it is flexible and forms a prototype for further house construction – the Tyes intend to build more houses in the future.

Structure

The upper floors are of lightweight construction rising from a concrete basement, partly set into the site and partly opening onto a sheltered sunken garden. The high performance fabric follows Scandinavian precedent, from the prefabricated panel construction of the basement through to the heavily insulated timber panel walls and the red pantile clad roof. The detailing of the boarding, the nailing, ventilation and so on, is very important and has evolved in Sweden over decades. A high degree of airtightness is achieved through the construction methods.

Materials

Much of the structure is wood, partly because of its sustainable credentials (not least because it ties up atmospheric CO_2) and partly because the clients liked the 'comfortable feeling in wood houses'. In this context, to be ecologically sound, the wood needs to be fast growing. This determines the timber species and longitude where grown, which has some effects on the properties of the wood, particularly its strength.

The exterior timber is treated with a matt red paint, 'Falu röd farg', characteristic of many Swedish farm buildings on which it has been used for over 200 years. Falu is a town in Sweden formerly renowned for copper mining of which the red pigment is a by-product. The finish:

- is water-based so brushes are cleaned in water
- is breathable so the wood can take in water and let it out again
- can be used fully exposed, for example on fencing
- protects from UV light and does not fade
- ages well and lasts up to 10 years before repainting is needed.

The Vittinge Lafarge red clay tile roof tiles were imported from Sweden where they are made today as they were 300 years ago. The tiles were not available in UK and the decision to import them was made because they are larger in size than UK tiles (and so compatible with the Swedish design of roof trusses etc.), have a more suitable colour for the design of the building, have good condensation-reducing properties and have simpler fixing details. For example, the ridge does not have to be bedded in cement.

The floors are Rappgo Swedish pine supplied by Anglo Norden UK. They are pretreated with 'lut', to keep the beautiful blond original colour, and then

Figure 2.8 Detail of the roof overhang showing the 'Falu röd farg' exterior finish.

treated with white oil which is a virtually invisible oil finish. Lut (lye in English) is a highly caustic solution of sodium hydroxide and/or potassium hydroxide. Although it is relatively environmentally benign it should be used with great care as skin and eyes can suffer serious burns on contact. The floors are cleaned and maintained with white soap diluted 1:20 with water. This cleans and seals the floor, including the joints, and adds a touch of whiteness.

Although floors treated in this way are used for public buildings in Scandinavia, the architect's experience suggests that they need careful maintenance.

The Lindab galvanised steel colour-coded gutters, down pipes, leaf collectors and flashings can be reused and are preferable to plastic goods.

Services

Thermal performance

The super-insulated Red House has very low U-values:

- 0.23 W/m^{2}K for walls and roof
- 1.00 W/m^{2}K for the Swedish Tanum gas-filled, triple-glazed windows (these are reversible for easy cleaning).

By way of comparison, even superior values – 'houses without heating systems' – have been built in Sweden with the U-values (W/m²K): roof 0.08 (48cm insulation), floor 0.09 (concrete on 25cm insulation), walls 0.10 (43cm insulation) and windows 0.85 (3 panes, 2 metallic coats, and krypton filled).

The house also uses Tri-ISO Super 9, a thin multi-foil insulation product from ACTIS; although only 25mm thick, its thermal performance is equivalent to 200mm of mineral wool.[37]

In order to achieve a balance between energy efficiency and air quality, a Villavent mechanical ventilation heat recovery system was installed. The heat exchanger can operate at efficiencies of up to 90%.[38] The system has been designed to operate all year round, with different fan settings for winter and summer use.

Clean air is supplied continuously to the living spaces via a pollen filter, which takes out particles down to 1 micron.[39] The clients are concerned about security, so being able to ventilate the house without the need to open windows is an advantage. Air is extracted from the services spaces. This has the advantage of extracting humid air, and air from the kitchen and bathrooms, while distributing the warmed incoming air throughout the house.

Because of the clients' concern about air quality, a Villavent central vacuum system was also installed, which exhausts to the outside. Traditional vacuum cleaners can sometimes redistribute allergens (for example, dust mite droppings) and dust around the house.

Light
Because of the shaded site, the windows are primarily for views of the surroundings. However, the majority of the rooms are sufficiently naturally lit, though there are some artificially lit storage spaces in the basement.

Water
Rainwater is collected for use in the garden. A tank, submerged pump and various filters developed by Polypipe Civils[40] were used. Ancillary gear is located in a cylinder above the water level and below the manhole cover and an ordinary garden tap automatically switches the pump on and off.

Energy supply
The house's location in an area of pine trees gives a local, renewable, fuel source for the built-in stone stove and bake oven. This was designed by ATD, and consists of over 300 diamond-shaped stone pieces. The stone is unique to northern Karelia (between Finland and Russia) and has truly excep-

Figure 2.9 The stone fire and oven

tional heat retaining properties; for example, it can retain 20% of its heat 36 hours after firing. The mass of the stove compensates for the relative lack of thermal mass in the upper storeys. The warmth from the stone is distributed throughout the house by the continuous ventilation air system, and there is a local adjustable fresh-air vent near the fire if required.

A chimney fan is used to avoid a long flue; this has the added advantages of avoiding the difficulties of creating a draught when lighting the fire, preventing rain damp in the flue and ensuring that the fire burns brightly. In practice, the fan only needs to be used for a few minutes until the natural draught takes over.

Source: Alan Tye

To get the most heat out of wood, and to reduce pollution, the latest Swedish advice is:

- Only burn dry, fine, split wood that has dried for at least 6 months, or 12 months if hardwood. Newly cut wood releases more 'tar' and it takes twice as much wood to get the same warmth.
- Maintain good ventilation. This gets maximum heat from the fuel and reduces carbon monoxide emissions.
- Smoke should be white or better invisible. Black or grey smoke indicates an unsuitable fire construction, wrong burning technique or inappropriate wood.
- Take a look at the chimney: it should not have black deposits, and wood ash should be fine and grey.
- Flues function better when swept and cleaned often.
- Do not burn household rubbish, plastic, painted or impregnated wood, chipboard etc. as poisonous gases may be released.

In addition to the stove, the house has an electric heating system – this can be a sustainable choice if a gas supply cannot be connected and the heat demand is low.

Figure 2.10 The Red House from the south-east, showing the secluded courtyard opening off the basement

A device enabling 'mains signalling' which uses the normal electricity mains wiring to transmit 'messages' to heaters (and other electrical equipment) is incorporated. Every connected heater can be individually programmed to be on or off at any hour of the day, and these times can be different for each day. For example, the bathroom might be programmed to be on more frequently or heaters to be on at different times at weekends when occupants may be at home more. It is also possible to give switching instructions by calling the system by phone, for example if the occupants wanted to turn on the heating just before arriving home after a weekend away.

Heaters also have their own thermostats to override the standard programmes chosen. The system is automatically frost protected.

Communications
An Allgood colour video entry system is installed so that visitors at the garden gate can be seen and allowed entry by a person in the entrance hall or basement studio.

Landscape
The grounds around the house have been kept as natural as possible, again following the Scandinavian example.

Transport
The clients work from home or in the ATD studio, which is adjacent to the house. The house is also within walking distance of a small town.

5.2 The Hawkes House, Cambridge, Case Study

Architect: Dean Hawkes, Greenberg and Hawkes
Design: 1990
Construction: 1991

Background
This is one of a series of designs for houses by Greenberg and Hawkes that began with the Golden House, Doughty Mews, London, 1983–5[41]. In each of these houses, the aim was to respond to the specific needs of the client and to the conditions of the site, while developing an interpretation of the modern house that, among other things, addressed the question of energy-conscious design. That said, the overriding concern was to produce designs in which the energy-related elements were wholly integrated.

Planning, form and construction

Site

The house at Gisborne Road, Cambridge, occupies a small infill site in an area of typical 1930s suburbia. The site dimensions are approximately 30 metres by 11 metres and the long axis runs almost exactly east–west.

The brief and design rationale

The house was designed to be inhabited by two people. It was to accommodate both professional and social life. At the time of construction, both occupants worked full-time and also worked at home in the evenings and at weekends. Since then they have retired from full-time work, but remain active in their professions, so more time is spent working in the house. In response to this, the former garden shed beyond the screen wall at the east end of the courtyard has been improved to provide a second study.

Design

The plan consists of a long, narrow, principal block built on the northern boundary of the site and running approximately east–west. This block has a monopitch roof, elevated towards the sun, and houses the principal spaces. To the south is a sequence of open and closed spaces defined by free-standing screen walls.

Figure 2.11 Axonometric of the house (not showing the new study)

A projecting wing contains a study space and defines the planted courtyard along with a second, recently built, workspace with a monopitch profiled metal roof lying to the east.

In the nomenclature of energy-conscious architecture the house is 'direct-gain, passive solar'. The principal rooms – living room, bedrooms and kitchen – face south and the south elevation of the living room and principal bedroom (facing the internal courtyard) is highly glazed. The main living area occupies the full height of the roof, with a bay providing full height windows that allow light to reflect off the curved timber ceiling and to project to the back of the living

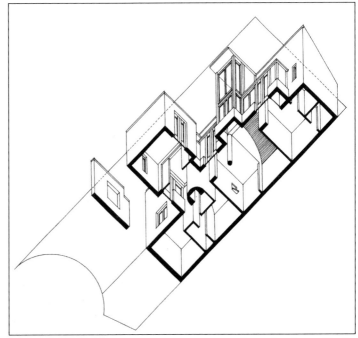

Source: Greenberg and Hawkes

room. The bedrooms, however, are relatively low-ceilinged and dimly lit. Storage spaces are designed as rooms within rooms, as are the bathrooms.

The environmental design of the house was to sustain both work and social life. For over 12 years it has done this in all seasons. The spatial and environmental diversity that it offers provides agreeable settings for the lives of the inhabitants. In winter, the living room is intensively used when it receives solar gains. At other times, the heating system is used frugally, spaces are only heated when they are in use. This habit, in combination with the inherently efficient design, achieves low energy consumption.

Structure
The construction is conventional load-bearing masonry supporting timber roof structures of rafters and joists.

Materials
The main living spaces are contained within heavily insulated roof and walls, which are of insulating blockwork, painted and rendered on the outside, and with a plaster finish on the internal face.

Services

Thermal performance
Insulation: The house is insulated to higher standards than the Building Regulation requirements of the time. At approximate U-values of 0.2 W/m^{2}K, for walls and roof, these are comparable with 2003 requirements.

Because the solar access at the site is relatively unobstructed, the section was made such that it allows wintertime solar admission while in summer the timber-framed circulation route, with its bay window which projects into the courtyard, is a sunlit space distinct from the inner carpeted area which remains shady and cool.

The kitchen is a high room, half vaulted and with clerestory windows, that ventilates well so that the fan extract hood at low level is rarely needed.

The natural servicing strategy of the house provides a variety of environments, allowing the occupants adaptive opportunities to withdraw to cooler areas away from the south façade in the heat of a summer day, or to bask in warming winter sunshine while being protected from chill air temperatures. A balanced distribution of low and high admittances is employed to create a thermally comfortable environment. The solid block walls surrounding the major spaces do, however, provide a degree of longer-term storage for solar heat.

Light

The tall bay window is a key element of the living room. It is used for informal dining and as a workplace, and is the principal source of daylight and of useful solar gains to the entire room. Light is distributed down a timber-clad half-vaulted ceiling. The kitchen has a similar ceiling vault – this time painted white – and is illuminated by a clerestory window located above the flat-roofed study and entrance. A mechanically controlled opening light provides high-level ventilation.

Energy supply

All mains services were available at the site, and the house has conventional connections to these. The systems are also conventional. Space and water heating are gas fired. A 'combi' boiler, with a simple timer control, serves the space heating and the hot water requirements of the kitchen and one bathroom. A secondary instantaneous gas water heater supplies the second bathroom. This decision was made to avoid the operational waste of a long 'dead leg' connection to the main boiler.

Heat is supplied to the rooms by a variety of radiator types, all with thermostatic valves. The electrical installation provides convenient power services for typical contemporary use, and the lighting is controlled by a relatively complex switching scheme to allow precise control in relation to specific uses.

Perimeter radiators are provided, but given that the heating loads are relatively small, so are the radiators.

Transport

The location of the site, not far from the centre of Cambridge, means that the owners can use bicycles rather than a car for most day-to-day trips.

Figure 2.12 The solar strategy in section (i) and in practice (ii)

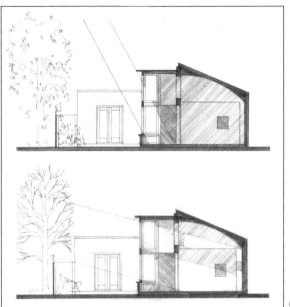

(i)

(ii)

Source: Greenberg and Hawkes

6 Notes

1. Final energy is the energy that is delivered to the end user; primary energy is the total amount of energy used, before losses occur in conversion processes (such as the generation of electricity) and in transmission.

2. DTI, *Digest of United Kingdom Energy Statistics 2004.* DTI, www.dti.gov.uk, London, 2004. p. 14.

3. Calculated through taking Building Regulations U-values (elemental method) and applying the areas of building elements for different housing types, and their proportional make-up in building stock. From Anderson, B.R., *Review of Part L of the Building Regulations: U-values, Heating efficiency, SAP and Index methods.* Oscar Faber and DETR, www.odpm.gov.uk, 1999. Table 4.2.

4. Houghton, J. *Global warming: The complete briefing.* Cambridge University Press, Cambridge, 1997.

5. Edwards, B. and Turrent, D. (eds). *Sustainable Housing – Principles and Practice.* Spon, London, 2000. p. 118.

6. Department of the Environment, Transport and the Regions (DETR). *Quality and Choice: A Decent Home for All.* DETR, www.odpm.gov.uk. London, 2000. Para 2.23.

7. *ibid.*

8. Rao, S., Yates, A., Brownhill, D. and Howard, N. *EcoHomes – The environmental rating for homes.* BRE, Watford, 2003.

9. BRECSU. General Information Report 89. *BedZED – Beddington Zero Energy Development, Sutton.* Energy Efficiency Best Practice programme (DETR), www.bioregional.com, London, 2002. p. 15.

10. Lazarus, N., *Summary: Beddington Zero (Fossil) Energy Development – Construction Materials Report – Toolkit for Carbon Neutral Developments – Part 1,* BioRegional, Surrey and www.bioregional.com, 2002. p. 5.

11. *ibid.*

12. FSC: www.fsc.org, ITTO: www.itto.or.jp, UKWAS: www.forestry.gov.uk

13. OFWAT, *Security of supply, leakage and the efficient use of water – 2003–4 report.* OFWAT, Birmingham and www.ofwat.gov.uk, Dec 2004. p. 47.

14. The more even the heating, the less the risk that areas where air stagnates (such as behind furniture) will form condensation. See Thomas, R. (ed), *Environmental Design – an introduction for architects and engineers.* Spon, London, 1999. pp. 24–26.

15. Radiation can only travel through substances that are transparent to the wavelength. The solid parts of insulation are usually both opaque and with low surface emissivities, so little radiant energy is emitted. Progressively, less heat is then emitted from each surface within the insulation towards the cold side of the insulation. Coating the material with a foil surface can reduce the amount of radiant heat loss still further. This layer may also serve as a vapour control layer.

16. Anderson, J. and Howard, N., *The Green Guide to Housing Specification.* BRE, Watford, 2000. pp. 8–9.

17. *ibid.,* p. 13.

18. *ibid.,* pp. 12–13.

19. *ibid.,* pp. 22–23.

20. The chlorine in PVC is responsible for dioxin formation.

23. *ibid.,* pp. 16–17.

24. *ibid.,* pp. 12–13.

27. Meteorological Office. *UK climate and weather statistics – 2004 Seasonal weather summary.* Meteorological Office, www.met-office.gov.uk, 2004.

28. EST, *Good Practice Case Study 441. Low-energy domestic lighting – 'looking good for less',* Energy Saving Trust, www.est.org.uk, 2002. p. 2. A useful discussion of energy-efficient lighting for housing is *Energy Efficiency Best Practice in Housing. Energy Efficient lighting – Guidance for Installers and Specifiers,* www.est.org.uk, EST, 2004. p. 2.

29. *ibid.,* 2002.

30. ODPM. *The Building Regulations 2000, Conservation of fuel and power – Approved document L1, conservation of fuel and power in dwellings,* 2002 edn, www.odpm.gov.uk, ODPM/HMSO, London, 2003. paras 1.54–1.57.

31. EST, *Energy Efficiency Best Practice in Housing. Energy Efficiency in New Housing,* Energy Saving Trust, www.est.org.uk, 2003.

32. Perera, E. and Parkins, L. 'Build Tight – Ventilate Right' *Building Services Journal.* Chartered Institute of Building Services Engineers, June 1992. pp. 37–38.

33. Lowe, R.J., Curwell, S.R., Bell, M. and Ahmad, A. Airtightness in masonry dwellings: laboratory and field experience. *Building Services Engineering Research and Technology,* 1994. 15 (3). pp. 149–155.

34. www.dwell-vent.com

35. Most efficient boilers from SEDBUK online (www.sedbuk.com) database, 1 July 2005.

36. SEDBUK online (www.sedbuk.com) database.

37. www.enigma-insulations.co.uk

38. The unit is VM-400. Technical details can be found at www.villavent.co.uk When specifying heat recovery units, a balance needs to be found between the potential energy savings from heat recovery and the pressure loss across the heat exchanger, with consequent increase in fan energy requirement.

39. This is with a physical filter. With an electrostatic filter, 97% of particles down to 0.1mm can be removed, see www.villavent.co.uk

40. www.polypipecivils.co.uk

41. 'Golden House, Bloomsbury, London', *The Architects' Journal,* 30 October 1985.

3   Housing Sustainable Communities

1 Discussion

The previous chapter was concerned with one-off, exemplary and (in the instance of the case studies) detached houses. Such 'pathfinder' projects point the way for the mass of housing; the affordable homes required in quantity over the coming years. Given a concern for the design of the local environment, the aim should be to achieve the wider goal of housing sustainable communities.

1.1 Climate change

Anthropogenic climate change – due mostly to CO_2 emissions from the (fossil-fuel-burning) energy supply industry – is a very good reason for considering both the design of new housing but also measures which can be taken to increase the energy efficiency of our current housing stock.

Not only do we need to minimise energy use to reduce our effect on global weather systems, we also need to take into account the changes that are going to happen as a result of our past greenhouse gas emissions.

Increasing or decreasing winter temperatures?

How our climate will evolve depends greatly on how successful we are at stemming CO_2 emissions. The different emission scenarios (see Box 3.1) have a significant effect on heating and cooling loads, something that is explored below.

Mostly, we think of climate change as being a result of the 'greenhouse effect', but there is also a chance that the Gulf Stream – which keeps the UK relatively clement in comparison to other areas of the same latitude – may be 'shut down'.[1][2] This would potentially make our winters three to five degrees colder,

By Dr Mark Gaterell; while at the Martin Centre for Architecture and Urban Studies, University of Cambridge

The domestic sector can potentially make a significant contribution to reducing the UK's energy consumption. Some of these potential reductions will be realised through improvements in energy efficiency standards, in both new homes and refurbishments, arising from the 2006 revision of the Building Regulations.

However, it is likely that existing dwellings will continue to be a significant proportion of the stock, at least for the coming decades. Over 85% of the current UK housing stock was built before 1985 and a high proportion was built to standards that required far lower levels of thermal performance than are obligatory under current building regulations.[1] While the performance of some existing dwellings has been improved through retrospective insulation, there are still likely to be considerable opportunities for reducing energy consumption.

Clearly, the main factor influencing the effectiveness of measures designed to improve thermal performance is the nature of the prevailing climate. Projected changes in the global climate could significantly affect this performance. However, there is considerable uncertainty regarding how projected changes in the UK climate might actually develop over the next 50 years or so.

In order to investigate the implications of such uncertainty, a number of thermodynamic building simulations were undertaken. These were designed to evaluate how projected changes in the UK climate might affect the performance of insulation measures applied retrospectively to an existing residential dwelling typical of the type built in the 1960s and 1970s. Climate data for the simulations were based on changes in heating and cooling degree days projected under the UK Climate Impacts Programme high and low emissions climate change scenarios.[2]

Results suggest that the performance of some measures designed to improve the thermal characteristics of buildings are likely to be sensitive to the precise nature of climate change experienced in the UK. Higher temperatures in some cases will reduce the amount of heating energy saved or introduce the need for a cooling load and thereby affect the cost-effectiveness of the insulation measures applied, see Figures 3.1 and 3.2. Moreover, while the relative performance of each of the measures does not change, the absolute amount of heating energy that can be saved varies considerably under the different climate scenarios.

Consequently, to ensure that energy policy measures designed to reduce energy demand remain effective, particularly in the domestic sector, they need to be informed by the longer-term impacts of climatic uncertainty.

1. *ODPM, Housing and households: 2001 census*, ODPM, London, 2003. p. 64.
2. Hulme, M., Turnpenny, J. and Jenkins, G., *Climate Change Scenarios for the United Kingdom: The UKCIP02 Briefing Report*. Tyndall Centre for Climate Change Research, Norwich, 2002.

continued …

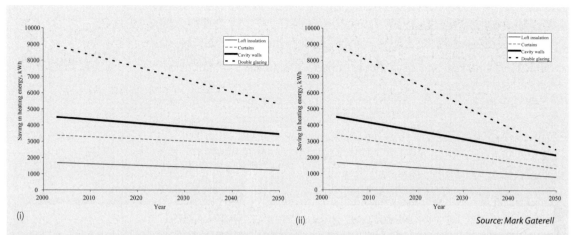

(i)   (ii)   *Source: Mark Gaterell*

Figure 3.1 Saving in heating energy demand under different climate scenarios:
(i) low emissions scenario and (ii) high emissions scenario.

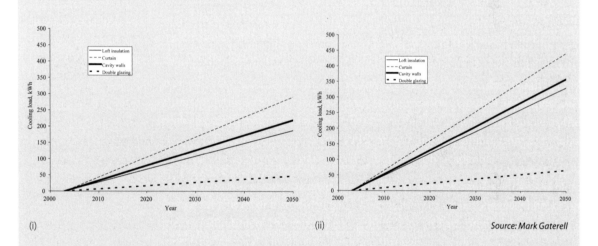

(i)   (ii)   *Source: Mark Gaterell*

Figure 3.2 Cooling loads under different climate scenarios:
(i) low emissions scenario and (ii) high emissions scenario.

despite a rising mean temperature,[3] and thus any extra insulation in buildings would save even more energy.

However, if the Gulf Stream remains active, we are faced with between a two degree increase in mean temperatures (for a low CO_2 emissions scenario) and a 3–3.5 degree increase (if emissions are high). Although warmer winters will reduce both the energy required for heating and cold-related deaths in the UK, there will be negative effects from an increase in 'extreme' weather patterns: heatwaves will increase heat-related deaths, infrastructure will be damaged by storms and flooding and, perversely considering in increase in flood events, water availability will be constrained with 'serious droughts' occurring more frequently.[4]"

The rule of thumb is that a one degree change in the inside–outside temperature results in an 8% change in the heating energy required.[5] Not only does this give us a sense of the scale of changes in energy demand that will result from climate change, but also how significant an effect poor use of heating controls can have.

Increasing summer temperatures

As we have seen in Mark Gaterell's research (Box 3.1), cooling demand in homes has been near nil in the past. However, the predicted increase in summer temperatures is quite large. Rather than the temperature exceeding 30°C for only 2% of summer days, there is the very real possibility that temperature could exceed it for 20% of summer days by 2080.[6] Unless really good passive cooling strategies are put into place, this will probably increase the demand for air-conditioning in domestic properties. In fact, it is not only heatwaves that will increase: an increase in mean summer temperatures of 2–5 degrees could be expected.[7]

With heatwaves here to stay, we also need to aim to prevent a repeat of the deaths during hot spells, as seen in Paris during the summer of 2003. This may mean that a change is needed in the way society works, as well as changes to building construction.

Cloud cover, solar radiation and wind speeds

Cloud cover is expected to decrease by 10–20%, with a consequential increase in solar radiation reaching ground level.[8] This has negative impacts in terms of the increased risk of overheating, but also an uncertain impact on the amount of energy available for renewable energy generation:[9]

- water heating arrays could be reduced in size
- the output from PV arrays could increase or decrease
- increasing wind speeds mean higher heat losses from (and wind loads on) buildings but also an increased potential for power generation.

Precipitation

Total rainfall and peak rainfall are both expected to increase[10][11] leading to:[12]

- an increased risk of flooding

- an increased risk of rain penetration and consequent damage to building materials and, if rain makes it through to the insulation, a decreasing effectiveness of insulation.

It is worth noting that these changes will affect not only the construction industry. Ecosystems and agriculture may be affected[13] changing humanity's ability to feed itself and affecting the diseases to which we are exposed.[14] With an increasing global population, we can ill afford to put even more stress on ecosystems.

1.2 Increasing population

We need more housing: the UK government estimates that there are going to be 190,000 additional households each year by 2021[15] and, if they are all to be housed, that means that over 3600 new homes will be needed each week. At the moment, the net housing supply is nearer 120,000[16] per year, and the rate of construction in the ten years to 2002 was lower than that in the previous ten years by 12.5%.[17]

The most obvious reason for the demand for new housing is population growth. In 2001, the UK population was just over 59 million, an increase of 4.7% over 20 years,[18] and the numbers are expected to keep on growing. The United Nations (UN) estimates a population of over 66 million by 2050.[19] Most of this is 'natural' growth, due to more births than deaths.[20]

Box 3.2 World population

It is not just the UK population that is growing. The UN predicts an increase from 6.07 billion people worldwide in 2000 to 8.9 billion (medium-level prediction) in 2050, considerably lower than the figure estimated in 2000 as 9.3 billion.[1] This is thought to be attributable both to deaths from HIV/AIDS and to lower fertility levels.

Human fecundity is dependent on very many variables. The age of first-time mothers, medical interventions to aid conception (including IVF), decreasing deaths rates for women during pregnancy and childbirth, decreasing infant mortality rates, plus social and economic pressures – to have larger or smaller families, all play a part. What seems to be certain is that we need to control birth rates: if fertility were to remain at current levels the world population could balloon to an incredible 12.8 billion by 2050[2] (the figures have, however, recently been revised downwards, partly as a result of the AIDS pandemic).

1. United Nations, *World Population Prospects: The 2002 Revision*, United Nations, www.un.org, 2003. p. 30.
2. *ibid.* p. vi.

To say "we need more houses" is simple; the question of where and how they should be built is less simple. Not all cities have the same demand for new housing, our existing building stock also requires attention and, at the beginning of the 21st Century, population growth is not the only demographic change that we are faced with.

1.3 Urban density and different geographical demands

Across the world the population of some countries is growing faster than others and the difference between national growth rates is increasing.[21] This is an effect that is seen in the UK too, see Table 3.1.

Table 3.1 UK population

	Mid-2002 population (% of total UK population)	% population growth, 1981 to 2002
England	49,561,800 (83.7)	+5.9
Northern Ireland	1,696,600 (2.9)	+10.0
Scotland	5,054,800 (8.5)	-2.4
Wales	2,918,700 (4.9)	+3.7

Source: *Population Estimates Webpage*, National Statistics, www.statistics.gov.uk. 2003. Crown copyright

Source: *Mid-2002 Population Estimates*, National Statistics, www.statistics.gov.uk. 2004. Crown copyright

We find ourselves in a situation where there are highly buoyant housing markets in some places and an oversupply of housing in other areas. It is estimated that around 730,000 dwellings – 3.4% of the total housing stock[22] – stand empty. This could supply the housing demand for over four years *if* they were suitable.

Obviously some of these houses would be unsuitable to be lived in: some will be unfit for habitation, some will be too remote from potential employment, some will be suitable only for seasonal occupation, some will be in areas with very high crime rates, and so on.

About 90% of properties classified as being in a 'low demand' area are in some 40 local authorities in the North and Midlands, with twice as many being social, rather than private sector, homes.[23]

The government is seeking to put pressure on the owners of empty properties. Through the New Empty Dwelling Management Orders allowed by the *Housing Act 2004* local authorities can take over the management of private properties without becoming the legal owner.[24]

1.4 Changing household types

The structure of society is changing: the make up of families and households has altered over the past few decades, and a different society has different housing needs.

Over the past 20 years, there have been great changes in the way we live, although the rate of change slowed, or stopped in some cases, from the late 1990s onwards. We are an aging society, having fewer children – with those we do have being brought up in a spectrum of different family types, rather than the 'traditional' nuclear family – and, increasingly, we are living alone, see Table 3.2.

Table 3.2 Changing households

	1971	2001
Average household size (persons per household)[a]	2.91	2.33
Households (% of each type)[b]		
one person	23	31
couple with dependent children	31	22
couple with non-dependent children	7	6
couple with no children	27	29
lone parent with dependent children	4	7
lone parent with non-dependent children	4	2
Family type (% of each type)[c]		
2 parents	92	75
lone mothers	7	22
lone fathers	1	3
Percentage of people of given age[d]		
65–74 years	8	8
75 and over	4	7

Source: Rickards, L., Fox, K., Roberts, C., Fletcher, L. and Goddard, E., *Living in Britain. No 31. Results from the 2002 General Household Survey.*, National Statistics and TSO www.statistics. gov.uk, 2004: (a) p18; (b) p21; (c) p22; (d) p24.

With changes like these, we will need to build fewer large family homes, more one-bed and studio dwellings, more retirement/sheltered housing plus associated crèches, after-school clubs, community centres and drop-in centres for the elderly.

It is not only the changing type of household that means we need different types of housing. Many people are now choosing to work at home for all or part of the time – seeking the elusive 'ideal' work/life balance.

Good housing design supports these types of change: the BedZED development is a good example of planning with changing working patterns in mind.

1.5 State of existing buildings – refurbishment

Empty dwellings aren't the only ones which may be in poor condition.

Britain's housing stock is old: half is more than 50 years old and a quarter predates the First World War.[25] Most homes have been renovated and improved since they were built but, while 90% are now centrally heated, and very few (less than 1%) lack basic sanitary arrangements,[26] many still fall below modern standards.

As time goes on we are demanding housing of higher and higher quality; indeed, the government recently changed the standard of thermal comfort needed for a home to be considered 'decent'.[27] As a result the number of non-decent homes increased from 32% prior to the revision, to 41% after[28] with more homes in the social sector failing to meet standards than in the private sector. It is clear that using our existing building stock responsibly is a question of much more than simply filling empty properties.[29]

While many houses that fall below modern standards can be repaired or renovated, many cannot, and need to be replaced. However, though we do not have large numbers of condemned bomb-damaged buildings, the rate of construction of new housing in 2001 was at its lowest level since World War II.[30]

1.6 Affordable housing

As might be expected, the people who are most likely to be living in poor quality housing are those with the lowest incomes. The situation is compounded by the decreasing affordability of homes, which results from strong growth in housing prices.[31] The increasing[32] number of households living in temporary accommodation (in 2005, it was 100,000[33]) is another symptom of the crisis in the affordable housing sector.

Rented accommodation

The number of social houses built has been falling – from *c.* 42,700 pa in 1994–5 to *c.* 21,000 in 2002–3[34] – but our need for them hasn't. The UK needs between 17,000 and 26,000 new social houses per year.[35] The government has responded by saying that it aims to increase the annual supply of new social housing to 45,000 pa by 2010–11, rising to 50,000 at the next spending review.[36][37] Plus they expect 95% of all social housing to meet decency standards by 2010."[38][39]

Home owners

In areas where there is high housing demand – such as the South East – lower income households are often priced out of the market. The Barker Report[40] concluded that the government could manipulate house prices by increasing the housing supply; in order to decrease house price growth to the European average, the annual supply would have to be increased by 120,000, i.e. a doubling of current construction rates.

The government has a number of schemes to increase home ownership, such as the First Time Buyers Initiative, the Homebuy, Right to Buy, and Right to Acquire initiatives, Key Worker Low Cost Home Ownership (LCHO) programmes and the £60,000 Home competition.[41]

Box 3.3 Demographic change and deprivation

A diverse spectrum of household types does not, unfortunately, automatically make for vibrant and thriving communities.<1>

If you live in social sector housing you are around twice as likely to be unemployed than if you owned your own home or rented privately. You would also have, on average, the lowest gross weekly income in the country. The type of household that is on the increase in the UK is precisely the type which is more likely to live in social sector housing. Lone parents, for example, are four times more likely to live in social housing than other families with children.

1. Rickards, L., Fox, K., Roberts, C., Fletcher, L. and Goddard, E., *Living in Britain. No 31. Results from the 2002 General Household Survey.* National Statistics and TSO, www.statistics.gov.uk, 2004. p. 32.

2. Construction issues – reducing environmental impact

2.1 Reducing environmental impact

We briefly considered the embodied energy of buildings in Chapter 1, noting that it is starting to account for a greater proportion of a building's total energy use.

The construction of new homes is thought to be responsible for 2–3% of the UK's total annual CO_2 emissions, while household energy consumption accounts for 29%.[42] This would seem to indicate that embodied energy is a relatively unimportant factor in housing's sustainability; however, it accounts for over half of our annual resource use by weight[43] and so is worth considering further.

Box 3.4 Heavyweight versus lightweight: scenarios for future housing

David Tompson, while at the Martin Centre for Architectural Urban Studies, University of Cambridge

A building's energy consumption is made up of four components:

- the energy to initially produce the building
- the energy to operate the building
- the recurring energy required to refurbish and maintain the building over its life
- the energy to demolish and dispose of the building.<1>

Until now, embodied energy has generally been found to be secondary to operational energy in studies of the whole life energy use of buildings. As building regulations become increasingly stringent, however, calling for extra insulation and thicker constructions, the relative importance of the last three components – the embodied energy – is increasingly significant.

My research set out to analyse how the projected demand for 3.8 million homes by 2021<2> can be met most effectively in terms of total environmental impact. Dynamic thermal computer modelling, and embodied energy analysis software, developed by the BRE, was used to assess the whole life energy impact of a likely future dwelling, over a 100-year lifespan.

Both operational and embodied energy were analysed for four different construction types. One is heavyweight (traditional brick and block construction) and three lightweight:

- timber frame construction
- LGSF (light gauge steel frame) volumetric modular construction
- timber based SIP (structural insulated panel) construction.

continued …

For each, I investigated the impact of orientation, glazing ratio and different building regulation scenarios, in the context of projected climate and demographic change.

A single-person apartment within a larger, three-storey block was analysed to reflect the demand for smaller households and more dense developments that are likely to be built in the 21st Century.

The apartment was assumed to have openable windows and an MVHR system to provide minimum fresh air requirements for use when the windows are not open.

Fabric U-values and airtightness levels were stipulated for two future scenarios, based on government consultation figures published in 2000,[3] and are given in Table 3.3.

Table 3.3 Assumptions for modelling

PRESENT (2000)	Building element	U-value, W/m²K	Construction type	Air-tightness (m³/hr per m² at 50 Pa)
	External walls	0.35	Brick and block	10
	Roof	0.2	Timber frame	10
	Ground floor	0.25	LGSF volumetric	1.3
	Windows and external doors	1.9	SIP	1
PREDICTED (2008)	Building element	U-value, W/m²K	Construction type	Air-tightness (m³/hr per m² at 50 Pa)
	External walls	0.2	Brick and block	3
	Roof	0.16	Timber frame	3
	Ground floor	0.2	LGSF volumetric	1.3
	Windows and external doors	1.6	SIP	1
FUTURE (super-insulated)	Building element	U-value, W/m²K	Construction type	Air-tightness (m³/hr per m² at 50 Pa)
	External walls	0.1	Brick and block	3
	Roof	0.1	Timber frame	3
	Ground floor	0.1	LGSF volumetric	1.3
	Windows and external doors	1.2	SIP	1

Source: David Tompson

Research findings

Given the assumptions for the model, for all of the proposed building types:

- Increasing thermal efficiency and airtightness reduces the relative effect of 'traditional' energy efficient design
- Embodied energy is the determining factor of total environmental impact.

continued …

- Embodied energy effects outweigh operational energy savings from increased insulation, see Figure 3.3.
- Embodied energy effects outweigh energy savings from orientation, glazing and thermal mass.

Moreover, heavyweight construction was found to suffer a greater operational energy penalty when not orientated due south than the other three construction types, and it suffered a relatively high operational penalty if the glazing ratio was not optimal for the orientation of the building.

These findings suggest that, instead of concentrating solely on operational energy, the Building Regulations should include standards for embodied energy too, reflecting its growing significance in the development of UK housing.

Figure 3.3 Operational and total building savings in Ecopoints

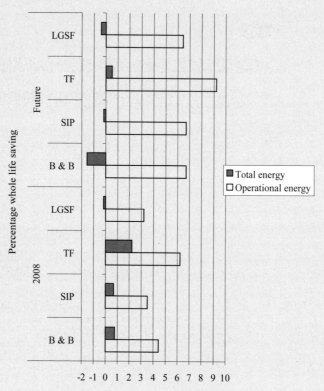

Source: David Tompson

If the future demand for housing were to be met by adopting timber frame or timber-based SIP construction rather than conventional brick and block, the UK could potentially save 4.4 million tonnes of CO_2 annually or over 400 million tonnes over a 100-year building life, see Figure 3.4. This is equal, annually, to 1.17% of the 60% target reduction in CO_2 emissions set by the government for the UK before 2050.[4]

continued ...

Ongoing research is needed to evaluate the effects of changing methods of construction and to investigate the interaction of embodied and operational energy in the refurbishment, demolition and replacement of existing housing.

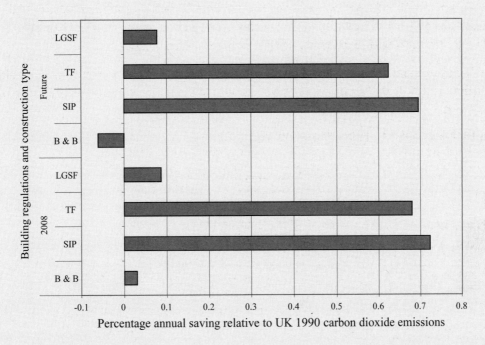

Source: David Tompson

Figure 3.4 Potential future CO$_2$ savings

1.   Cole, R. and Kernan, P., 'Life-Cycle Energy use in Office Buildings', *Building and Environment,* Vol. 31, No. 4. 1996. p. 307.
2.   BRECSU, *General Information Report 89. BedZED – Beddington Zero Energy Development, Sutton.* Energy Efficiency Best Practice programme, Watford, www.bioregional.com, 2002. p. 8.
3.   ODPM, *Current thinking on possible future amendments of energy efficiency provisions,* ODPM, www.odpm.gov.uk, Nov 2000.
4.   ODPM, *Proposals for amending Part L of the Building Regulations and Implementing the Energy Performance of Buildings Directive – A consultation document.* ODPM and www.odpm.gov.uk, London, July 2004. p. 5.

It is possible to justify an increase in embodied energy, over standard practice, if it improves operational energy efficiency sufficiently to decrease the overall energy consumption of a building. This can be the case with thermal mass, which has the potential for moderating room temperatures in passively heated buildings.

However, as can be seen from David Tompson's comments (Box 3.4), increased mass does not always deliver sufficient energy savings to be worthwhile, and so careful design is needed. When deciding on the amount of thermal mass to provide, considerations to be taken into account might be:

- The energy consumption of thermally massive buildings is highly dependent on orientation.

- As insulation levels increase, so does the embodied energy due to insulation materials and the structure needed to support it, with diminishing returns in terms of operational energy savings.

- There will be a step decrease in embodied energy as insulation levels reach that which allows a traditional heating system to be omitted.

For a building type that is more or less in continuous occupation, there are considerable advantages in using the mass of the construction to store solar energy inputs and to buffer the internal environment from the diurnal (and to a lesser degree longer period) external temperature fluctuations. Whether housing can still be considered to be a continuously occupied building type is open to debate. Households where all the adults leave the home to work are increasingly common, as are households where one or more people work from home.

At the same time, there is a move towards the production of more prefabricated building products, with the resulting possibility of increased quality control and decreased time on site. This mitigates in favour of lightweight building components such as the growing use of timber stud panels, with an outer skin of brick, or the more recent introduction of steel stud panelling in housing construction. These methods result in buildings with relatively low thermal mass and a consequently fast thermal response.

Given the increased tendency of heavily insulated buildings to overheat, and the inability of the construction to damp down the variations in temperature, the debate of 'heavyweight vs lightweight' is set to continue.

Table 3.4 Sustainability at BedZED

Site:	An overall density of 47 homes per hectare on site.
Structure:	6.3 m crosswalls with clear spanning pre-cast slabs gives flexibility in internal accommodation.
Materials:[i,ii,iii]	15% of construction materials at BedZED were reclaimed or recycled, and were cheaper or the same price as the conventional products.
	95% of structural steel on site was reclaimed,[1] with a cost saving of 4%.
	Reclaimed softwood joist and floorboards were used for mezzanine floors.
	Reclaimed timber was used for internal partitions.

	52% of construction materials were sourced from within a 35 mile radius of the site.
	The average material sourcing distance was 66.5 miles – 40 miles less than the national average.
	In situ concrete came from a batching plant just a few hundred metres away.
	Internal staircases are of locally sourced softwood.
Cost:[i,ii]	The overall expected cost was 1370–1470 £/m², 3.4 to 4.7% greater than that of a typical Peabody development (1000–1100 £/m²).
	Recycled aggregate and sand were cheaper than virgin products.
	Pre-stressed concrete saved time, money and materials.
	FSC certified green oak weatherboarding was cheaper than brick and, over its lifetime, imported preserved softwood.
Thermal performance:[i]	Passive solar design.
	Most housing glazing is placed for maximum sunlight penetration.
	Glazed sunspaces become open air balconies in summer to reduce the risk of over heating.
	Workspaces (with the greatest over-heating risk) are to the north of the houses (which have the least over heating risk).
	The construction is thermally massive, with concrete ceilings and tiled floors to store solar energy.
	North, east and west facing windows are low-e triple-glazed.
	Sunspaces are double glazed.
	Walls contain 300 mm of insulation.
	Two piece wall ties, able to span larger insulation gaps, were developed for the project.
	Airtight, super-insulated construction.
	Natural ventilation with heat recovery is used on site.
	Heat recovery, integrated into the wind cowls, is around 60% efficient.
Water:[i]	Low water use appliances and WCs are installed.
	Water-saving spray taps and showers are installed.
	Mains water for drinking, cooking and washing is metered.
	Water meters displayed in the kitchens of dwellings to encourage frugal water use.
	Rainwater is harvested and stored on site.
	Rainwater, grey and black water are treated on site and used for watering gardens and flushing WCs.
	Green water (rainwater and treated waste water) is coloured green to distinguish it from drinking water.
	18% of the BedZED residents' water consumption was estimated to be met by rainwater.

Energy:[i,iii,iv]	The total embodied energy was reduced by 12.5% by using timber windows rather than uPVC.
	PV panels are integrated into the construction.
	Heat and power come from a 135 kW CHP plant.
	Fuel for the CHP plant comes from carbon neutral tree waste from nearby London Boroughs.
	Theoretical SAP(1998) rating of 150.
Transport:[i,iv]	PVs feed electric car chargers on site, are sufficient for 40 cars.
	A car ownership pool reduces private car ownership.
	Parking is on the perimeter of the site, keeping the centre for pedestrians and cyclists.
	Cycle racks and shower facilities are provided for cyclists.
Lifestyle:[i,iv]	Residents are encouraged to recycle household waste.
	There is easy access to locally grown food.
	Two thirds affordable housing.
	Healthy living centre, sports pitch, crèche, café etc., on site.
Landscape:[i,iv]	A residents' handbook advises on the planting of garden spaces to promote bio-diversity.
	The planting on the roof gardens has been chosen to be to the liking of butterflies during the day, while night scented plants encourage bats.
	Roof gardens contain 300 mm of soil over a two-layer bituminous felt roof system.
	The buildings themselves have been detailed to provide habitat for sparrows and bat roosts within the weatherboarding, the sedum covered roofs encourage insect life (providing food for birds).
	Around the buildings existing features such as trees have been retained, while ditches have been developed to provide habitats for dragonflies and water voles.
	The eco-park, which is proposed for the adjoining site, is to include wetland and wooded habitats, park and play areas, and commercial horticulture such as the growing of lavender.

Note:

1. Reclaimed steel is preferable to recycled steel, where quality allows, as it is dismantled and then re-erected on site, whereas recycled steel undergoes energy intensive re-melting.

Sources:

i. *The BedZED Exhibition*, currently (2005) Bill Dunster Architects, available from www.surreycc.gov.uk, 2002.

ii. Lazarus, N., *Summary: Beddington Zero (Fossil) Energy Development – Construction Materials Report – Toolkit for Carbon Neutral Developments – Part 1*, BioRegional, www.bioregional.com, 2002.

iii. Lazarus, N., *Summary: Beddington Zero (Fossil) Energy Development – Toolkit for Carbon Neutral Developments – Part II*, BioRegional, www.bioregional.com, 2003.

iv. Dunster, B. & Carter, G., *General Information Report 89. BedZED – Beddington Zero Energy Development, Sutton*, Watford and www.bioregional.com, Energy Efficiency Best Practice programme, 2002.

In some cases, it may be possible to use some high-embodied-energy materials, while still reducing, or at least stabilising, the total embodied energy of a building. This is the case at the Beddington Zero (Fossil) Energy Development, BedZED. Here, not only is the demand for energy low (through the use of high levels of insulation etc.) but all the site's energy demands are met from carbon neutral sources. At the same time, the embodied CO_2[44] for the buildings is 675 $kgCO_2/m^2$ – in the lower half of the range for typical values for volume housing construction of 600–800 $kgCO_2/m^2$.[45] This reduction was made through the careful choice of all materials used, with local, recycled and low environmental impact ones being favoured.

BedZED addresses many of the issues regarding sustainable housing – materials, energy use, housing density, mixed uses, demographic and social change, transport and so on. Some of the measures taken to make the project more sustainable are listed in Table 3.4.

One of the main features of the site is that it is mixed use: 82 homes and 3000 m^2 of office space occupy the same area.[46] Having commercial space on site gave the Peabody Trust a source of potential income, on the promise of which they could develop the sustainable housing design[47] – a design which has been largely successful and has attracted awards such as RIBA's housing design award.[48]

For example, in terms of resource use reduction, the BedZED development has exceeded nearly all of its targets. During the first year, there was a reduction in space heating of 88% over the national average (the target was 90%).[49] Hot water consumption was reduced by 57%, electricity by 25% and mains water use by 50% – the target for all these had been to achieve one-third reduction – and fossil fuel car mileage was reduced by 65% (the target had been to halve it).[50]

Central to achieving sustainable communities is the question of transport. Already responsible for a third of the nation's energy consumption, transport is a growing energy use while the consumption of other sectors appears to have peaked. In addition, there are the many environmental effects of pollution, the stress caused by traffic noise, and the growing incidence of asthma (now affecting one in four school children) and traffic accidents which injure 1 in 15 children before reaching school leaving age.

The controversy about the appropriate pattern of development, given the seemingly inexorable growth of car usage, is ongoing. Mixed development that reduces the number of journeys, by creating the potential for work and home to be at the same location, and reducing the number of shopping journeys by encouraging smaller stores as a partial alternative to supermarkets, and facilitating home deliveries, are all measures that have been adopted at BedZED.

The architects believe that if all urban fabric that is replaced was built to BedZED standards the UK "could be carbon neutral by the start of the next century."[51] With the government aiming to reduce CO_2 emissions by 60% by 2050[52], and for new housing in future to be 'zero carbon', the ongoing development of ZEDs can only be welcomed.

2.2 Planning for climate change

Regulatory changes

As we saw in Chapter 2, domestic buildings account for about a third of the UK's annual energy consumption. The government maintains that the 2006 amendment to the Building Regulations will produce around a 25% increase in a new dwelling's energy efficiency and a concomitant reduction in CO_2 emissions.[53][54]

The new Regulations are to increase efficiency not only through decreasing U-values – for which there is an optimum value which depends on the monetary value that society gives to CO_2 emissions savings – but also through other measures, such as MVHR, improved controls, solar shading and solar water heating and improving the existing standards for artificial lighting and airtightness.[55][56] Obviously there are social benefits, such as decreasing fuel poverty, that go beyond the climate change benefits.

The regulations have therefore moved away from showing compliance through the old elemental method and target U-value method to proof of performance being assessed by the SAP.[57] A similar move is being made for showing compliance for non-domestic buildings as is required by the EU's Energy Performance of Buildings Directive (EPBD).[58] Like the UK, other European countries have an old, inefficient, building stock – hence the EPBD.

Improving the energy efficiency of new buildings is not the whole answer, however, so the Regulations will ensure that:

- the majority of new domestic boilers will be high efficiency condensing ones (with a SEDBUK rating of A or B)[59]
- the energy efficiency of an old dwelling will have to be increased when renovation/refurbishment happens (depending on a cost-effectiveness assessment).[60][61]

In the future it is likely that the Building Regulations will come to cover embodied energy[62] as well as increasing requirements for existing buildings.[63] The government is likely to look for an increase in performance of around 20–30% at each review of Part L.[64] This might mean a change in indicative U-values from:

- 0.27 to 0.20 W/m^{2}K for walls, between 2005 and 2010
- 0.13 to 0.10 W/m^{2}K for roofs
- 0.22 to 0.20 W/m^{2}K for floors
- 1.80 to 1.40 W/m^{2}K for windows.[65]

Airtightness and other standards are set to become more stringent too.[66] We should also note that refurbishment of existing buildings can be very efficient in terms of embodied energy, although the gains in terms of performance are lower.

Living with flood risks

The damage caused by recent flash floods (thankfully mostly to property rather than people) has served to highlight their enormously destructive force and potential to cause havoc, not only in the UK[67] but around the world.[68] Changing storms patterns are set to cause widespread damage as a result of climate change,[69] with both the depth of the water and the speed of the water producing damage.

Obviously the most sensible thing to do is not to build on land that is on a river's flood plain or which is at risk of coastal flooding; but, of course, life isn't that simple. Existing communities lie on land at risk, with around 1.7 million homes being affected.[70] When considering housing, the danger posed by flooding can be reduced by employing a sustainable urban drainage system (SUDS), for example:

- stopping floods before they start (or reducing the severity), i.e. reducing the peak storm-water load on surface water drainage, either by reducing the run-off to begin with (e.g. by reducing hard surfaces in landscaped areas) or by intercepting water before it reaches the storm drains, through the use of catchment ponds, water meadows etc.
- stopping the flood water from getting to the buildings, through the use of flood defences. This may be as simple as locating the building on the higher part of a site or with more complex flood barriers (though be wary of increasing the risk of flooding elsewhere, and take into account the great speed[71] of flood water that will occur if the defence is breached or the flood waters rise above the level of the defences)

- planning buildings so that minimal damage is caused; this might be by making sure the main accommodation (and services equipment such as electricity meters and distribution boxes) is well above ground level, plus ensuring that finishes in areas which will be inundated aren't likely to be damaged; or, as a final resort
- moving existing developments to a safer area.

2.3 How much insulation?

In an 'ideal' climate we wouldn't need insulation at all. We would need roofs – to keep out the rain and bird guano – and walls to keep our possessions in (by keeping burglars out), but insulation would just lead to any heat gains staying in the building and presenting an overheating risk. Any deviation in outside temperatures away from the 'ideal' would make insulation progressively more useful: if it's colder outside, you want to keep the heat in and if it's very much warmer, you want to keep it out. This is a huge oversimplification, of course, but it illustrates why some people think that the warming of the UK climate (i.e. a move towards a warmer 'ideal' climate) means that we should be putting less, not more, insulation in our walls. However:

- depending on the construction, insulation can be difficult to install in existing buildings (loft insulation is easy, cavity wall insulation is limited by the existing cavity width)
- the thermal risks of over-insulation are low
- the thermal risks of under insulation are high (since peak summer temperatures are set to increase and mean winter temperatures may decrease)[72]
- insulation is relatively inexpensive and can be low in embodied energy, although very thick insulation can have structural implications (which can be overcome – for example, the bespoke wall ties at BedZED).

Insulation thicknesses should therefore probably be of the order of those in the 'ZED' standard, i.e. 0.10 W/m^{2}K.[73] For a brick and block wall, the insulation thicknesses for various materials is given in Table 3.5.

Table 3.5 Approximate insulation thicknesses to achieve 'ZED' standard (i.e. 0.1 W/m²K)

Insulation material	Insulation thickness required,(mm) for a 102 mm brick, 50 mm cavity, insulation, 100 mm lightweight concrete block, 12.5 mm lightweight plaster wall.
Mineral wool, rigid slab	550
Sheep's wool	500
Expanded polystyrene board	410
Polyurethane foam	290
TRI-ISO SUPER 9	3 sheets*

Notes: All thicknesses were calculated using data from *CIBSE Guide A - Design Data*, 5th Edn, St Albans, 1988, except for * which is a very approximate value deduced from www.enigma-insulations.co.uk

Box 3.5 The Hockerton Project

In 1996,[1] construction began on the Hockerton Housing Project, the UK's first[2] earth-sheltered autonomous housing project. The 10-hectare site, owned by a sustainable housing cooperative of five families, is used to provide organically grown food, and contains a lake for aquaculture.

The terrace of houses is dug into a south-facing slope, with the excavated earth being used on the green roofs. The houses are designed as solar houses, and have no heating system as such.[3]

In front of the houses runs a long sunspace, separated from the main accommodation by a series of pairs of glazed doors. This is part of the solar heating strategy, which relies on the building having low fabric and ventilation heat losses and high thermal mass.

Fabric and ventilation heat losses

The buildings have 300 mm of CFC-free expanded polystyrene.[4] The sunspace is glazed in low-e double glazing, with softwood frames, with aluminium glazing bars in the roof. The doors between the sunspace and the rest of the building are argon-filled, triple-glazed and have two low-e coatings.

The houses have mechanical ventilation with heat recovery (MVHR) which is intended to be used mostly in winter. Fresh air is drawn from the conservatories and so has solar pre-heating during the day.

Thermal mass

The inner faces of the external envelope of the buildings are of 300 mm thick concrete, while the internal walls are of 200 mm concrete, providing plenty of thermal mass to store solar thermal energy. Usually, thermal mass is used to even out diurnal temperature fluctuations. At Hockerton, not only does the thermal mass mean that daily temperature fluctuations are less than half a degree but the mass (around 2.3 tonnes/m²) is also used to store warmth garnered in the summer to heat the building in winter. Winter temperatures drop to no lower than 18°C while summer temperatures do not exceed 23°C.

continued …

The concrete used for thermal mass has a relatively high embodied energy, but this was minimised by using concrete blocks that were made just six miles away.[5] Other materials for the houses were sourced locally, and much of the labour came from the future residents. Several hundred native trees were also planted on site, which slightly mitigates the effect of the embodied energy in, and pollution caused by, the construction materials.[6]

The impact of the buildings on the environment is also reduced by careful servicing design.

The only water supply to the houses is rainwater, with the glass conservatory roofs providing drinking water, which is filtered and treated with UV light. Hot water is generated by a heat pump. Wastewater is treated on site by a septic tank and water treatment pond.

The site has two 5 kW grid-connected wind turbines (this removes the need for batteries) and a 7.6 kW PV array. These charge the site's electric car.

1. Vale, Robert, *Housing project – Hockerton*. www.greenhouse.gov.au, Australian Greenhouse Office – Department of the Environment and Heritage (2004). p. 6.
2. *An Index of Initiatives for Building Homes as if Tomorrow Matters*, London, RIBA, 1997. p. 31.
3. Some houses have wood-burning stoves in the conservatories to provide occasional heating for parties, etc., see *op. cit.* Vale, 2004, p. 3.
4. Polystyrene is an organic polymer with the chemical formula $(C_8H_8)_n$.
5. *op. cit.* RIBA, 1997, p. 31.
6. *ibid.*
7. www.hockerton.demon.co.uk

2.4 Increasing density – reducing physical footprints

Incredibly, one of the greatest changes in terms of different housing types has been that a greater proportion of households now live in detached houses: an increase from 16% in 1971 to 22% in 2002.[74] Yet this is a country where over 80%[75] of us live in cities!

Is the increase in the proportion of detached homes an inevitable consequence of the aspirations of the increasing number of homeowners?[76] Certainly, at the moment, flats/apartments are more likely to be inhabited by households in the social sector than by either private renters or owner occupiers: a tiny 7%[77] of homeowners live in flats.

When one thinks of flats, it is easy to think of the failure of mass housing projects in the 1960s and 1970s rather than of the highly desirable mansion flats of Kensington. But this is a prejudice that we need to overcome: on our crowded island we are rapidly running out of space in which to put low-density housing, quite apart from the environmental damage caused by cars which take people from their suburban home to work. We only need to look at the sophisticated apartment lifestyles that we see on the continent to see that denser cities are a viable possibility.

That this chapter follows the one concerning single houses is deliberate. Rather than looking at houses in isolation, it is vital that we look at houses in context: a house's location and surrounding built environment can have an enormous effect on the way in which it is used and its consequential environmental impact.

In fact, both of the case studies in Chapter 2 do take account of wider issues. The Hawkes house increases urban density by occupying a site which previously provided gardens for nearby houses. It is also within easy cycling distance of Cambridge town centre, with its shops and services.

The Red House occupies part of the site where Alan Tye's home and studio already stand. It is an excellent study in the live–work principle: the occupants need only walk across the garden to reach the design studio, and there are facilities within the house for a home office too.

The Hockerton Project, though it consists of five houses, is perhaps nearer to the original philosophy of autonomous houses (discussed in Box 2.6), than either of these. The difference between 'autonomous' schemes and 'sustainable' communities is that, while the first aim to be as self-contained as possible, 'sustainable' schemes aim to reduce their environmental footprint.

The problems for housing design in the future are both environmental and societal. We need to find a way of decreasing our 'environmental footprint' and we need to find it fast. At the same time, we need to find ways of doing it that don't hinder flourishing communities.

2.5 Eco-footprinting

The embodied energy/CO_2 of their homes is obviously not the only impact that a home's residents will have. A person's 'eco-footprint' is the proportion of the Earth's surface that is required to support them, not just in terms of energy, but for oxygen, food, water, pharmaceuticals, space and the materials to make the consumables they buy.

Bill Dunster Architects looked at the idea of 'eco-footprinting', when they were working on the BedZED project, and they concluded that if all of the people on the planet were to have an equivalent lifestyle to those in the UK, three Earths would be needed to support them. This is clearly unsustainable, so two solutions – one light green (a transitional lifestyle, with an eco-footprint of two planets) and one dark green (an ideal lifestyle, with an eco-footprint of one planet) – were proposed, see Table 3.6.

Table 3.6 Green lifestyles – reducing our eco-footprints

	Light green:	Dark green:
Home	Live in a sustainable development, such as BedZED.	Live and work in a sustainable development, such as BedZED.
Travel	Commute to work by public transport. Limit travel by private car. Only use air travel once a year for holidays.	Use only a car-pool electric car for car travel. Use air travel for holidays only once in every two years.
Waste	Recycle 60 % of waste.	Recycle 80 % of domestic waste. Recycle office paper.
Food	Moderate meat consumption.* Limit consumption of imported foods. Eat local food, in season.	Low meat diet. Eat local food, in season.

Notes: * Meat takes a greater area of land to produce than vegetables and grains

Source: Adapted from data from *The BedZED Exhibition*, Bill Dunster Architects, www.surreycc.gov.uk, 2002.

2.6 Volumetric

The forms of buildings which are emerging from the sustainability debate differ greatly. On one hand are heavyweight buildings, with construction that relies on local skills and materials, typified by the Hockerton Project and BedZED. On the other are lightweight buildings (which may be preferable in terms of overall energy use – see earlier in the chapter), produced with an increasing degree of prefabrication.

History

As we will investigate the use of standardised and prefabricated components has great potential in the building of sustainable housing, though it has a slightly chequered history.

The industrial revolution was fuelled in part by technological advances that allowed for the mass production of products of increasing complexity and of assured quality. This move away from fabrication by artisans has allowed the production of items as intricate as the computer and the modern car at prices that consumers are willing to pay. In 2002, more than half of all households in the UK had access to a computer at home (most of these have internet access) and nearly three-quarters have access to a car or van.[78]

Although modern houses will contain relatively sophisticated items, such as condensing boilers, they have almost all been built by skilled tradespersons. A construction site offers nowhere near the potential for quality control or standardisation that can be achieved in a factory, even when a number of 'identical' houses are being built.

Despite this, there has been interest in increasing mechanisation of the construction process since quite early in the 20th century. Lightweight system designs were investigated by designers such as Jean Prouvé and Buckminster Fuller, and modern examples include crane-installed bathroom/kitchen pods.[79]

Changing perceptions

Many of the post-war prefabs are well loved, even today. However, poorly designed products of 1960s 'system building' badly marred the reputation of housing prefabrication and this has given rise to a lingering perception that the

---

Box 3.6 Murray Grove

Murray Grove in Hackney, designed by Cartwright Pickard architects for the Peabody Trust, occupies a corner site flanked by busy roads. It consists of 30 key-worker flats with one or two bedrooms, with a striking lift tower at the intersection of the two wings of the building.

The kitchens, bathrooms and entrances to the flats face the roads and protect the living rooms and bedrooms from traffic noise and pollution. Each flat has a balcony, off the living areas, overlooking the communal garden.

All the units were steel framed 'boxes' which were bolted together on site. Each module provides support for its upstairs neighbours and together they form the structure of the building. The internal walls were pre-finished with plasterboard on the inside and galvanised steel sheet on the outside, with foam insulation injected between. On the roadside façades, a rainscreen of terracotta tiles was fixed on site to an aluminium support grid, while on the garden side the cladding is western red cedar. Here, full height sliding doors bring light and air into the rooms and allow access to the balconies. This form of construction led to a nearly scaffold-free site.

The access walkways were made separately: storey-high steel tube columns (at 3190 mm centres[1]) were spigot jointed above floor level where a welded steel plate is bolted to parallel flange channels (PFCs) supporting the outer edge of the precast concrete walkways. The inner edges have pockets which allow them to be bolted to the modules, and conduit for the walkway's lighting was cast in too. The balconies were made in a similar way to the walkways.

1. Larger spans can be made, such as at Raines Dairy where the modules are on a 3805 mm (w) by 11802 mm (l) grid, although here the balconies are part of the module. Measurements from plans supplied by Yorkon.

prefabrication concept itself was at fault. Owner-occupiers, for whom a house is an enormous purchase and investment, have been particularly chary even though many of the earlier problems have been overcome, a reluctance that has also been seen in the European market.

Housing associations, however, seem cautiously optimistic: for their large projects, the advantages of the use of repeatable units are clear. There are many recent examples of developments with varying degrees of prefabrication, such as the Cartwright Pickard designed Murray Grove (Hackney), and Sixth Avenue Apartments (York) and Alford Hall Monaghan Morris' Raines Dairy (Hackney for the Peabody Trust).

It seems that in the future the market is likely to take its cue from the car industry and move towards 'mass customisation' and 'lean production' to make inroads into the housing market, where consumers wish to customise their investment to their own taste. The expectation of consumer choice has already permeated the Japanese housing market where kit houses manufactured by car companies such as Toyota have the range of options expected of Toyota's cars.

Advantages of prefabrication

Affordability and key-worker housing
Hastening the progress of prefabrication is about much more than a desire to improve build quality. It is seen as a way of quickly building affordable key-worker housing and of helping to solve the housing crisis in the South East.[80][81]

The linchpin of the government's recent programme to increase the number of homes being built for what it calls 'key workers' – those on whom we depend but whose incomes are unlikely to allow them to live near their place of work – is the proposal for prefabricated homes.

Build where others can't
Because factory-produced housing is relatively light in weight, recent proposals have included inhabited bridges over waterways and railway lines[82] – an ancient idea revisited.[83]

Fast construction
For example, at Cartwright Pickard's 6th Avenue in York construction took less than half the time the client would normally expect, with a consequential saving in land finance costs.[84] Plus the off-site construction means that vulnerable interiors and insulation[85] are only exposed to the vagaries of the British climate for a minimal period.

Reducing time on site also reduces the impact of the construction on the site and the neighbours. Traffic to the site is decreased as is the impact of noise. Because foundations can be less extensive than with traditional construction, the building impacts less on the drainage patterns on site.

Increased space

James Pickard believes that using modular construction allows Cartwright Pickard Architects to design homes with 10% more usable interior space than the norm.[86]

Increased thermal efficiency

The projected decreased running costs (due to increased insulation – Yorkon estimates their 2002 housing system should use 20% less energy than those designed to meet the 1995 Building Regulations[87]) should be taken into account when considering the, currently, higher construction costs.

In fact, thermal efficiency is not the only sustainability aspect of factory housing, as Lizzie Babister explores (Box 3.7).

Box 3.7 Sustainable aspects of modular housing

Lizzie Babister, while at the Martin Centre for Urban and Architectural Studies, University of Cambridge

Modular construction has a number of characteristics that lend it to being a sustainable construction method.

Efficient use of materials through repetition of units

Modular construction is appropriate to buildings that require a high degree of repetition. This can be sustainable because repetition demands an efficient supply system. Orders can be placed for a large amount of the same material formed into the same shapes.

Efficient use of materials through highly controlled processes

The repetition of construction processes can lead to high quality results, because workers are able to become specialists, and tolerances can be improved. However, the removal of the construction process from site can lead to a lack of understanding about how the modules relate to the final building, unless those involved are familiar with building construction. In practice, workmanship and the efficiency of materials use are only as good as the worker and the supervisor: factory production itself is no guarantee of high quality.

continued …

Efficient use of site area owing to narrower wall and floor sections

Modules can be built so that structure and insulation are integrated so narrower wall and floor sections can be achieved than with traditional construction. This allows for more usable space in plan and section, and potentially more efficient use of the site. However, not all modules are built in this way, so the assumption cannot be made that space will be saved simply through modular construction.

Reduction in wet trades

Factory construction usually uses dry trades that, in conjunction with waste management, can be very efficient. Dry alternatives to wet processes can use less energy, but the embodied energy of the materials, and their contribution to overall energy consumption, should also be taken into consideration.

For example, cement mixing for brickwork uses a higher level of energy than installing lightweight steel framing. However, the embodied energy involved in making brick is less than that involved in making steel so this may cancel out the energy saved at construction stage. Also, pressure from a planning authority may result in the use of brickwork as cladding, the installation of which re-introduces wet trades.

Lightweight units using less energy to lift them into place

Modular units made from lightweight steel sections are designed to be transported on articulated lorries and to be craned into place. This repetitive method enables very rapid erection of the building. Savings in energy are even greater with larger projects.

Recyclable

Modular units can usually be recycled in part or as a whole. A significant amount can be salvaged from any one building, depending upon the materials and how they have been joined. A steel structure can be dismantled easily. Windows can also be detached if they are screwfixed. However, interiors are often finished in a similar way to traditional buildings so their recycling may be no easier.

Whole modules are generally bolted together so they can be taken apart easily, allowing for the recycling of entire rooms. An entire hotel was once dismantled in this way and transported on the back of lorries to a different site, where it was rebuilt and reclad.

Summary

Modular construction has certain characteristics that lend it to being a sustainable construction method, but is not inherently sustainable. For this reason, it is important that sustainability is a key aim so that the modular process can be partnered with a carefully chosen workforce and suitable materials to exploit its sustainable characteristics.

Disadvantages of prefabrication

Societal

There are, of course, disadvantages to prefabrication. Some are physical, and so may be addressed by new technology and good design, and others are social and are more difficult to quantify and to resolve. Certainly, there are some who view increasing mechanisation and a decreasing involvement of skilled crafts-people in much the same way that William Morris and his contemporaries viewed the increase in mechanisation of the production of other consumables.[88] This is something of a chicken-and-egg situation: increasing mechanisation means a decrease in the demand for skilled labour which means the number of craftspeople decreases and the price for them increases, which leads to calls for increasing mechanisation!

Research has identified a number of consumer views which are hostile to the success of prefabrication methods in relation to housing:[89]

- The housing market appears to be inherently aesthetically conservative.
- People equate 'prefabs' with poor quality (an apparently historical association).
- Traditional construction appears to be seen as more 'durable'.

However, given that the modular housing at Murray Grove is valued to be more expensive than the average for the area,[90] there is certainly hope that these negative perceptions can change. On the continent, prefabricated housing is much more accepted, for example the Ikea/Skanska-developed 'Bo Klok' housing,[91] and in Japan up to 40% of housing is built using prefabricated units.[92]

Physical

Thermal risks: There are inherent thermal bridging and vapour control issues to be addressed when working with steel framed and clad units. Manufacturers such as Yorkon believe they have solved the major problems through materials choice and detailing, which was the subject of a research contract at Oxford Brookes University.[93]

Prefabricated buildings tend to be low in thermal mass, partly because of the transport mentioned above. Because of this, and the good standards of insulation, there is a danger of summer overheating. These risks can be reduced by careful design. Cross-ventilation, such as at Allford Hall Monaghan Morris' Raines Dairy development in London,[94] and at Murray Grove,[95] can help as can shading windows with projecting balconies or overhanging roofs.

Price: The price differential between traditional and factory construction, currently favouring traditional construction by around 10%, can be expected to reduce if increased demand leads to an increase in manufacturing capacity. It could be argued that prefabricated buildings already represent better value because building costs for traditional construction do not automatically take into account the making good of defects etc.[96]

Inflexibility: A significant problem is also the perceived inherent inflexibility of prefabricated units – the modifications that changing family needs might require would not necessarily be possible, nor would much of the customisation that building occupants seek to stamp on their own home.

However, prefabrication does not necessarily mean modular units. Building components of various sizes, from window frames and bathroom 'pods' through to large chunks of buildings, can all be prefabricated and so could be incorporated into a more traditionally built home. An increase in demand for prefabricated components would also be likely to stimulate manufacturers to provide a wider range of designs too.

Transport embodied energy: Having building parts assembled in a factory setting, though good for build quality, has implications for transportation emissions. The potential change in transport energy required during manufacture (and so the component's embodied energy) has not been reliably enumerated.

This is also an issue that is likely to be addressed by an increasing number of manufacturing plants, but the limited potential for using reclaimed materials is unlikely to change. There is also a legal restriction on the size of units which can be transported by road, which also potentially limits design.[97]

2.7 Framed and clad

A framed and clad building is just what it says: both framed and clad. The underlying construction can be used to support a number of different building layouts and façade treatments. In some types, such as structural insulated panel system (SIPS), discussed below, the framing and cladding are combined.

Reusing office buildings

Older office buildings, constructed before the 1980s, had only domestic scale floor-to-floor heights, making them unsuitable for the volume of servicing (cable, ducts and pipes contained within suspended ceilings and raised floors) that modern air-conditioned offices demand. During the recession in the early 1990s pressure was taken off the office market. As a result, many unsuitable, empty and redundant existing offices, and some half-finished buildings, were converted to housing.

Because of their heritage as office buildings, where space needs to be flexible to accommodate changing tenants, these structures can contain many different types of dwelling. Compared to the rigidity of volumetric construction, which combines dwelling plans from a repetitive module, frame structures have the great advantage of being inherently reconfigurable:

- A frame stripped back to the structure can readily be reclad to transform the building from business to home.
- In the same way, a frame initially used for family housing could be further converted to starter flats or sheltered housing.
- Small studio flats can become larger apartments.
- Concrete columns can easily be concealed within blockwork partitions.
- The 16-metre standard depth of these blocks readily lends itself to a double-loaded corridor with artificially serviced kitchens and bathrooms at the centre of the block.
- Housing requires relatively little pipework and few ducts. These can be concealed (above a false ceiling) under the flat plate concrete structure commonly used for office buildings.

Every time the frame is reclaimed/reused in a new re-embodiment of the building, an embodied energy equal to that of the underlying structure is saved. This saves more energy, and reduces more environmental impacts than just reclaiming (or recycling) the materials themselves.

With reuse of any resource, you need to cut your clothes to suit your cloth: an air-conditioned office is unlikely to have been planned with passive solar, or other low-energy strategies in mind.

The concrete slab floors also have a great deal of thermal mass. This may be useful in an office with high heat gains from ICT equipment, but is not necessarily useful for dwellings with variable access to solar gains. We will consider the servicing implications of non-optimum solar orientation later in the chapter.

An existing building may also have other problems such as proximity to a noisy main road. As this can be an issue with any brownfield (or indeed greenfield) site, we should probably not stress this as too much of a disadvantage in comparison to other construction options.

Structural insulated panel systems (SIPS)

For traditional construction, increasing insulation means accommodating ever-increasing thickness in walls and roofs. New types of components are then needed, such as the longer wall ties that are required to bridge the expanding width of cavity.

SIPSs adopt a different approach. Instead of the functions of the wall being separated out between different materials and components, SIPSs are composite stressed panels, having inner and outer surfaces made from a timber sheathing board such as orientated strand board (OSB), with a bonded layer of insulation between them.

The resulting construction is remarkably slender and lightweight in comparison to traditional constructions, meaning that foundations need not be so extensive.[98]

Box 3.8 Reclaimed materials

Of the 70 million tonnes of waste that leaves building sites each year, approximately three-quarters is recycled, but as lower grade material.[1]

While this does reduce the amount of waste that goes to landfill, recycling can be an energy intensive process (such as when steel is re-melted). It is better if the waste can be reused (reclaimed) with relatively little processing – although the best solution would have been to take steps to reduce the amount of waste from the outset.

A flourishing architectural salvage trade exists for high value components: fireplaces, staircases, reclaimed wood panelling and even sanitaryware. Salvage for bulk materials such as bricks, timber, steel sections and concrete aggregate is less well developed.

Despite this, reclaimed materials are being used in housing projects. At BedZED, 95% of the steel used was reclaimed. The overall savings were a 3.8% reduction in the development's total eco-footprint and a 4% cost saving (compared to using new steel).

The engineers specified a range of sizes for steel members, that could be used according to availability, with varying connection details. When steel comes from an existing building that is being demolished, quantities of any given size of component may be limited, and lead times may be long, so it pays to be flexible. It turned out that most of the reused steel was in good condition, requiring just one extra pass through the grit blaster before being zinc coated.

Recycled materials can also give cost savings. The crushed glass used at BedZED, as a substitute for sand was 15% cheaper, and the 2002 aggregates tax would give even greater cost savings today.

1. Lazarus, N., *Summary: Beddington Zero (Fossil) Energy Development – Construction Materials Report – Toolkit for Carbon Neutral Developments – Part 1*, BioRegional, www.bioregional.com, 2002, p. 5.

Typically, these systems use expanded polyurethane foam (now manufactured without CFCs and HCFCs) to easily achieve a U-value of 0.2 W/m²K. Although the panels have low thermal mass, this can be overcome, where needed, by thermally heavyweight floors, for example concrete beam and block. Patent jointing methods ensure that a high level of airtightness is achieved, down to 1.6 ach (at 50 Pa), and reduce ventilation heat losses too. However, this is a new type of product, and the long-term airtightness isn't yet proven.

At present there are a limited number of manufacturers of SIPS in the UK, but this can be expected to increase if the concept proves popular.

Rendered insulation

The market pressure that created SIPS is for wall systems that simplify the construction process. Polymer-modified render, introduced from the continent, also does this. The insulation is fixed to a blockwork structure and is then sealed with a thin layer of impervious render. This avoids both the frequent panel joints required in render façades, and space-consuming wall cavities.

Care does need to taken to design out condensation problems with this, as with any impervious coating. Render, in conjunction with timber frame is common in the US,[99] but the humid climate of the UK and the extent of timber's differential movement must raise concerns about the durability of these composite constructions.

Stud panel construction

During the 1970s, timber framing captured an increasing proportion of the new housing market, but negative publicity about its standard of site assembly reduced its popularity in the 1980s.[100] However, during the 1990s the market share increased again, approaching 20% in 2002,[101] with the method being particularly well established in Scotland.

Box 3.9 Timber engineering products

Timber engineering products are gradually achieving acceptance in the UK. Since the panels can be used to construct roofs, as well as walls, the system offers an alternative to the space-wasting trussed rafters that have been the norm.

Trussed rafters are themselves an established factory prefabricated technology: it is common to see them on the back of a lorry trundling from factory to building site. With the increasing use of roof spaces as rooms they have the disadvantage of extreme inflexibility, with elements of the truss intruding into the roof space.

The latest versions rely to a greater extent on the prefabrication of panels in a factory. Panel jointing details are particular to each manufacturer, resulting in closed systems that can accommodate design requirements for window and door openings, and can be combined with beam and block floors, and alternative roof structures.

A parallel development has been the increasing use of steel cold-formed studs as an accurate and higher strength alternative to timber framing. Already much used for internal partitions, light gauge steel framing (LGSF) is the preferred option for the manufacture of modular units because of its stiffness and reduced weight, but it is also used for roof extensions, overcladding and infill walling. Obviously, care needs to be taken to design-out cold bridging risks.

Box 3.10 Sealed wall vs breathing wall

Condensation problems can be the Achilles heel of housing. There are two potential problems: structural damage and health risks. The risks to health are relatively slight, although there are some worries about a possible link with asthma.[1]

The risks of structural damage depend on where the condensation forms. Surface condensation, such as the misting that forms on bathroom windows does not usually have major structural implications. Finishes may need to be renewed more frequently, although damage can be minimised by good ventilation.

Although the surface condensation is relatively harmless, interstitial condensation can corrode through fittings, potentially causing structural collapse. Because interstitial condensation has particularly damaging effects on timber-framed walls the 'breathing'[2] wall may be a suitable alternative.

The usual plywood outer sheathing to timber framed walls is highly vapour resistant, and this prevents the escape of moisture. With a breathing wall the most vapour resistant layer, logically, moves to the inside face of the wall. For example, in the form of foil-backed plasterboard. A alternative, breathable, outer sheathing (such as bitumen-impregnated fibreboard) is substituted for the plywood. This provides structural bracing while allowing water vapour to escape.

The same principle can be applied to a variety of constructions including where timber frames form the inner leaf of a brick-faced cavity wall. The term 'breathing' is, however, typically associated with stud walls comprising shredded newsprint insulation within masonite or plyweb studs. The studs provide the width required to accommodate the insulation. The 'Warmcell™' insulation is blown wet between the studs and adheres to them when dry, achieving a surprisingly airtight construction.

1. *The Building Act 1984, The Building Regulations 2000, Review of Approved Document F – Ventilation, A consultation package*, www.odpm.gov.uk, ODPM/HMSO, London, July 2004, p. 31.
2. The term 'breathing' is used here in the same way as for breathable clothing, and has nothing to do with respiration.

Small unit cladding systems

As a result of the advantages of prefabricated systems – reduced thickness of the structural envelope and fast construction – new types of dry cladding using small units are being developed.

Often attempting to replicate the appearance of brickwork, these brick, or brick-and-render tiles are hung from a support panel with fixing at the centres of the cladding units. Although involving individual fixing, these methods can contribute to a fast-track building programme.

...and underneath, a precast foundation system

Precast and prestressed concrete ground beams are designed to span between concrete piles. The resulting substructure can be combined with beam and block flooring, and it achieves accurate and fast construction with only a limited amount of ground disturbance. This make it particularly suitable for brownfield sites where there are likely to be obstructions in the ground.

3. Generic construction methods

3.1 Typical UK mass housing construction

Figure 3.5 Typical UK housing construction

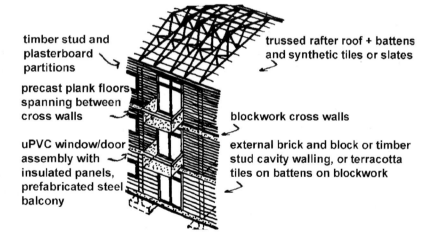

timber stud and plasterboard partitions

precast plank floors spanning between cross walls

uPVC window/door assembly with insulated panels, prefabricated steel balcony

trussed rafter roof + battens and synthetic tiles or slates

blockwork cross walls

external brick and block or timber stud cavity walling, or terracotta tiles on battens on blockwork

- *Blockwork cross walls, or loadbearing walls of brick and block*
- *or timber/steel stud + brick cavity walling,*
- *or terracotta tiles on battens on blockwork*

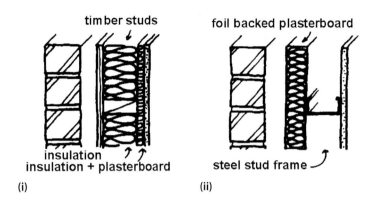

timber studs

foil backed plasterboard

insulation
insulation + plasterboard

steel stud frame

(i)

(ii)

Figure 3.6 (i) Timber stud + brick cladding, (ii) steel stud/frame + brick cladding

Both of these framing structures are light and consequently have an advantage over heavy masonry. They are also quick to install on site, because inner walls can largely be prefabricated in a factory before fitting on site.

Where steel stud is used, aluminium-foil-backed insulation is located to the outside of the frame. The foil acts as a vapour control layer on the room side and to control radiative heat loss to the cavity on the external side. Flexible wall ties are required because of the different expansion characteristics of the various components. These bridge both the insulation and the foil backing, forming cold bridges.

Cold bridging is a disadvantage where timber studwork is used too: insulation is installed between the timber members, which then act as cold bridges. This can be overcome by using an insulated lining bonded to the back of the plasterboard. The vapour control layer in this case is also bonded to the back of the plasterboard. Unfortunately, this is liable to be damaged by nails and during the installation of electrical outlets.

Both frame types are therefore at risk of condensation damage, though careful detailing and installation can minimise risk.

Again the type of insulation has little effect on the overall rating of the structure (with the usual proviso regarding ozone depletion).

The BRE rating for both structures is an 'A'.[102]

- *Roof: Trussed rafter roof + battens and synthetic tiles or slates*

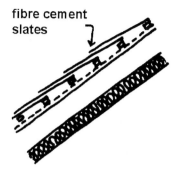

fibre cement slates

Figure 3.7 Fibre cement or polymer resin slate pitched roof

Neither fibre cement nor polymer slates perform particularly well in terms of their environmental rating, mostly because of the relatively large amount of energy used in their production.

Fibre cement is economical in terms of cost, though life expectancies are lower than for traditional tiles. They may be recycled, but currently few are. The environmental rating is a 'B'.[103]

Polymer/resin bonded slates have a low rating ('C'[104]) because of their poor performance in terms of recycling and because of the large amounts of fossil fuels used in their manufacture.

- *Floors: precast planks/block and beam spanning between cross walls for separating floors*

Figure 3.8 Concrete floors: (i) beam and block, (ii) prestressed concrete planks

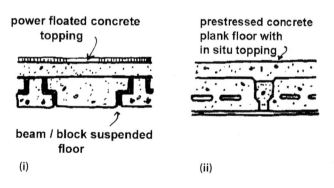

power floated concrete topping

beam / block suspended floor

(i)

prestressed concrete plank floor with in situ topping

(ii)

- *Glazing: u-PVC windows/insulated panels, prefabricated steel balcony*

u-PVC windows have won an increasing proportion of the market in recent years; indeed, they dominate the replacement window market. Their perceived advantages are the potential for very low maintenance requirements and an increased thermal performance.

In practice, the thermal advantages are unimpressive. The material lacks structural stiffness and so the frame becomes bulky, resulting in a smaller glazed opening and lower daylight levels. Steel is used within the window as reinforcement, and this impairs their thermal performance.

Their overall performance rates a 'C',[105] which is explained by their energy-intensive manufacture along with heavy metal and potential dioxin pollution from the process. (The chlorine in PVC is responsible for dioxin formation.) In addition, PVC is not recyclable, and recycled materials cannot be used in its manufacture. Indeed, PVC's environmental credentials are so poor that many pressure groups are campaigning for a ban on its use altogether.

- *Internal partitions: blockwork or stud + plasterboard*

Table 3.7 Ecopoints evaluation of generic constructions for houses, using BRE's Envest tool

Generic house type: 12m × 6m (ground and upper floors each 72 sq m); no. storeys: 3; storey height: 2.8 m; % cellular: 80%; location: S.E. England; soil type: firm clay		Ecopoints	%
		Ecopoints	**%**
Ground floor	Precast concrete 150mm + 50mm topping + 80mm rockwool	170	10.5
Upper floor	Precast concrete 150mm + 50mm topping	238	14.7
External walls	Inner leaf of 75 x 38mm studs + 12.5mm plasterboard + rockwool + outer leaf of brick	167	10.3
Internal partitions	75 x 50mm stud + 12.5 mm plasterboard	12	0.7
Windows	u-PVC double glazed	115	7.1
Roof	Pitched timber with gables + purlins 1.4m c/c, 0.75kN/m² loading	5	0.3
	Synthetic slates + 150mm rockwool insulation	119	7.4
Floors	10% 2mm vinyl	18	1.1
	90% 5mm composite wood block	289	17.8
	Sub-total	307	19

Wall finishes	10% 6.5mm ceramic tiles		25	1.5
	90% skim plaster + emulsion		44	2.7
		Sub-total	69	4.3
Ceiling	Plaster + emulsion		26	1.6
Sub-structure	450 x 300mm strip foundations		132	8.2
Total embodied including material replacements over 60 year lifespan			1620	
Total embodied per sq m of floor area			11.25	

Source: based on Anderson, J., Shiers, D.E., Sinclair, M., *Green Guide to Specification*, (3rd Edition), BRE, Watford, 2002.

Commentary: Compared with the evaluation in the previous chapter for houses the embodied energy per sq. m. of floor area is greatly increased. The incorporation of concrete floors, ground and intermediate is responsible for this greater impact. Elements such as composite wood block flooring also score very highly, which would argue in favour of using the natural alternative.

3.2 An alternative

Following the example of Bill Dunster Architects at BedZED can be a sustainable path.

Structure

Dense concrete block cross-walls, 6.3 m centre to centre, were used as an element of the scheme's thermal mass strategy, to even out diurnal temperature variations to reduce the likelihood of overheating in summer, and store solar heat in winter, while compensating for overcast days.

Walls

External walls have a 300-mm cavity filled with mineral fibre insulation. The stretcher bond outer brick skin is fixed across the cavity to the inner leaf of blockwork by two-part stainless steel wall ties, achieving a U-value of 0.1 W/m^2K, and achieving 2 ach when pressure tested to 50 Pa. At the upper walls, local oak weather-boarding was nailed to softwood stud frames, the timber cladding aligning with the face of the brickwork below.

Floors

Self-centring prestressed concrete floor panels form permanent shuttering to the in-situ floor slab which has a tiled finish to expose the thermal mass of the slab to the room. In the workspaces, recycled steel beams achieve clear span floors, and reclaimed softwood joists and floorboards are used for construction of the mezzanines.

Roofs

Sedum-planted landscape roofs consist of two-layer bituminous felt water-proofing on timber decking supported by curved laminated timber beams.

Windows

Windows are Danish triple-glazed windows with a low-emissivity coating, in durable hardwood frames. Conservatories are double-glazed with photo-voltaic cells to south-facing roofs. The extent of opening windows is sufficient to turn the sunspaces into balconies in summer obviating the need for shading. Rooflights are aluminium framed and triple glazed.

4 Issues regarding typical servicing strategies

Why is the servicing for mass housing any different from services in individual houses? The basic differences between housing and houses are shape, diversity and proximity. 'Shape' is fairly obvious – a terrace or block of flats is very different to a simple detached house – as is 'proximity'. 'Diversity' is a term which covers the fact that, say, 50-odd households are all going to be drawing on services at slightly different times. Diversity is the reason that an electricity substation isn't sized to meet the peak loads of all of the buildings served by it at the same time.

4.1 Shape: heating and ventilation

By 'gluing' houses together to form 'housing', you decrease the surface area to volume ratio; this decreases the total heat lost by each dwelling in the conglomeration. However, it also means that fewer outside walls are available to each dwelling through which it can be ventilated (Figure 3.9), and that it is less possible to give each flat an optimal orientation with regard to solar gains.

This ties in nicely with David Tompson's findings (Box 3.4): heavyweight construction is not generally appropriate for apartment buildings because solar gains cannot usefully be exploited, and low heat losses mean that capturing solar gains is not quite as important anyway. Low heat losses mean that options other than the usual default boiler-plus-rads (such as underfloor heating and MVHR), can become attractive.

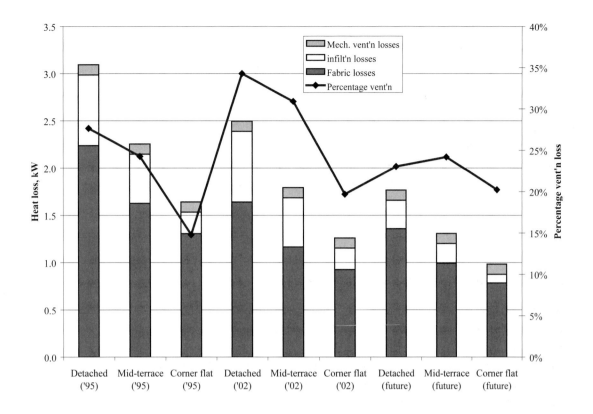

Figure 3.9 Fabric and ventilation heat losses for different housing types. (In all cases, infiltration was sufficient to act as background ventilation.)

Source: author, based on data from: *The Building Regulations Conservation of fuel and power, Approved Document L1*, 1991 and 2002, www.odpm.gov.uk; and *The Building Regulations 2000, Review of Approved Document F – Ventilation, A consultation package*, London and www.odpm.gov.uk.

Underfloor heating can be appropriate because:

- a warm radiant environment means that comfort can be maintained with lower air temperatures – a benefit because lower air temperatures lead to lower ventilation heat losses

- heating loads are smaller so floor temperature can be lower – overcoming the objections of some users of older systems where the floor could feel uncomfortably warm underfoot

- the screed around the pipework provides some thermal mass to help even out diurnal temperature variations, but remains relatively warm, thus overcoming the problem of cool radiant surfaces in thermally heavy buildings without optimal solar gains

- low water temperatures mean that the system can take advantage of low grade heat from CHP plant.

Table 3.8 Advantages and disadvantages of natural ventilation strategies.

Advantages of natural ventilation...	Disadvantages of natural ventilation...
Control of simple systems is 'intuitive' to building occupants. Simple systems are simple to maintain and clean. Driving force for ventilation is free – wind or stack effect. Generally low capital cost (however natural ventilation can be relatively expensive in non-domestic buildings).	Risk of draughts if ventilation is not well controlled. Pressures developed are generally small, so items that add a large pressure loss, such as heat exchangers, usually cannot be installed, though see note below.

Passive Stack Ventilation (PSV): air is extracted from kitchens and bathrooms through the stack effect in vertical ducts. Incoming air is drawn in from trickle vents.

...additional advantages of PSV	...additional disadvantages of PSV
Vertical vents remove humidity, or cooking smells, near to source by stack effect. Ducting is relatively short. No intake ductwork needed.	PSV works less well when the inside/outside temperature difference is reduced – in summer and some days in spring and autumn.

Notes: At BedZED the extract and intake cowls, designed to be wind assisted, incorporate a 70% efficient heat exchanger. See Dunster, B., and Carter, G., *General Information Report 89. BedZED – Beddington Zero Energy Development*, Energy Efficiency Best Practice Programme, Watford and www.bioregional.com, 2002. p. 12.

Table 3.9 Advantages and disadvantages of mechanical ventilation strategies.

Advantages of mechanical ventilation...	Disadvantages of mechanical ventilation...
• Air intake can be located at the point with least pollution. • Humid air, or cooking smells, can be removed near to source. • Heat recovery can be incorporated relatively easily.	• Higher capital cost. • Ductwork needs to be kept scrupulously clean in order to minimise risk from pathogens and allergens – a maintenance issue. • Noise (from fans and crosstalk) can be an issue.

Mechanical ventilation with heat recovery (MVHR): in addition to intake and exhaust ductwork and fans, a heat exchanger recovers heat (or coolth) from outgoing air passing it on to incoming air. Heat exchangers can be, for example, a plate heat exchanger or thermal wheel.

...additional advantages of MVHR.	...additional disadvantages of MVHR.
• Adding MVHR means higher ventilation rates do not incur a heating energy penalty (in comparison to standard mechanical ventilation). • Any additional heating required can be provided by a heat exchanger after the heat recovery in the supply air ducts.	• The UK has a temperate climate: if the winter climate warms then energy savings become more marginal. • A constantly running fan can be seen as wasting energy by householders. As a result they sometimes switch the system off and the air quality deteriorates.

Positive input ventilation (PIV): A fan draws air from the loft space into the stairwell/hallway putting the whole house at positive pressure. Air exits from trickle vents.

...additional advantages of PIV	...additional disadvantages of PIV
• Little ductwork needed. • No need to balance supply and extract duckwork.	• Risk of water vapour being driven into the building structure and hence posing an interstitial condensation risk if detailing is poor.

Dynamic insulation: Incoming air is filtered through the building fabric itself. Vitiated air is mechanically extracted.

...additional advantages of dynamic insulation	...additional disadvantages of dynamic insulation
• Incoming air moves heat, which would otherwise be lost through the walls, back into the building.	• As with PIV, interstitial condensation is a risk. • Technology is proving hard to get right. For example, the effect of differing wind pressure on different elevations upsets the functioning of the system.

Dwell-vent: Air enters through 'supply air windows' and is expelled through passive stacks. Air enters at a vent at the bottom of the outer frame and rises by the stack effect to the head of the window where it enters the room. Fan exhaust can be used where a hybrid solution is required but dwell-vent is essentially a passive alternative to MVHR.

...additional advantages of 'dwell-vent'	...additional disadvantages of 'dwell-vent'
• Supply air recaptures some heat that would otherwise be lost through glazing – low effective U-values for glazing are possible. • Little ductwork needed. • In temperate climates extract air can be driven by the stack effect. • Draught-free ventilation.	• Heat reclaim is below the efficiency of MVHR, though this is to be addressed through ongoing development of the system.

The main drawback is that underfloor heating needs to run near continuously in the heating season as it takes time for the floor to reach running temperature and this can be an issue where this hasn't been impressed upon the occupants. Covering the floor with carpet (an insulator) decreased the system's efficacy, which again is a user education issue.

Heat loads can be low enough that a heating coil can be incorporated into an MVHR system meaning that a traditional heating system can be omitted altogether. If a traditional system is desired there are also benefits:

- Radiators can be smaller (as we saw in the Hawkes House, Chapter 2).
- Thermally efficient glazing means that radiators no longer need to be automatically banished to beneath windows to counter cold down draughts.
- Pipework can be smaller (although there are practical limits on this).
- A smaller boiler can be considered, see Box 3.12.

While considering the sizing of heat emitters it is helpful to note that moving from a heavyweight to a lightweight building also has a potential effect. When specifying radiators, it is usual to specify one with a larger heat output than needed for the steady state heat losses for the design day. This is so that, if the house has been unoccupied for a while, the system won't take days to achieve a comfortable temperature. Some of the additional heat goes into the air in the rooms, and some into warming up the fabric of the building; with a heavyweight building this takes a fair amount of energy. Lightweight buildings have a much faster thermal response so the heat emitters need not be over-sized to the same extent.

Natural ventilation vs mechanical ventilation

A home requires ventilation to provide fresh air for the occupants to breathe, and to dilute and expel pollutants. Since a pollutant is simply a chemical that is harmful when in the wrong place, water vapour and CO_2 are included in this category as well as NO_x, SO_2, CO (from incomplete combustion), VOCs, radon (in certain areas of the country), ETS (environmental tobacco smoke) and odours. A good ventilation scheme strikes a balance between ventilation heat loss (especially through unwanted infiltration through gaps in the building fabric) and maintaining indoor air quality (IAQ), i.e. 'build tight – ventilate right'.

Since the 1970s, the predominant method of domestic ventilation in the UK has been to install trickle vents above windows. Trickle vents can either supply or extract air, depending on wind conditions. In addition, mechanical extract fans in kitchens and bathrooms are used to expel humid air and thus reduce the risk of condensation and mould growth. Extract fans also control the combustion products and odours from cooking.

The 1995 Approved Document Part F was mainly concerned with IAQ, possibly pre-empting the 2002 revisions to Part L which asked for airtightness to be better than 10 m³/h per m² (cubic metres of air per hour per square metre of building fabric) at a pressure difference of 50 Pa.[106] It is worth noting that BRE believes that the best airtightness that can be achieved currently, using conventional techniques, is 3–4 m³/h per m² at 50 Pa.[107] This reduces heat lost through uncontrolled infiltration.

The 2006 revision of Part F has emphasised the need for controlled ventilation with set performance standards, so that energy efficiency and IAQ can both be maintained, rather than simply setting increased free areas for trickle ventilators. It was argued that the move towards performance-based building control assessment would result in novel ventilation schemes being easier to achieve. These requirements should result in a background ventilation rate of 0.5 to 0.75 ach.[108]

The final thing to note is that it is important that all newly built dwellings are thoroughly flushed with clean air before occupation to disperse pollutants, such as VOCs, that are a result of the construction process.

4.2 Shape: lighting

In terms of natural and artificial lighting for housing most of the factors that affect their sustainability are the same as for individual houses, but we will discuss some of them further here.

Firstly, the move to a lifestyle where working from home is more prevalent has big implications in terms of natural light. In well spread out suburban houses, as long as the windows are large enough, and the garden isn't shaded by leylandii, it should be possible to provide daylight to office standards. In urban situations, however, it can be more problematic, as explored in Box 3.11.

This is one area where lessons can be learnt from the past. Historic weavers' cottages are a useful example: the work rooms on the first floor benefited from a larger sky view (and thus an increased daylight factor) with large ribbon windows letting in as much light as possible. In the weavers' cottage, the floor-to-ceiling heights were relatively low so that the area with really good daylight was confined to the area by the windows.

In the Georgian town house, taller rooms and elongated sash windows allowed light to penetrate into deeper plans. Thus good daylighting and clever ventilation were combined, even if the windows do tend to let in a draught. Splayed window reveals with shutters (painted in a light colour) and facetted glazing bars all helped to maximise light within rooms while limiting glare. Light shelves,[109] as are seen in many traditional buildings on the continent, are useful too.

In some recent low energy schemes, where to save energy the windows have been reduced in size, the same strategies have been applied. For example, in Rick Mather's student housing at the University of East Anglia splayed reveals act to counter some of the effects of the trend towards smaller windows.[110]

One of the side effects of solar design guidelines has been to limit the area of window orientated towards the north. Anecdotal evidence suggests that north-facing kitchens can be gloomy with the result that lights are left on during the day.

An example of a development where thought has been given to making lighting sustainable is at the Greenwich Millennium Village. Here, floor-to-ceiling heights were determined by the need to allow daylight to the back of rooms, and light shelves were installed. Downstand beams (which could reduce light penetration into occupied spaces) were avoided. External shadings and internal blinds control solar gain and glare, respectively.[111]

Box 3.11 Daylighting for live–work apartments

Jessica Hrivnak, while at the Martin Centre for Architectural and Urban Studies, University of Cambridge

The widespread use of computer technology means that working patterns are undergoing reform, and homes are increasingly also used as offices. The ideal apartment is seen as one that offers maximum adaptability: a big neutral space that brings with it all the connotations of the 'loft-living' ideal. However, achieving such flexibility has structural implications. There is a developing trend in housing construction, where as well as densification, a typology similar to that of office buildings is being adopted.

The housing block with an inner courtyard has, in the past, been popular in European cities, and the increasing pressure to create denser urban residential housing developments has led many architects to return to the form. Yet, increasing urban density raises problems, not least the provision of private space and daylight. What do these changes to the home and working environment imply for architects and their designs?

Office deskwork should be carried out with a daylight factor of 5%, whereas recommendations for domestic rooms lie around 2%. Can dense urban courtyard housing schemes fulfil the day lighting needs of modern live–work apartments?

Scale model tests of recently built urban courtyard schemes were used to investigate the daylight conditions in modern apartments. The study highlighted the problems of daylight penetration and the use of compact courtyard housing blocks as live–work dwellings.

continued ...

Figure 3.10 Scale models for daylighting analysis, (i) without walkways, (ii) with walkways

Source: Jessica Hrivnak

Depending on the height and width of the courtyard, the light from the sky vault may be completely absent because of the proximity of the facing buildings. Therefore, the reflective properties of materials within the courtyard are significant, and affect the availability of daylight in rooms in the lower storeys of the building. Using light and reflective materials such as glazed tiles in the courtyard can be beneficial, see Figure 3.11.

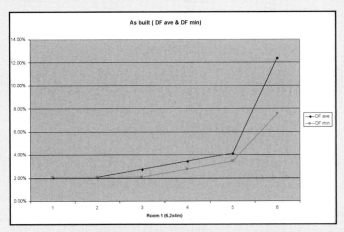

Figure 3.11 Average daylight factors in test model for sample room

Source: Jessica Hrivnak

The results show that there is a balance between the size and efficacy of windows. In such instances where the sky-view in the courtyard is restricted by overhanging walkways, the scale model tests found that even increasing the glazing by 50% (thus also increasing heat losses) did not improve the daylight factors in the lower areas of the building. The use of walkways in courtyard schemes should therefore be avoided, and internal access cores used when daylight is at a premium.

Moreover, adopting a strategy of equal maximum glazing on all floors and façades can result in considerable overheating problems in the uppermost storey. Incrementally, increasing window sizes towards the ground floor achieves a balance between the problems of heat gain/heat loss and daylighting. However, it should be noted that deep, single-aspect rooms opening off a courtyard should be avoided, as even wall-to-wall glazing will rarely achieve satisfactory effects. Moreover, it can be seen that inappropriate glazing results in glare and privacy problems. It is observable that this causes widespread use of curtains during the day, which negates the benefits of the glazing, and increases artificial lighting and energy use.

4.3 Diversity: water

Earlier, we discussed controlling the amount of rain run-off from hard surfaces (roofs, roads and hard landscaped areas) as a method of reducing flood risk. We can think of water usage in a very similar way to how we considered thermal mass in buildings. In a building (ecosystem) with little thermal mass (water storage) if the heat inputs (rainfall) are 'peaky' then the occupants may either find the conditions too hot (wet – floods) or too cold (droughts). This explains the apparent paradox of how a country notorious for wet weather can also suffer from water shortages and, hopefully, will prompt us to change the way in which we interact with the natural water cycle – disrupting it as little as possible.

Many of the water-saving measures for housing are the same as for individual houses, such as low-flow appliances and water meters. However, in housing developments, designers can make use of water-conscious measures that might not be suitable for single-family dwellings.

These include storing and treating rainwater and/or greywater for non-potable use, which becomes more attractive as plant sizes and running cost are affected by economies of scale. For example, if you are storing and treating rainwater for watering plants, you need one larger storage tank, rather than many smaller ones, which can be installed in one shot and which may save on the total materials used. Likewise, micro-sewage treatment, such as the reed beds that treat waste water from the community at the Centre for Alternative Technology (CAT, www.cat.org.uk), become a viable option.

Box 3.12 Hot water demand and boiler choice

In a well-insulated building, lower heating loads potentially allow a smaller (lower output) boiler to be installed. A boiler is sized on whichever is the larger out of heating demand and hot water generation demand. This in turn depends on how the hot water is generated.

With a combi-boiler, the peak hot water demand far exceeds the heating demand, by say a factor of ten, so the boiler will be oversized for its usual load. Since boilers have tended to operate at peak efficiency over a relatively narrow range of outputs, this can waste energy. Modern boilers are much better at maintaining efficiency over a range of outputs, but this is still a factor that should be considered.

If hot water is stored in a calorifier – a hot water tank – this can be less of a problem. The boiler simply builds up the temperature in the tank over the course of the day, so the instantaneous energy demand is smaller.

There is also greater opportunity to explore options for soft landscaping, such as the gravel car parking at BedZED, which allows water to percolate away into the surrounding soil rather than rushing away through storm drains,

4.4 Diversity: energy supply

People draw off power at different times, so the power load for a number of dwellings will tend to be more steady, especially if some of the houses are live–work units where the electricity demand will be during the day when most residents are away at work. This can make CHP an attractive option: high grade heat from burning fuel (preferably a bio-fuel) generates electricity, and lower grade heat (waste from power generation) goes to heat homes and water. Because the power demand is more constant there will be fewer periods when a shortfall needs be made up from the generally fossil-fuel-powered grid system and, likewise, fewer periods when excess electricity needs either to be stored in batteries or exported to the grid.

An example of this approach can be seen at BedZED where a 130 kW (of electricity) wood-fired CHP plant is installed.[112] Here PVs are also installed, again with advantages of scale for plant selection. Micro-wind generators can also be a viable option, as seen at Hockerton and CAT.

4.5 Proximity: sound

The mechanism for noise-induced hearing loss – damage to the inner ear as a result of exposure to very loud noises – appears to be well understood.[113] But this is not the only health risk associated with noise. Lower levels of noise, while they may not damage the structure of the ear, can still be damaging to health. Noise at night is thought to be of greatest concern.[114]

Reported effects of increased levels of ambient noise exposure include: impaired cognitive function,[115] disturbance to deep and REM sleep (which, regardless of cause, carries health risks),[116][117][118] risk of cardiovascular disease (as a result of effects on the neuro-endocrine systems), annoyance/stress plus a large range of health problems where the causal relationship is not so clear, including migraine, asthma and other allergic diseases. [119]

In 1991, a study showed that around 30% of households had negative experiences of ambient noise with 1% saying that their home life was 'totally spoiled'.[120] Increasing the density of dwellings is likely to exacerbate noise problems perhaps with a move from road noise being the primary concern[121] to community noise

– such as from TVs, crying infants, boisterous parties or even washing machine spin cycles – being equally problematic. People need to be able to go about their daily lives without being unduly disturbed by noise from their neighbours, or having to worry that they will be making too much noise themselves. This means that any sound-reduction measures in housing are likely to have a huge benefit in terms of quality of life.

Table 3.10 Common acoustic terms

C_{tr}	A correction term to take account of a specific sound spectra.*
dB (decibel)	Logarithmic scale to measure sound power, on which zero dB is the threshold of hearing and 130 dB causes pain.[†,§]
$D_{nT,w}$	Characterises the sound insulation between rooms, based on the difference in sound level between a pair of rooms, in a stated frequency band, corrected for the reverberation time.*
$L_{nT,w}$	A single number used to characterise the impact of sound insulation of floors, in terms of the sound pressure level, in a stated frequency band, with reverberation time correction.*

Sources:

* The Building Regulations 2000, The Building (Approved Inspectors etc) Regulations 2000, Resistance to the passage of sound, Approved Document E, TSO, London and www.odpm.gov.uk, 2003. pp. 74–75.

† CIBSE Guide C, Reference data, Oxford, Butterworth-Heinemann for CIBSE (2001). p. 6–4.

§ Burberry, P., Mitchell's Environment and Services, London, 6th edn, Mitchell Publishing Co. 1988. p. 120.

Sound insulation regulations for housing

For new housing, the walls, floors and stairs (between separate dwellings) must have a minimum $D_{nT,w} + C_{tr}$ value of 45 dB (i.e. airborne sound resistance).[122] Floors and stairs must also have, for impact sound insulation, a maximum $L_{nT,w}$ value of 62 dB.[123]

Internal walls and floors should have a minimum weighted airborne sound reduction index (Rw) value of 40 dB.

Some ways of reducing the impact of noise:

- Site the noise sensitive areas (bedrooms) away from noise sources, using less sensitive areas (hallways, kitchens and bathrooms) as a buffer, e.g. Coopers Road (see Case study, below).

- In flats, try to avoid putting a 'quiet' room in one dwelling next to a 'noisy' room in an adjacent dwelling.

- Select low-noise plant and keep it in an acoustic enclosure rather than siting it on the roof. Also, ensure that service risers have good sound insulation.

- Make sure that, where pipes, ducts, cables etc., pass through walls, the gap is acoustically sealed.

As with many measures for sustainable buildings, acoustic insulation can have other benefits. For example, retrofitting double glazing to an existing building can help acoustically as well as thermally. Likewise, because of the way sound travels, walls with thermal mass (thermally massive materials are usually dense) can reduce sound transmission. If the mass per surface area of a wall doubles there is a 5 dB – i.e. noticeable – reduction in noise.[124]

5. Case studies

5.1 Coopers Road Estate regeneration: Southwark, London

Architects: ECD Architects Ltd
Client: Peabody Trust and London Borough of Southwark Housing
Service engineers: Max Fordham LLP
Structural engineers: Price and Myers
Landscape architects: Jennifer Coe Landscape Architects
Cost consultants: BPP
EcoHomes Assessor: Faber Maunsell
Design: 2001
Construction: started 2003 (completion of Phase One; early 2005

Background
In 1999, the Peabody Trust joined forces with Southwark Housing and appointed ECD Architects to prepare a masterplan for the redevelopment of the Coopers Road Estate.

Planning approval for the new design was obtained in November 2001, and construction work started on site in February 2003 under a Design and Build form of contract. Phase One of the works was completed in early 2005 and has achieved an EcoHomes rating of 'very good'.

Planning, form and construction

Site
The Coopers Road estate was built in the 1960s and occupied a 1.69 hectare site north of the Old Kent Road. It consisted of 196 dwellings in five blocks, varying in height from three to eleven storeys. A central stair served each block, with deck access to front doors. The site density was 358 habitable rooms per hectare.

The surrounding area is dominated largely by council housing estates, with the London Borough of Southwark Astley Coopers estate to the west and the Corporation of London's Avondale estate to the east, with its three distinctive high-rise towers. The Old Kent Road itself is a busy thoroughfare – historically the main road into the capital from continental Europe – bounded in the main by an assortment of undistinguished retail 'sheds'.

The open spaces on the Coopers Road estate consisted mainly of grassed areas with a few trees. There was no sense of ownership of these spaces, and they provided minimum amenity value. The play areas were not well maintained and had limited equipment. Generally, the open spaces were intimidating and underused.

The site is about 15 minutes walk (approximately 1.3 km) from Bermondsey station on the Jubilee Line. It is also well served by bus routes to the Elephant and Castle, the West End and St Paul's Cathedral.

The brief

The Coopers Road estate was in need of considerable investment and its 1960s design was increasingly unpopular and unsuitable. The communal spaces were abused by sections of the community; the rubbish chutes were blocked with furniture causing a fire hazard and the open spaces had poor visual surveillance. In 1999, Southwark Housing made the radical decision to demolish the estate and redevelop it. In doing so, they formed a partnership with the Peabody Trust, who would acquire and manage the majority of the new housing.

Figure 3.12 The existing site

Source: ECD Architects

Despite some antisocial elements, the original estate had a strong sense of community, which was an essential ingredient for the long-term success of the project. The local residents were fully engaged in the development of the proposals at every stage, from the initial master planning through a series of design workshops, to selection of the main contractor and tenant choice items on internal finishes.

The brief for the new estate was for a mixed tenure development of 154 new homes. When completed, the new estate would have 121 affordable rent units and 33 shared-ownership units. All homes are designed to Lifetime Homes standards (see Box 3.13), with five units being fully wheelchair accessible. The scheme would be built in two phases to allow the gradual decanting and demolition of existing blocks. The density of the new development is 355 habitable rooms per hectare.

Design

The new build scheme is based on four courtyards and aims to have a major impact on the lives of those used to the failed 1960s housing model it replaced. The courtyard form, evolved in consultation with the residents, encourages a sense of community and engenders a strong sense of identity. It also creates a clear hierarchy of private, semi-private and public spaces and provides a good model for urban regeneration.

Each courtyard consists of approximately 40 homes in a mix of one- to three-bedroom apartments and three- or four-bedroom family houses, providing a balanced community with a composition of four-storey flats and three-storey houses. This arrangement has been designed to be flexible to meet future changing needs and developments in living patterns.

The design principles for Coopers Road were:

- to restore the fabric of the city, with streets, courts, mews and gardens – the form of the courtyard housing continues an urban design theme from the 19th Century, when local maps show a pattern of streets with houses grouped together in short terraces

- to integrate architecture and landscape to provide attractive, legible and easily maintained private and public spaces – large- and small-scale vegetation are located in response to the scale of the surrounding archi-tecture, while robust materials are combined with generously planted semi-mature trees to create a sense of greenness across the site

- to develop a sense of community ownership – individual houses and ground-floor flats have gardens to the front and rear, which create well-defined private space, and the rear gardens face onto the larger communal garden, which measures 21×34 m, comparable in size to a small London square.

From the outset, both client and design team shared a commitment to make Coopers Road a model of sustainable urban regeneration. First and foremost this meant designing a scheme that would provide good quality, appropriate accommodation not just in the short term but 100 years from now. Another main aim was to design buildings that could feasibly achieve zero CO_2 emissions in the long term without major modifications to the fabric, services or infrastructure.

Orientation and solar access were foremost in the consideration of the planning of the courtyards:

- The lower three-storey houses are placed to the south of the higher four-storey flats.
- Roofs are designed to face south wherever possible, for the future retrofit of solar or photovoltaic panels.

Box 3.13 Lifetime Homes

Since 1999 the access requirements given in Part M of the Approved Documents have applied to new dwellings as well as other building types.[1] The Lifetime Homes standards, however, go beyond the requirements of Part M.[2] They cover:

- external access: wider parking spaces; minimal distances from parking to dwellings, with low gradient approaches; entrances that are covered, level and well lit; specific dimensions for stairs and lifts; specific widths of corridors and doorways
- internal access: turning space for wheelchairs in living accommodation, e.g. a turning circle of 1.5 m; an entrance-level living room; a room that can be used as a bedroom on the entrance level in dwellings over a number of storeys; space for a stair lift or traditional lift; a route for a hoist from main bedroom to bathroom
- sanitary accommodation: (a wheelchair-accessible WC on the entrance level and provision for future shower installation; walls in bathrooms and toilets that can take handrails; easy access to bath, WC and basin
- environment: low-level living room windows for view from wheelchairs
- services: mid-level – between 450 and 1200 AFFL – sockets and controls.

1.   See DETR, *The Building Regulations 1991 – Access and facilities for disabled people, Approved Document M*, 1999 edition, TSO, London and www.odpm.gov.uk 1999. Also ODPM, *The Building Regulations 2000 – Access to and use of buildings, Approved document M*, 2004 edition, TSO, London and www.odpm.gov.uk, 2004.
2.   Carroll, C., Cowans, J. and Darton, D. (eds), *Meeting Part M and designing Lifetime Homes*, Joseph Rowntree Foundation, York, www.jrf.org.uk, 1999, p. 6.

Figure 3.13 Typical
floor plans

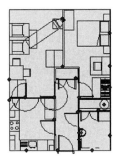

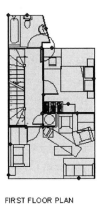

GROUND FLOOR PLAN
Typical 3 Bedroom House

FIRST FLOOR PLAN

SECOND FLOOR PLAN

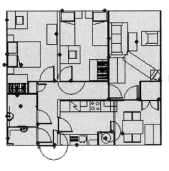

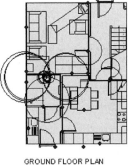

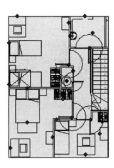

Typical 1 Bedroom Flat

Typical 2 Bedroom Flat

GROUND FLOOR PLAN
Typical 3 Bedroom Maisonette

FIRST FLOOR PLAN

Source: ECD Architects

Structure

Materials

Material choice: Materials were typically selected for their low embodied energy content, recyclability and impact on the environment when disposed of. This meant a preference for timber and masonry rather than plastics and steel. 'A'-rated construction materials were used for the windows (softwood frames) and the upper floors of the houses (timber joists with plywood finish). HCFC-free insulation was used throughout, and timber cladding was specified from sustainable sources. The contractor was encouraged to source materials from within a 50-mile radius, to minimise CO_2 emissions released through transportation.

The inner-city environment of the new estate required a range of robust finishes to surfaces and boundaries, particularly for the public realm, including porous paving and brick paviors. Garden walls in conjunction with the architectural form present a secure perimeter to the blocks. The walls create a protected and beneficial environment for the healthy growth of evergreen hedges and climbers.

Recycling: On-site waste was minimised through material choice, prefabrication of some elements, careful detailing and scheduling. The main contractor also recycled on-site construction waste. All dwellings are provided with recycling bins within the kitchens, designed to separate household waste. Houses have an individual external recycling store, and communal stores are provided for the flats.

Services

Flexibility and adaptability were also key issues for the design team. Service risers in Coopers Road are located on the outside of the building for ease of access and have also been oversized to facilitate the installation of future technologies as they become more economically viable.

Thermal performance

Orientation and solar access were foremost in the consideration of the planning of the courtyards. By maximising the daylight into the homes, the demand for artificial heating has been reduced. This has been further reduced by good insulation: the weighted average U-values for the development are 16% better than the unadjusted Building Regulations (2002) target U-value.

Light

The design reduces the need for artificial heating, through sunlight and daylight access. Energy-efficient light fittings are provided in internal rooms. All external feature, security and communal lighting are dedicated compact fluorescent lamp fittings. Security lighting also has movement detection and daylight cut-off.

Water

Water consumption has been minimised by specifying dual-flush WCs (6/4 litre), aerated taps and small baths (less than 150 litres to overflow). The water consumption is 44 m^3/bedspace/year according to the EcoHomes methodology. The communal garden areas have rainwater butts for irrigation purposes.

Figure 3.14 Three-storey houses to the south

Energy supply

As well as making provision for future installation of PVs, CO_2 emissions have been reduced significantly by the incorporation of a gas-fired community heating system with combined heat and power (CHP). This system has been selected both on its own merits, for its 'environmental showcase' value and as part of the client's ongoing commitment to the environment. During the design process it was very helpful for the design team to show some existing CHP installations in London to occupants from Coopers Road, to reassure them that the technology was safe and reliable.

A gas-fired CHP plant has been installed which provides approximately 11% of the heat demand of the development and approximately 12% of the electricity demand – the unit has a 30 kW electrical output. Average CO_2 emissions for each dwelling are estimated to be less than 25 kg/m^2 pa.

Landscape

The aim of the landscape design for the new estate was to create both a physical continuity between the four new courtyard blocks and a highly legible space that is easy to understand. The grain of the new estate allows long views and an ease of orientation that creates a sense of physical security. In addition the landscape scheme aims to achieve a sense of wellbeing at many levels. It provides the essential contact with the natural world and the changing seasons.

Source: ECD Architects

Figure 3.15 Artist's impression of the new scheme

Within each courtyard all the properties at ground-floor level have a small patio garden, which opens into a communal garden for the use of the courtyard residents only. Residents will become involved in the management of these spaces, the idea being that they will become a focus for community pride. Properties above ground level have private balconies or sky gardens. Within the communal gardens there are designated areas for gardening, children's play, cycle storage, composting, seating and rainwater harvesting.

Trees are planted within the streets and define the edge of circulation spaces, home zones (described below) and car parking. Their location, to the northern side of the blocks, prevents overshadowing and does not limit the passive solar gain to the south-facing elevations. The street trees have been selected from native species or cultivars of indigenous species – hornbeam, ash, pear and sorbus. Fruit trees and useful plants that attract wildlife are planted within the back gardens and courtyards. Trees assist the health of the environment, with intake of CO_2, emission of oxygen, filtering of dust and other contaminants, and also support a range of wildlife species, particularly birds and insects. A hedge of native species – willow, elder and hawthorn – is proposed adjacent to the eastern and northern boundaries as cover and food for birds and insects. Planting elsewhere has been specified to be robust and drought resistant.

Transport

Access roads are designed as 'home zones' to enable pedestrians to have priority over vehicles. A home zone is a street or group of streets designed primarily to meet the interests of pedestrians and cyclists rather than motorists, opening up the street for social use. Legally, neither pedestrians nor vehicles have priority, but the road may be configured to make it more favourable to pedestrians.

In addition, the roads are designed as short runs, intersected by squares and traffic-calming measures. Vehicles will also be restricted to 20 mph.

5.2 White City

Architects: Cartwright Pickard and BC Architects
Client: CABE and French equivalent DAPA (the Direction de l'Architecture et du Patrimoine)
Structural engineers: Campbell Reith
Services engineers: Atelier Ten
Landscape architects: Grant Associates
Design: 2003

Background

The White City project is the result of a winning entry for an international design competition to develop best practice in affordable housing, launched in the spring of 2003. This competition is the first of a series of Anglo–French collaborative projects with sites in London and Paris, aimed at bringing new thinking to the design of affordable housing in both countries.

Sponsored by CABE and its French equivalent DAPA (the Direction de l'Architecture et du Patrimoine), the scheme is a collaboration between Cartwright Pickard Architects and French architects BC Architects together with Octavia Housing and Care Housing Association.

The scheme has collected a CABE Festive Fives 2003 Award and was a winner of the schemes with detailed planning permission of the Housing Design Awards 2004, promoted by the RIBA, RITP, ODPM and NHBC.

Planning, form and construction

Site

The scheme occupies a site between a massive retail development and mixed fabric of Victorian, Edwardian and later terraced housing.

Part of the site was occupied by a bus depot, leaving areas of contaminated ground which needed to be dealt with prior to construction. Trials indicated that the contaminated soils were not sufficient to be reused to provide a suitable engineering base for the roadways. However, providing a suitable capping layer for the landscaped areas was viable. This would allow for a reduction of the amount of material that would need to be removed from the site because it could be mixed with lime to provide a suitable growing medium to enhance the landscaped areas.

The brief and design rationale

One of the principal objectives of the design was for the new housing and external spaces to establish a real sense of place and wellbeing for its residents, to provide a development to delight both residents and passers-by. The development incorporates 27 houses and 51 flats and maisonettes for rent or shared ownership.

As well as aiming to move the design of affordable housing forward, the project has defined sustainability objectives. An EcoHomes rating of very good or excellent is to be achieved through, among other proposals, improvements upon the Building Regulations in terms of thermal and acoustic performance of the construction.

Design

The site has offered a number of challenges to be overcome. The retail development is bounded by a seven-storey 'citadel' wall forming the northern boundary to the site from which extend a series of timber-clad blocks, up to four storeys in height, providing a succession of mews spaces alternating with private gardens.

The blocks have been orientated perpendicular to the main boundary wall with the fingers protruding to the south; although this does not make use of a south-facing façade, the design intent was to focus on the quality of the intermediate spaces between the blocks. This also allows dwellings to be accessed from the mews spaces and from shared stair cores allowing for efficient distribution of services.

In all cases each of the units has direct access to some form of external space, be it a balcony, external terrace or rear garden. These provide private external spaces to augment those provided in the public mews spaces. A pedestrian-friendly access road, over-sailed by dramatic cantilevers, separates the housing from a landscaped parking strip.

Despite the minimal length of south-facing façade, the dwellings have been designed with the reduction of energy use in mind, through passive means. The spaces have been designed to meet and exceed the requirements for daylight but with standardised window openings, minimising the number of bespoke components. The depths of the units have been considered to allow for natural cross-ventilation through the dwellings.

Structure

Precast pile foundations were considered to be the most appropriate for the site given the unsuitability of the founding stratum and the proximity of the adjacent housing. Above this, the ground-floor slab consists of a beam and block floor on ground beams, forming a ventilated sub-floor void.

A number of structural options were considered for the project, with a steel frame with precast concrete hollow plank floors being chosen to facilitate speed of erection, minimising the loadings on the pile foundations and giving the required material density so as to achieve a suitably high acoustic separation between dwellings.

A number of external wall constructions were considered in terms of their thermal, acoustic and material make-up. Light gauge steel frame and timber structural insulated panels offer significant thermal improvements on the Building Regulations requirement. A breathable construction comprising an infill walling system was proposed to fit within the steel frame to provide a thermal envelope upon which a timber rain screen cladding system is to be fitted.

The systems reviewed were typically made of an internal lining board, vapour barrier framing system with insulation, and an external weather board covered by a fully lapped breather membrane.

These panels were either pre-formed, or site manufactured with windows pre-fitted prior to offering up the wall panel to the façade from cherry pickers or hoists, negating the need for scaffolding, while reducing erection times and site wastage.

The roofing proposed is a built-up standing seam system with a mill-finished aluminium top layer to facilitate recycling of the materials at a later date. The built-up system was chosen as it provided a clear strategy for providing airtightness and gave a finished roof with minimal maintenance requirements over the design life of the project.

Precast concrete stairs were installed to the common areas, timber staircases being constructed within the dwellings themselves. The thinking was to install the domestic stairs as early as possible, to enable their use as site access.

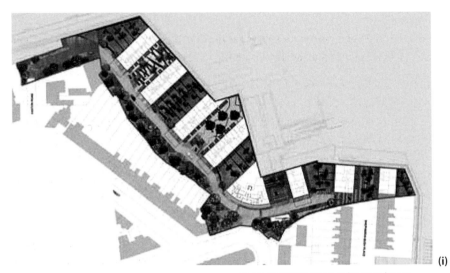

Figure 3.16 (i) site plan and (ii) schematic showing relationship between access areas, private and semi-private spaces and dwellings

Source: Grant Associates Landscape Architects

(i)

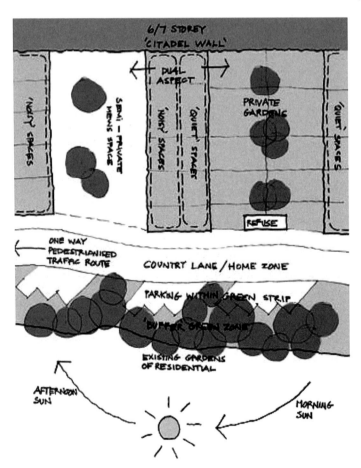

(ii)

Materials

All materials and products were assessed for their longevity in use and their ability to be recycled after the design life has been exceeded.

A particular concern were to balance the specification against the requirements of the Housing Association in terms of maintenance and life expectancy of the project as a whole. The cladding of the façades is a case in point; numerous products were assessed before settling on kiln-dried European Oak which provides a durable, sustainable material requiring minimal maintenance in keeping with the design aspirations of the scheme, which has been detailed to accentuate the geometry of the blocks and to provide a suitable rainscreen to the façade.

The scheme has been considered from the outset as providing an invigorating place in which to live and providing a sustainable, efficient method of construction which allows for effective use of resources in use throughout and beyond the design life of the project.

Services

Thermal performance

In response to the desired environmental quality of the dwellings, a whole-house ventilation system was used. This comprises a heat exchanger with heat recovery to reduce heat loss from the dwellings. Air is supplied from a central hall and extracted via a unit over the cooker. The system also extracts from the bathroom areas. The only penetration of the façade is thus a concentric duct providing intake and exhaust.

Light

Though all dwellings have been designed to make good use of daylight, there will always be a need for some artificial lighting, especially to establish a sense of security for the residents.

All shared area and external lighting is switched by dusk-to-dawn sensors to balance energy requirements against achieving the recommendations of the 'Secured by Design' principles that are deployed across the site

Sound

All internal partitions and separating walls are designed to improve upon the Building Regulations with regards to sound transmission; using plasterboard on metal stud. A raised acoustic floor comprising sustainably sourced flooring-grade ply on acoustic battens is to be employed to maintain the acoustic requirements and to provide a service area for pipework runs.

Source: Cartwright Pickard Architects

Energy supply

A centrally located energy centre was installed, comprising gas-fired condensing boilers with a combined heat and power plant. This serves a district heating system, having buried LPHW mains, for the individual flats via local valve assemblies with integral heating meters in each apartment.

Water metering is an effective way of encouraging users to limit water use. Likewise heating meters are a way of decreasing energy use where communal heating is installed, where there may be a temptation to use heat profligately. The BedZED development also uses this strategy.

Figure 3.17 View of mews showing façade treatment and transition from public to semi-private spaces

6. Notes

1. Schneider, S.H. and Lane, J. 'An overview of 'dangerous' climate change', in H.J. Schellnhuber (ed.), *Avoiding dangerous climate change.* Cambridge University Press, Cambridge, 2006.

2. ODPM, *Proposals for amending Part L of the Building Regulations and Implementing the Energy Performance of Buildings Directive – A consultation document.* HMSO/ODPM, London, www.odpm.gov.uk, July 2004. Section 9 pp. 5–6.

3. *ibid.*

4. Stern, N., *The Economics of Climate Change – The Stern Review.* Cambridge University Press, Cambridge, 2007, p. 144.

5. *op. cit.* ODPM 2004, pp. 14–15.

6. *ibid.* p. 7.

7. *ibid.* p. 14.

8. *ibid.* p. 17

9. *ibid.*

10. *ibid.* p. 18.

11. Though possibly not uniformly across the country, see 'Experts blame it on the jet stream'. www.timesonline.co.uk, *The Times*, 21 June 2005.

12. *op. cit.* ODPM, July 2004, Section 9 p. 18.

13. A possibility discussed in 'Climate change hits base of food chain'. *New Scientist*, No 2461, 21 August 2004, p. 18.

14. Malaria could be reintroduced to the UK as warmer conditions favour insect life, although the risk of outbreaks is low. See *Health Effects of Climate Change in the UK. An update of the Department of Health report 2001/2002.* www.dh.gov.uk, Department of Health and Health Protection Agency, London, 2007, p. 35.

15. ODPM, *Sustainable Communities: Homes for All.* HMSO/ODPM London, www.odpm.gov.uk, 2005. p. 16.

16. ODPM, *Sustainable Communities: Building for the Future.* ODPM, www.odpm.gov.uk, 2003. p. 8.

17. Barker, K., *Review of Housing Supply. Delivering Stability: Securing out Future Housing Needs. Final Report – Recommendations.* HM Treasury, www.hm-treasury.gov.uk, 2004. p. 3.

18. ONS, *Mid-2002 Population Estimates.* National Statistics, www.statistics.gov.uk, 2004.

19. UN, *World Population Prospects: The 2002 Revision.* United Nations, www.un.org, 2003, p. 35.

20. Natural change accounted for nearly three-quarters of the total population change between 1981 and 2002. *op. cit.* ONS, 2004.

21. *op. cit.* UN, 2003, p. vi.

22. *op. cit.* ODPM, 2003. p. 11.

23. *ibid.* p. 49.

24. *op. cit.* ODPM, 2005, p. 45.

25. DETR, *Quality and Choice: A Decent Home for All – The Housing Green Paper.* DETR, London, www.odpm.gov.uk, 2000. p. 7.

26. "...less than 1% lacks any of the basic amenities of a kitchen sink, a bath or shower in a bathroom, a wash hand basin, hot and cold water to each of these and an indoor toilet." *ibid.* p. 7.

27. The government defines a 'decent' home as one that: is above the current statutory minimum standard for housing is in a reasonable state of repair provides a reasonable degree of thermal comfort has modern facilities and services. *National Statistics Website, Housing: Percentage of households living in non-decent housing: Sustainable Development.* National Statistics, www.statistics.gov.uk/statbase, 2002.

28. Figures refer to housing stock in 1996. *ibid.*

29. The Government has aims to make all social housing 'decent' by 2010. *op. cit.* ODPM, 2003. p. 13.

30. *op. cit.* Barker, 2004.

31. In 2002 37% of new households could afford to buy, whereas in the late 1980s 46% could. *ibid.* p. 3.

32. *ibid.* p. 1.

33. *op. cit.* ODPM, 2005. p. 40.

34. *op. cit.* Barker, 2004. p. 8.

35. *ibid.* p. 5.

36. *op. cit.* ODPM, 2005. p. 40.

37. Department for Communities and Local Government (DCLG), *Homes for the future: more affordable, more sustainable.* TSO, London, www.communities.gov.uk, 2007, pp. 72–74

38. *op. cit.* ODPM, 2005.

39. *op. cit.* TSO, p. 72–80.

40. *op. cit.* Barker, 2004.

41. *see op. cit.* ODPM, 2005.

42. Lazarus, N., *Summary: Beddington Zero (Fossil) Energy Development – Construction Materials Report – Toolkit for Carbon Neutral Developments – Part 1.* BioRegional, Surrey, www.bioregional.com, 2002. p. 4.

43. *ibid.* p. 5.

44. If the energy used in the manufacture and transport of building materials is derived from fossil fuels then the embodied CO_2 is equivalent to the embodied primary energy. This assumption doesn't hold if the energy comes from hydro-electric power, or other renewables.

45. *op. cit.* Lazarus, 2002, p. 4.

46. *ibid.* p. 3.

47. *The BedZED Exhibition,* Bill Dunster Architects, www.surreycc.gov.uk, 2002. p. 17.

48. Dunster, B. and Carter, G., *General Information Report 89. BedZED – Beddington Zero Energy Development,* Energy Efficiency Best Practice programme, Sutton, Watford, www.bioregional.com, 2002, p. 3.

49. *op. cit.* Lazarus, 2003, p. 3.

50. *ibid.*

51. *op. cit.* Bill Dunster Architects, 2002, p. 16.

52. *op. cit.* ODPM, 2005, p. 62.

53. *op. cit.* ODPM, July 2004. Letter to consultees. p. 5.

54. *ibid.* Section 1, p. 1.

55. *ibid.* The social cost of CO_2 emissions was assumed to be £70 per tonne per year. Section 1, pp. 33–39.

56. *ibid.* Section 2, pp. 5–30.

57. *ibid.* Section 2, p. 3.

58. Energy Performance of Buildings Directive 2002/91/EC, *EU Official Journal L001*, europa.eu.int/comm/energy/ demand/legislation/buildings_en.htm, January 2003, pp. 65–71.

59. *op. cit.* ODPM, July 2004, Section 1, p. 15. Also see www.SEDBUK.com.

60. *ibid.* Section 1, p. 16.

61. *ibid.* Section 3.

62. *ibid.* Section 6, p. 6.

63. *ibid.* Section 6, p. 7.

64. *ibid.* Section 6, p. 8.

65. *ibid.* Section 6, pp. 9–10.

66. *ibid.* Section 6.

67. BBC website, *Residents clear flooded gardens,* http://newsvote.bbc.co.uk, BBC (18 April 2005), and BBC website, *Flood cuts power to 2500 homes,* http://newsvote.bbc.co.uk, BBC (20 June 2005).

68. BBC website, *East Australia hit by flooding,* http://newsvote.bbc.co.uk, BBC (30 June 2005).

69. BBC website, *Storm costs 'could rise by 66%',* http://newsvote.bbc.co.uk, BBC (28 June 2005).

70. ODPM, *Planning Policy Guidance 25: Development and flood risk,* www.odpm. gov.uk, ODPM, July 2001, Introduction, para. 3.

71. *ibid.* para. 69.

72. *op. cit.* ODPM, July 2004, Section 9, p. 10.

73. Bill Dunster Architects, *ZED scheme specification 2004,* Bill Dunster Architects, www.zedfactory.com, 2004. p. 11.

74. Rickards, L., Fox, K., Roberts, C., Fletcher, L. and Goddard, E., *Living in Britain. No 31. Results from the 2002 General Household Survey.* TSO, London, www.statistics.gov.uk, 2004, p. 30.

75. *ibid.*

76. Home ownership increased from 49% in 1971 to 69% in 2002. The biggest increase was in the 1980s under the 'right to buy scheme'. *ibid.* p. 7.

77. *ibid.* p. 31.

78. *ibid.* pp. 32–33.

79. Powell, K., 'Core values', *The Architects' Journal,* 3/10 August 2000, pp. 28–37.

80. 'Homes fit for heroes', http://society.guardian.co.uk, *The Guardian,* Leader Column, 7 March 2002.

81. Housing Corporation, *London Housing Statement 2002 – Delivering Solutions,* The Government Office for London and the Housing Corporation, London, www.housingcorplibrary.org.uk, pp. 9, 28.

82. Dilley, R., 'Build castles in the sky', BBC News Online, http://news.bbc.co.uk, 18 July, 2002.

83. There were houses on London Bridge prior to the mid 1700s (www.bbc.co.uk/history), and Firenze's Ponte Vecchio is still occupied by buildings, as is Bath's Pulteney Bridge.

84. Pickard, J., 'Sixth Avenue – "A Very Handsome Building"' *Connections (Yorkon Magazine)*, Issue 5, 2002. p. 4.

85. Wet insulation does not perform as well as dry – just as a wet sweater performs worse than a dry one.

86. *op. cit.* Pickard, 2002, p. 6.

87. Blackwell, P., 'Improving energy efficiency through off-site construction', *Connections (Yorkon Magazine)*, Issue 5, 2002. p. 13.

88. Berge, B., *The Ecology of Building Materials*, Architectural Press, Oxford, 2001, Chapter 3, pp. 43–52.

89. Laing, R., Craig, A. and Edge, H. M., *Prefabricated Housing: An Assessment of Cost, Value and Quality*. www.rgu.ac.uk, The Robert Gordon University, Aberdeen, 2001. pp. 8–10.

90. It also has 'traditional' terracotta cladding, which may have helped its image.

91. www.skanska.com

92. Richards, D., 'The Smarter Way to Build', *OSC – Off Site Construction*, April 2004. p. 8.

93. *op. cit.* Blackwell, 2002, pp. 12–13.

94. As shown by plans supplied by Yorkon.

95. Plans are given in 'Houses from the Factory', *Architecture Today*, AT 96. pp. 60–64

96. Cole, M. and Stevens, N., 'Is Off Site In Sight?', *OSC – Off Site Construction*, April 2004, p. 5.

97. 'Here's one I built earlier', *Guardian Unlimited*, http://society.guardian.co.uk, 18 November 2001.

98. BRE, *An Introduction to Building with Structural Insulated Panels (SIPS)*, BRE Information Paper IP13/04, Building Research Establishment, Garston, 2004.

99. Callender, J.H., *Time Saver Standards for Architectural Design Data*, McGraw Hill, New York, 1974, p. 551.

100. Cook, G.K. and Hinks, A.J., *Appraising Building Defects: Perspectives on Stability and Hygrothermal Performance*. Longman Scientific and Technical, Harlow, 1992, p. 48.

101. BRE, *Multi-storey Timber Framed Buildings*, BRE BR454, BRE, Garston, 2002.

102. Anderson, J. and Howard, N., *The Green Guide to Housing Specification*, BRE, Watford, 2000, pp. 8–11.

103. *ibid.* pp. 12–15.

104. *ibid.*

105. *ibid.* pp. 22–23.

106. ODPM, *The Building Act 1984, The Building Regulations 2000, Review of Approved Document F – Ventilation, A consultation package*, www.odpm.gov.uk, ODPM/HMSO, London, July 2004, p. 18.

107. *ibid.* p. 19.

108. *ibid.* p. 37.

109. A useful pictorial representation of the effect of light shelves and blinds on daylight distribution can be found in Baker, N. and Steemers, K., *Energy and Environment in Architecture – A Technical Design Guide.* Spon, London, 2000, Chapter 6.

110. Photographs of Rick Mather's housing at UEA can be found in: Dormer, P. and Muthesius, P., *Concrete and Open Skies: Architecture at the University of East Anglia.* Unicorn Press, London, 2001, p. 20–21.

111. Greenwich Millennium Village, *Quality of Environment and Construction – Datasheets, Greenwich Millennium Village,* London (date unknown)

112. *op. cit.* Dunster and Carter, 2002, p. 13.

113. Ising, H., with Babisch, W., Guski, R., Kruppa, B. and Maschke, C., *Exposure and Effect Indicators of Environmental Noise,* WHO, http://www.euro.who.int, 2003, p. 21.

114. WHO, *Report on the second meeting on night noise guidelines,* WHO, Geneva, http://www.euro.who.int, 2004.

115. Hygge, S., *Noise exposure and cognitive performance – Children and the elderly as possible risk groups.* WHO, http://www.euro.who.int, 2003.

116. *op. cit.* Ising et al., 2003, pp. 1, 4–12.

117. Sleep is, of course, an important part of home life, and important for health. The WHO is drawing up guidelines for night-time noise. http://www.euro.who.int/Noise

118. *op. cit.* WHO, 2004.

119. *op. cit.* Ising et al., 2003, pp. 2–4, 12–21.

120. DEFRA, *Towards a National Ambient Noise Strategy – A Consultation Paper from the Air and Environmental Quality Division,* www.defra.gov.uk, DEFRA, London, Nov 2001, p. 19.

121. EU standards mean that noise from vehicles has been reduced. Also measures have been taken by the UK government to reduce noise due to the roads themselves, such as the erection of 'noise barriers' or quieter road surfaces. *ibid.* pp. 43–46.

122. ODPM, *The Building Regulations 2000, The Building (Approved Inspectors etc) Regulations 2000, Resistance to the passage of sound, Approved document E,* London and www.odpm.gov.uk, 2003 edn., TSO, 2003. p. 8.

123. For housing formed by change of use, the requirements are less onerous: for airborne sound, 43 dB and for impact 64 dB. ibid.

124. Sneider, A., *Noise Pollution Issues in Dwellings,* IMBM, www.imbm.org.uk, 2005.

6 Further reading

RCEP, *Royal Commission on Environmental Pollution 22nd Report*, www.rcep.org.uk.

Hacker, J. and Twinn, C., *UK Housing and Climate Change – Heavyweight vs lightweight construction*, Bill Dunster Architects with Arup Research + Development, October 2004.

Environment Agency, www.environment-agency.gov.uk, is a useful source of information on flooding and sustainable damage, and provides maps of flood plains.

'Houses from the Factory', *Architecture Today*, AT 96. pp. 60–64.

Partington, R., 'Prefab Sprouts', *The Architects' Journal*, 25 November 1999. pp. 25–34.

4 Offices: the Working Environment

The office building is a type which, perhaps more than any other in the 20th Century, embodied the economic imperatives of the age, its own characteristic technologies (the raised floor and suspended ceiling, for example) and consequent environmental impacts. Whereas contemporary UK housing, at least superficially, isn't at a great remove from pre-modern types, the office block is very much the outcome of recent history. But just as with dwellings, offices are responsible for greenhouse gas emissions that have repercussions on the environment. Because energy saving strategies are not 'one size fits all' it is important to look at the ways in which patterns of energy use differ in these buildings types. So, how and why do the CO_2 emissions from offices and dwellings differ?

1 Similarities and differences across building types

Figure 4.1 shows calculated CO_2 data for dwellings and offices, based on data from the Movement for Innovation (M4i)[1]. In terms of operational energy, although the average office emits less operational $kgCO_2/m^2$ than the average dwelling, the range is much, much greater. For embodied CO_2 the trends are reversed: the average office has greater embodied CO_2, but a smaller range — although the difference in ranges is smaller than with operational emissions. We can postulate some reasons for these results:

- There is likely to be less diversity in lifestyles than there is in business practices.
- However, a greater proportion of households are likely to undertake energy intensive activities such as washing clothes and taking baths, while most offices do not.

- There may be less diversity in building forms for offices as a result of speculative offices driving space and servicing standards towards homogeneity.

- Offices are likely to contain a higher proportion of high-embodied-energy items (such as data networks, power trunking and specialist luminaires) at fit out than houses.

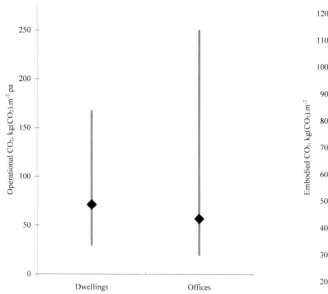
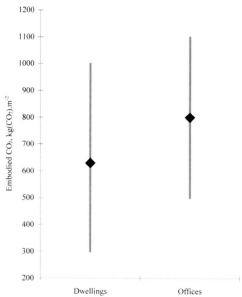

Source: author, adapted from[1]

To really understand these trends we need to look at offices in more detail.

At the beginning of the 1990s a comprehensive survey of energy use in office buildings was summarised in the Energy Consumption Guide 19[2]. This government-funded publication has been regularly updated and is referred to alternatively as ECON 19 or ECG019.

The document is based on statistics from 200 offices that were the subject of the case studies carried out during the development of ECG019 (Table 4.1).

The data was used to establish benchmarks for the typical energy consumption patterns of a broad range of office buildings, and good practice benchmarks for buildings achieving a better standard of energy efficiency.

Four categories of office type were distinguished from the data contributing to ECG019, each having markedly different energy consumption characteristics, and benchmarks for their energy use:

Figure 4.1 Range and 50th percentile for operation and embodied CO_2 for dwellings and offices

Type 1. Naturally ventilated with cellular offices between 100 and 3000 m^2 in area.

These tend to be smaller, more technologically straightforward buildings, relying on the use of daylight, with simple control systems for artificial lighting, and limited common spaces, the catering within the building being restricted in all probability to a tea kitchen.

Type 2. Once again naturally ventilated with some cellular offices and conference rooms, normally in the range of 500 to 4000 m^2. They are predominantly open plan, having higher light levels than the previous example but with their deeper plans limiting the access of daylight. In this case, artificial lighting is commonly switched on across a wider office area, and there tends to be a higher concentration of office equipment including vending machines.

Type 3. Air-conditioned, standard – these are usually purpose-built speculative developments with deeper floor plates than type 2. Benchmarks are based on variable air volume (VAV) air-conditioning. Typically, sizes range from 2000 to 8000 m^2.

Type 4. Air-conditioned, prestige – these purpose-built buildings may be a head office or regional office, including a staff restaurant, a central computer suite, and generally more extensive IT capability using a wide range of equipment and more centralised facilities.

Across the range of buildings that contributed to the survey, the annual delivered energy consumption varied widely from under 100 to over 1000 kWh/ m^2. It was found that, in good practice offices, energy costs could be 30–50% below the level of the average. To make a comparison between different types entailed making some assumptions: for example, the gross to net ratio for these different types of office varied from an average of 76% for type 1 buildings to 68% for type 4.

The 'good practice' benchmark is equal to the lowest quartile of the energy consumption data collected. A 'typical' office in the 1990s might produce a little under twice the CO_2 that a 'good practice' one would[3], something that can start to be remedied as offices become ready for refurbishment. ECG019 suggests that new offices should improve upon 'good practice' from the 1990s.

Table 4.1 ECG019 Office building types and benchmarks

Office types	CO$_2$ emissions (kgCO$_2$ per m^2 per year)
1. Naturally ventilated, cellular Typically 100 m^2 to 3000 m^2. Services of domestic type. Kitchens usually limited to tea-making facilities.	56.8 (typical) 32.2 (lowest quartile)
2. Naturally ventilated, open-plan Typical size 500 m^2 to 4000 m^2. Though mostly open plan, there are a few cellular offices. There is more office equipment. Lights and shared equipment switched in larger groups and may often be left on.	72.9 (typical) 43.1 (lowest quartile)
3. Air-conditioned, standard Typically 2000 m^2 to 8000 m^2. Largely purpose built and often speculative. Similar to type 2, but with deeper floor plates. Benchmarks are based on VAV air-conditioning.	151.3 (typical) 85.0 (lowest quartile)
4. Air conditioned, prestige Typically 4000 m^2 to 20,000 m^2. Purpose built, possibly a head office. Will include catering kitchens and air-conditioned rooms for mainframe computers and communication equipment. More extensive ICT capability.	226.1 (typical) 143.4 (lowest quartile)

Notes: floor area is 'treated floor area', i.e. excluding car parking and the like. All data from ECG019 are derived from measurements of buildings, taken in the 1990s. Source: data adapted from: *Energy Consumption Guide 19 – Energy use in offices*, 2003 edn, Action Energy/The Carbon Trust, www.thecarbontrust.co.uk, 2003. pp. 7–21.

Although the data sets are not directly comparable, we can see the same large variation in CO$_2$ emissions across the office types (Figure 4.2) as we did in Figure 4.1. Breaking the results down we see that:

- The greatest increase across the groups is accounted for by an increase in energy required for air-conditioning and for electrical equipment.
- The increase across the groups in the amount of energy needed for heating, hot water and lighting is negligible in comparison.
- Because of conversion and transmission losses, electrical loads produce a disproportionate amount of CO$_2$.

With the enormous increase in ICT use over the 1990s, the energy load due to electrical equipment for the smaller office types will probably be greater than shown here and the increase across the building types more gentle.

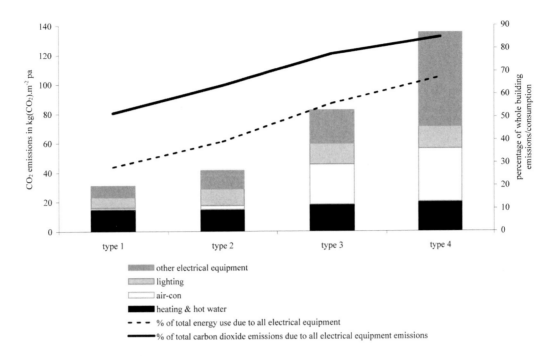

Figure 4.2 Carbon dioxide emissions from ECG019's office types, plus percentage of energy vs CO$_2$ due to electricity use

Notes: The category 'air-con' here includes pumps, fans and controls as well as cooling and humidification which explains why non-conditioned types 1 and 2 do consume some energy in this category. Energy used for catering is omitted in this comparison.

Source: author – data adapted from Energy Consumption Guide 19 *(2003), pp. 20–21*

ECG019 established benchmarks or standards for office buildings with the intention that new constructions should aim to improve on the good practice benchmark relating to each type. To this end, its recommendations were refined further to address the components of buildings, their environmental services for heating, lighting and air conditioning, and the components of those services, in particular the lighting efficiency and air handling systems (including the office computer equipment consumption, in relation to the typical working hours of a weekday).

The benchmarks are directed principally at developers and managers of offices in excess of 1500 m². What was found, perhaps not surprisingly, is that type 4 'prestige offices' are the largest energy consumers among the four varieties. A typical office might be expected to consume up to 600 W/m², and a good practice office up to about 400 W/m². Whereas the equivalent numbers for a type 1 building would be 250 W/m² on average, down to 130 W/m² for a good practice naturally ventilated type 1 building.

The itemised figures for the consumption of energy show that fossil fuel consumption was similar in all four cases, but slightly more for the prestige office because of it occupants tending to have longer working hours, and on account of the likelihood of its having a centralised kitchen and restaurant. On the other hand, electricity consumption increases rapidly from the simpler to the more heavily serviced types of office. In particular the air-conditioned types 3 and 4 which use a lot more electricity to run fans, pumps and controls for their air handling systems.

Similarly, as office buildings get larger and deeper, lighting electricity consumption rises, making effective lighting controls a necessity to stop lights from being left on all the time. The more sophisticated office types use more office equipment, and their equipment loads are a function of growth in ICT. Heat production by computers, which used to be thought a particular problem, has diminished over time, as desktop computers have become more energy efficient. As office buildings grow in size and complexity, however, telecommunications equipment and lifts consume more energy, so that electricity in air-conditioned offices can account for 80 to 90% of their total energy costs and carbon dioxide emissions.

Having established benchmarks for typical buildings, and good practice buildings, it was then possible to pinpoint those aspects of a building's environment that are conducive to achieving energy savings. For example, it was shown that heating costs could be reduced by 50%, and electrical costs by at least a third, by using readily available techniques such as making the building better insulated, using more efficient boilers, improving control systems, and improving the hot water system's efficiency. Substantial savings were shown to be possible by making modifications to plant and management. Lower electrical costs for air-conditioning systems can be achieved by the use of better controls, from designing systems with lower pressure drops requiring less powerful fans, and using modern fluorescent tubes in light fittings, which can make delivery of artificial lighting a lot more economical.

ECG019 explains a methodology that enables building owners and contractors to compare the efficiency of their buildings with the benchmarks by gathering together information from electricity bills, and other fuel bills. This entails isolating those parts of the building, which are particularly energy intensive such as kitchens, computer rooms, and HVAC plant. Then to establish a target for reductions based on priorities, and having decided on a list of measures to be taken, to timetable them in relation to future plans for maintenance[4].

1.1 CO_2 emissions

In 2002 changes were made to Approved Document L2 (AD L2) of the Building Regulations to introduce a new method for the control of carbon emissions during the lifetime operation of buildings. This is called a 'carbon performance rating' (CPR).[5] It is directed particularly towards types 3 and 4 offices, which make use of air-conditioning and mechanical ventilation in addition to space heating and lighting.

ECG019 was principally concerned with energy and cost, but it contains information, derived from the building surveys, about the extent of CO_2 emissions from office buildings. These were quoted in kgC/m^2 (kg of carbon per m^2, as opposed to kg of CO_2 which is sometimes used) of 'treated floor area' – the heated areas of the building only, i.e. excluding car parking etc. To relate the 'good practice' and 'typical' energy benchmarks for the four office types, the conversion factors relating delivered energy to CO_2, reflect the fact that electricity is responsible for much larger amounts of CO_2 than either gas or oil.

Calculation of the carbon performance rating is based on the method contained within ECG019, as follows.

It uses the power ratings of the services plant in addition to factors relating to controls and management, in order to predict levels of CO_2 emissions that can be measured against the ECG019 benchmarks.

The actual performance of mechanical systems depends on a range of variables, which are anticipated within the carbon performance rating estimates. For example, such factors as the orientation of the building, the form of the plan, the detailed design of the external envelope, and whatever internal heat gains are generated within the building.

The annual quantity of carbon in kgC/m^2 per year is calculated in the same way as previously, being equal to the power rating of the plant multiplied by the number of hours in a year that the plant is in operation, multiplied by the conversion factors for the different delivered fuels.

The aim that new buildings should reach 'good practice' emissions levels has now been incorporated within amendment AD L2.

The expectations for office refurbishments are that emissions may be 10% higher than for new buildings, because of the compromises that are probably inevitable when designing within an existing structure.

The regulations apply only to those parts of the building given over to typical office activities, i.e. excluding areas such as swimming pools, computer rooms, kitchens and restaurants.

Adjustments have to be built into the calculations if heat recovery equipment and thermal storage devices (such as ice storage for cooling) are to be used, and similarly for space heating using heat pumps, CHP and renewable energy which is offset against the CPR.

Heating and hot water using gas or oil has about a two-to-one ratio between the CO_2 produced by a 'typical' type 4 and a 'good practice' type 1 office. A computer room was assumed to exist in type 4 offices but not in type 1, and was responsible for approximately one quarter of the building's emissions. More dramatic was the spread between a 'typical' type 4 and a 'good practice' type 1 in terms of the electricity consumed by fans, pumps and controls, at approximately 25 to 1. The lighting bills, given that type 4 is anticipated to be a much deeper building, have a ratio of 4 to 1. This bears out the considerable reductions that can be achieved by making the best use of natural light and avoiding air-conditioning.

1.2 The journey to work

Whereas the construction and operation of buildings is responsible for 50% of the CO_2 emissions from the UK into the atmosphere, transport between buildings accounts for 22% of the energy used. The growth in transport year on year is, however, running at 4%, mainly due to an increasing number of car miles.[6]

Not surprisingly, the need to limit the use of personal transport is one of the aims of the BREEAM for Offices assessment. It has been shown that the amount of energy used by the population of the building for commuting is about the same as the amount of energy used within the building itself, though there are considerable variations from place to place. In London, although staff tend to travel further than in other cities, the important difference being the smaller number of people that use cars, particularly cars occupied by only one person.

The extensive use of public transport in London is responsible for the capital's relatively favourable figures. As a result BREEAM regards operational energy and embodied energy as being two sides of the same coin. It encourages the use of public transport, and other low-energy alternatives to the car, such as bicycles. Credits are awarded if the amount of car parking relative to new buildings is limited, if the building is close to public transport, and if bike parking and park-and-ride facilities are provided; also if organisations permit practices that reduce

Box 4.1 Work practices

The space planners DEGW, observing different patterns of contemporary office organisation, have described the corresponding types of office layout. These can vary from the open plan typing pool, or present day call centre, where individuals may have limited control over their environment, to the smaller scale group work spaces commonly found in advertising agencies, for example, where teams are formed to undertake particular projects, spaces are reconfigured for each project, and there is localised control of environmental conditions. Office spaces may have to change between these plan types over quite short time spans.

Contemporary offices are designed with sufficient inbuilt flexibility for these frequent changes to be made. The use of demountable partitioning enables the demarcation of space to be altered at will, raised floors and suspended ceilings allow services to be re-routed at the same time. The relatively short life of furniture layouts in offices is, in turn, responsible for the short life of finishes, such as carpets and paintwork, and the rapid replacement of building services, and can have a major impact on the lifetime energy consumption of the building.

As a result of the PROBE[1] studies, the relationships commonly found between the complexity of a building's technology, and the level of management it requires, have been identified. In this way, a good match can be achieved between the level of maintenance expertise that will be brought to the building on completion, and its design brief. There is the complex type of building that requires a well-resourced management strategy. The organisation has to be sufficiently large and sophisticated to recognise environmental management as an investment – one that increases staff productivity and satisfaction, and achieves business advantages as a result of the company's enhanced image.

1. Bordass, B., Field, J. and Leaman, A. Probe 14: Elizabeth Fry Building. *Building Services Journal*, April 1998. p37. and Bordass, B., Field, J. and Leaman, A. Probe 7: Gardner House. *Building Services Journal*, October 1996. p39.

Further reading:
    Energy Efficiency Best Practice Programme, *The Design Team's Guide to Environmentally Smart Buildings: Energy-efficient options for new and refurbished offices*. BRECSU, Garston, 1999.

commuting, such as tele-working, give incentives to staff for the use of public transport, and encourage cars to be shared, or provide a dedicated bus service.

Benefits accrue for reduction in car parking requirement, particularly since it is provided at great cost on city centre sites. BREEAM lists several other advantages derived from reduced car dependence: financially in that staff productivity increases when travel times are reduced, and in terms of staff health benefits as a result of reduced exposure to traffic fumes; also, being seen to be 'green' can enhance the organisation's public image.

1.3 Embodied energy vs operational energy

Embodied energy in office construction is a small proportion of the overall energy consumption of the building over its lifetime. The debate as to whether a concrete frame or a steel frame has the higher embodied energy, is something of a sideshow because, although it can be shown that CO_2 emissions resulting from construction of a timber frame will be 450 m³, for concrete around 1300 m³, and increasing to 2000 m³ for steel, this is small compared with the cumulative operational emissions over the whole life of the building (some 1500 m³ per annum if the building is air-conditioned).

This might suggest that embodied energy is not worth considering, but it is important to remember that embodied energy and operational energy both contribute to the total CO_2 emissions over the whole life of the building. For instance, if extra insulation is incorporated within the building, this will increase the embodied energy (because extra materials have been used), but the operational energy will be reduced. This would indeed increase the ratio of embodied energy to operational energy, but over the whole life of the building might reduce total CO_2 emissions.

When BREEAM guidelines are implemented, the greater efficiency of the building will reduce the operational energy but increase the first cost. For example, it has been calculated that for a 10,000 m² office building having a usual level of services provision of 30W/m² for power, 20W/m² for lighting and 20±1°C design temperature for the air-conditioning, BREEAM recommendations would increase the first cost by about 3%, but achieve worthwhile reductions in annual operational costs and CO_2 emissions.

If the energy consumption of services was reduced, power for example to 22W/m², lighting to 14 W/m², and if the air-conditioning temperature were relaxed to 22±2.5°C the effect upon operational costs would be dramatic. Should air-conditioning be eliminated entirely in favour of a stack ventilation and night cooling strategy, both the initial cost and the operational and CO_2 emissions reduction would be very significant.

Building to the standards set out in BREEAM for offices tends to increase a building's capital cost while lifetime costs are reduced. This means that the incentive for its adoption by developers is limited – all the advantages fall to the tenant! The correction of this significant disincentive has yet to be addressed; it will require the use of both legal and taxation measures by government.

1.4 High rise vs medium rise development

The most usual type of city office development throughout the 1980s and 1990s was medium rise with medium to deep floor plates. The recent spate of applications to build towers in London implies an increase in energy consumption as a result of their less favourable volume to surface area ratio, and the increased lift power they require, though these may be offset by the transportation advantages of locating tall buildings over public transport nodes. So far, the construction of low energy office buildings relying on shallower, naturally ventilated and daylit floor plans has been overwhelmingly the preserve of out-of-town and suburban locations, but the newest towers in London are incorporating innovative features (e.g. St Mary Axe).

Box 4.2 Size of floor plates

In the City of London a predominant form of office development has been the deep plan associated with dealing rooms. Not only are the dimensions of dealing rooms inimical to natural servicing but also the occupant and machine loads are very high. Although in terms of winter heat loss such a building is likely to perform well, there will be a large energy requirement for cooling and artificial lighting. The perimeter spaces may benefit from a view out and daylight, but air-conditioning is the norm not only for the deeper sections of the plan, but also at the perimeter.

The growth in tall buildings would appear to be inevitable given the anticipated demand for office space, and the pressures of land availability that are exacerbated in the centre of the City by the St Paul's height restrictions. To make these new developments environmentally sustainable will be a challenge because, although buildings with a shallow plan are suitable for natural lighting and ventilation, the continuing trend is for buildings to become deeper; floor plates having increased from the 5–8 metre column spans common in the 1980s, to the 10–15 metre spaces usual in more recent developments.

Tall buildings are, however, capable of achieving some sustainability criteria because of their economies of scale. Repeated floor plans can often result in savings in the quantities of materials being used, standardisation results in manufacturing processes that are more efficient with cheaper unit costs, and a tall building can have a small enough footprint to occupy only part of the site, allowing public space to be created at street level with associated retail development.

There are of course the offsetting disadvantages: the safety hazards involved in working at considerable heights; the large amount of surface area which tall buildings have compared with those of medium height and medium span; their relatively low efficiency of space occupation; more structure particularly at lower floors; more electrically driven services, particularly lifts; and the wind and shading effects that tall buildings can have at ground level.

Source: Pank, W., Girardet, H. and Cox, G. *Tall Buildings and Sustainability*. The Corporation of London, February 2002 (unpublished).

A report commissioned in 2002 by the City of London Corporation, and called 'Tall Buildings to Sustainability', describes current trends in office development in the City.[7] It estimates that, in order to meet the levels of economic growth that are predicted, 4–6 million m^2 of office space will be needed over the next quarter of a century, equivalent to five new Canary Wharfs.

The expectation is that the towers of the future will be of mixed use with shopping and recreational uses at lower levels and offices above.

It will be a considerable challenge to make these sorts of developments sustainable, not least because the usual mechanism for development is market driven by developers rather than end users, and developers have very limited interest in the construction of low-energy buildings.

The lesson from cities such as Hong Kong and Singapore is that the clustering of towers around transportation nodes is very efficient in terms of the journeys to work. Statistics suggest, however, that the energy consumption per area of office space is growing at a faster rate than new floor space is being provided, and in the UK the rate of services sector energy use is growing faster than anywhere else in Europe and, unfortunately, energy is being used less efficiently than on the Continent.

2. Environmental issues

2.1 Daylighting vs artificial lighting

Because working hours in offices are principally the hours of daylight, there are considerable advantages in maximising an office building's potential use of daylight. The major difficulty in achieving this goal is the unequal distribution of daylight levels. Illuminance levels fall away sharply as room depth increases away from windows. This not only means that light levels will be insufficient at the back of deeper office spaces but also that the relatively bright surfaces adjacent to the windows will be a source of glare.

Advanced daylighting systems are most useful in the generally overcast sky conditions of the UK in allowing a more even distribution of light within rooms, partially by redistributing light, but mostly by suppressing excessive light levels within the immediate vicinity of windows.

Daylight is the medium to which the human eye is biologically adapted. For the best perception of objects, and optimum colour rendering, the quality achieved by daylight is preferable to any artificial light source. In addition, the artificial lighting used in offices can account for up to 50% of primary energy use, but because there is a close correlation between office working hours and hours of daylight availability, the efficient use of daylight can lead to a reduction of between 35% and 75% of the amount of lighting power which is consumed. The extent of savings depends on the use of controls that dim artificial lights according to light levels out of doors.

The success of daylight design does, however, require consideration of other environmental parameters. Daylight admits heat into the building, so a shading system may be necessary in order to avoid summertime overheating. In winter, extensive areas of glazing not only result in heat loss but also result in the window surface being a source of radiant cooling and discomfort. Potential glare problems are a particular concern in rooms which are lit from one side only, and where the room surfaces are not of sufficient reflectivity.

Box 4.3 Switching systems

The use of dimmable lamps, including fluorescent lamps within contemporary installations, enables artificial lighting to be used as a complement to daylighting rather than as a substitute. Daylight can then be sufficient for a proportion of working hours and can be topped up by artificial light as needs be. Automatic controls are worthwhile even in small cellular offices. Once they have been turned on, lights tend to be left on throughout the day, and so switching systems have been developed to enable the lighting system to respond to the actual availability of natural light:

1. Occupancy sensors are designed to register movement in rooms and turn lights off when they are empty. They detect reflected beams within a room either by infrared, radar or ultrasound. Presence detectors turn all the lights off when the room is unoccupied, and are most effective when it is left to the user to turn the lights back on again when re-entering the room, otherwise the lights are likely to be switched on by the wind or other small movements in the space. The reaction of users to these systems is important because if they cannot be overridden, there is the danger that the occupants will become irritated and block the sensors so that the lights stay on constantly. Presence detectors can be very efficient: in one UK installation the payback period for presence controls was six years as compared with 20 years for light-level sensors.

2. Light-level sensors dim or elevate levels according to ambient daylight levels. They rely on the use of photoelectric cells. There are three different types, the first of which is for small offices: it turns all the lights off once daylight levels are sufficient. The second is suitable for larger rooms having light fittings with multiple lamps: the sensor turns the tubes off sequentially according to the availability of daylight. The third system uses dimmers to adjust the lights up and down, but this is not suitable for use with all types of lamp.

3. Timed switches can, for example, turn lights off at lunchtime, making it unlikely that the users will turn lights on when they return at the beginning of the afternoon since natural light is likely to be sufficient.

One of the most common ways to introduce daylight to the interior of office buildings is by the use of an atrium. An atrium designed to achieve reasonable daylight factors at the atrium floor in wintertime may be too brightly lit, causing glare, in the summer, so moveable shading at the roof of the atrium is very desirable. The upper floors of offices surrounding the atrium can be directly lit from the sky, but the lower floors will be mostly reliant on reflections from the floor surface of the atrium bouncing light back into the surrounding rooms.

From a daylighting point of view the use of extensive planting within the atrium, which is of relatively low reflectivity is not helpful. The changing daylight conditions from the top to the bottom of an atrium suggests that windows lighting rooms need to be designed in specific localised ways, according to their height above the atrium floor and below its roof; as a result the design of atria within office buildings can be of considerable architectural interest.

2.2 Air-conditioning vs natural ventilation

The 1980s Orbit Report[8] forecast that future machine loads in office buildings would preclude the use of natural ventilation and make air-conditioning inevitable. In fact, the efficiency of computers, in terms of their heat production, has increased markedly since that time but, over the same period, air-conditioning has become an industry standard for higher-grade office accommodation. In Germany meanwhile, the enthusiastic pursuit of a green agenda has resulted in the construction of large office developments that have successfully demonstrated how natural ventilation and passive servicing can deal with the majority of office situations. Some UK offices have been built with the intention of achieving the same result, most notably the BRE Environmental Office 'Building 16' at Garston, designed by Feilden and Clegg.

A primary aim, along the way to sustainable development, must be the avoidance of air-conditioning by making the best use of the outdoor environment, and utilising sustainable technologies, passive and natural cooling, passive solar gains, and daylight rather than artificial lighting. Given favourable local conditions, and a suitable location and pattern of use, then an office building should be able to function without air-conditioning and with limited use of mechanical services such as fans, but in a lot of cases these ideal conditions cannot be met.

There are always days in summer when there is insufficient buoyancy for stack ventilation to be effective. For inner city development, noise and pollution is a major problem if buildings are to rely on the use of opening windows, so in many cases air-conditioning has become the norm. This trend is also the result of changing market standards generated by higher user expectations in conjunction with more stringent regulations, increasing internal heat gains not only on account of increasing numbers of computers but also other office machines, and the tendency towards lightweight building construction.

In the UK, there are two principal reasons for the growing use of HVAC in offices, the first being the difficulty of keeping room temperatures within the thermal comfort zone due to internal heat gains, and the second is the reluctance to rely on passive measures (such as opening windows) because of concerns over security.

This is particularly true of spaces that are in dense occupancy such as conference rooms where air-conditioning is difficult to avoid, and because they tend to be located within the inner zone of the building.

The other reasons are to do with indoor air quality and the difficulty of drawing air into the building from streets that are heavily trafficked, because of the pollution issuing from car exhausts. Internal pollution sources such as carpets, and photo-copying machines compound the problem. This is a major issue because, in a well-insulated office building, ventilation and cooling loads may account for more than 50% of its overall energy use. To achieve low energy consumption requires a ventilation system that is well controlled and energy efficient.

Natural ventilation may gain user acceptance if the accompanying control systems are capable of responding to the vagaries of the outdoor climate, but it is difficult to achieve a consistent level of performance from natural ventilation. Natural ventilation airflows are driven by temperature differences between the indoor environment and outdoor ambient, and wind effects. These pressure differences across and through the building envelope are responsible for random air admission in the form of infiltration through gaps in the construction, as well as planned ventilation through windows and other ventilation openings.

There is a huge variation in the extent of these pressures and, in order to adequately control the amount of air passing through the building, leakage has to be limited by making the building envelope as airtight as possible, and the ventilation openings in the building being environmentally engineered for their purpose. This becomes more difficult in tall office buildings because wind velocities increase with height above the ground. The frictional resistance of the ground and other obstructions is negated with sufficient height, depending on the surrounding topography and whether the location is urban, or open landscape. The direction and distribution of wind pressure can be very variable if other tall buildings are in the vicinity, and tall trees can also have an effect.

In the UK, wind becomes the predominant driver for natural ventilation at wind speeds in excess of around 4 m/s. In wintertime, the stack effect, caused by difference in density of air at different temperatures, can provide significant air movement, but this is less successful in summer when the temperature difference between inside and outside is less marked.

Consequently, natural ventilation is not just about having operable windows within the façade of an office but rather a whole design concept for the sectional organisation of the building. Atria and internal stairwells have often been used as components of a natural ventilation strategy, to supply fresh air to the interior of the building even when its windows are shut. An engineered ventilation system requires that consistent and healthy conditions are maintained for the building's occupants, by 'building tight and ventilating right', i.e. by reducing the levels of infiltration using airtight construction, and by introducing fresh air in a regulated fashion.

The principal design criterion is that ventilation levels have to be appropriate so as to satisfy the requirements of the occupants. Assuming that smoking is banned within the building, fresh air ventilation has to supply sufficient oxygen for breathing (about 0.3 l/s per person), to remove body odours (requiring 5 l/s per person) and to allow enough indoor air for comfort.

In most cases, for the majority of the year, wind and stack effects can be used together to induce natural ventilation flows through the building, providing that wind pressure is acting in the same direction as stack pressure. For that reason, the outlets from the building should be on the leeward side. Special arrangements will have to be made in noisy or polluted areas and in hot and humid climates. Solar control will often be required to avoid excessive solar gain, and internal heat gains have to be anticipated.

Window design becomes an important issue, particularly in respect of the building's thermal mass and its utilisation for night cooling. Requirements in summertime will be different from those in winter. In summer, the main issues are the control of temperature and achieving sufficient velocity of air movement past the skin to achieve a sensation of comfort. The rate of airflow does not have to be as carefully controlled as in winter, when there is the problem of draughts to consider, but the flow rate in summer will be considered excessive when papers start to be blown off desks. To avoid overheating in summer, air flow rates will probably exceed those necessary to merely achieve good indoor air quality, and the sizes of openings required will be a lot larger than needed in winter.

It is, however, summertime overheating problems that initiate demands for the introduction of air-conditioning. In the UK, there are some days when the outdoor air temperature is higher than comfort temperature indoors (and some models of climate change suggest that this is likely to increase) in which case windows are best kept closed and a draught induced by the use of fans, but these occasions are usually limited to a few days or a couple of weeks a year. The internal gains are a problem to be considered at the design stage. Solar gain is the major external source of overheating; accordingly, shading systems for office buildings have become usual, components that have to be designed in relation to the orientation of the glass, and the amount of glass within the façade.

For buildings designed to achieve passive solar heating in winter, the majority of the glazing will be in a southerly direction, so the shading can be in the form of projecting louvres or gridded walkways that may double as window-cleaning access. Southern elevations will have less solar gain in summertime when the elevation of the sun is higher in the sky so overhangs and projections above windows will function well, but east and west elevations, and particularly west facing elevations, pose a real problem for the prevention of overheating since the sun is then shining into the building after its fabric has already heated up. External fins or extra deep reveals to the windows may help overcome the problem. Another possible solution is to have over-sailing upper floors, each floor jutting over the one below.

However, it is particularly difficult to prevent shading devices reducing daylight levels at the back of rooms in wintertime. Adjustable shading is beneficial from this point of view though it may entail external moving parts and their long-term maintenance problems.

Although sunlight passing through windows is the principal source of overheating, shading the external walls of the building in summer also helps keep the building cool.

This can be achieved by the use of light-coloured and reflective finishes, and careful disposition of external landscaping. Once heat gains have been reduced as far as possible, ventilation can be used as a summer cooling strategy; the aim should be to reduce the indoor temperature in working hours to be not more than 25.5°C for more than 100 hours a year and not more than 28°C for more than 25 hours a year.

For natural ventilation to work when the weather is warm outside, but cooler than within the building, a sufficient quantity of air should be supplied through opening windows, or from an atrium, to dissipate hot air from within the building. In this way, both evaporative and convective cooling of the building's occupants can be achieved; ceiling fans operating at low speeds are also effective.

Deciding whether or not outside ambient air temperature is above or below comfort level is a function of the 'dry resultant temperature'. At low air speeds the dry resultant temperature is the mean of the air temperature and the radiant temperature of the space. Generally, 27°C is regarded as the maximum temperature for naturally ventilated buildings. The standard technique for naturally ventilated buildings is to make best use of the building's thermal mass in combination with a night cooling strategy. In this way, the construction of the building, its environment and the envelope of the building all combine together to make a passive environmental strategy.

Thermal mass depends on the admittance of the internal surfaces of the building, but this needs to be coupled with the air space of the room, so it is important not to conceal the thermal mass behind suspended ceilings or raised floors. Thus removing or eliminating raised floors and suspended ceilings, and their detrimental consequences for architectural space, is the logical benefit of an environmental construction strategy.

Shading the façade: integration of shading devices

Office buildings designed to utilise solar energy are likely to have most of their windows facing south. In offices, unlike housing, the energy penalty for departing from an exactly south-facing orientation is not marked, but the danger of aggravating the threat of summertime overheating remains. As a result, it has become very usual, both for naturally ventilated and air-conditioned office buildings, that windows facing towards the sun incorporate a solar shading system.

Box 4.4 Advanced glazing systems

Light shelves have long been employed in the US where summer sunshine is generally more intense than in the UK. The specular upper surface of the shelf reflects light onto the ceiling and then to the back of the room. The result is to redistribute light to where it can be useful, and the shelf also serves to shade the area adjacent to the windows, which would otherwise be over illuminated giving rise to problems of glare.

In the UK, light redistribution is unlikely to be successful but instead light shelves help reduce the extent of contrast between the back and front of rooms which can help provide the perception of greater uniformity of illumination. As a rule of thumb, the depth of the light shelf should be equal to the height of the light shelf above the working surface.

Other advanced glazing systems, such as prismatic glazing, utilise plastic panes or glass cut to form prisms that, by total internal reflection, direct a proportion of the light towards the ceiling and then to the back of the room. Only the upper part of windows can be used in this way since they obstruct the view out, but the lack of intense direct beam radiation means that prismatic glazing (and alternatives such as those made from holographic film) is unlikely to be cost-effective in the UK.

Perforated overhangs are preferable since they will allow warm air to escape rather than channelling it into the building when windows are open during summertime. They will, however, draw the 'no sky' line towards the front of the room and reduce daylight levels at the back of the space in wintertime. A possible compromise is to contain Venetian blinds within the cavity of the windows, which may be operated by the user or the BEMS.

Hybrid ventilation

Entirely passive systems of ventilation are not suitable for some situations, because of the difficulty of achieving satisfactory indoor air quality and comfort conditions throughout the year, so hybrid ventilation (also known as mixed mode ventilation) is becoming widely adopted.

Natural ventilation systems can have problems with draughts in wintertime and overheating in summer, whereas air-conditioning systems are often the cause of user complaints because of their lack of individual environmental control. Hybrid ventilation provides access to the appropriate characteristics of each mode according to the prevailing weather conditions. The reduced use of fans and other mechanical plant achieves substantial overall reductions in energy consumption.

Hybrid systems make use of natural ventilation when appropriate, but have control and mechanical systems that enable artificial 'active' technologies to be utilised when required. Part of the cost of the plant is transferred into the building costs associated with the construction of passive stacks, intelligent window systems, and a building section conducive to airflow.

Hybrid ventilation may incorporate other low-energy characteristics such as advanced daylight systems, passive solar heating and night cooling. Consequently an integrated approach to the overall design of the building is required. They make use of different features of mechanical and natural ventilation at different times of year, or day, or season. The intelligent controls that are an integral part of hybrid ventilation switch between natural and artificial modes in order to save energy. Mechanical and natural systems have developed separately over the years with limited potential for substantial gains in efficiency, but their combination offers the potential for further improvements, and for the considerable savings that can be achieved by eliminating air-conditioning.

Hybrid ventilation requires both components of an artificial servicing system and building elements such as windows to be under the command of the building management system. The intention is to maximise the extent of natural servicing and reduce the mechanical component, implying that a broader tolerance to variable room temperatures will be required. Where local requirements and standards are very prescriptive, the proportion of mechanical provision may have to be increased. Studies have shown, however, that a degree of variation in indoor conditions, as influenced by the weather conditions out of doors, can be popular with office workers.

Case study installations, constructed in the late 1990s and investigated within the IEA Energy Conservation programme, suggest that hybrid ventilation has the capacity to meet human comfort criteria but without the uniformity of provision that is characteristic of fully mechanical systems. The majority of the case study buildings incorporated air extract/intake chimneys or turrets that became a visible component of their architecture and allowed air distribution at low pressure drops, reducing the power rating of fans, where required. In most cases, sensors registering temperature and indoor air quality, controlled the building management system. High insulation and the use of high performance glazing were consistent features. Heat recovery, external sunshading, and artificial light levels controlled by occupancy sensors, were used in some of the buildings according to their specific climate conditions.

Box 4.5 Sick building syndrome

Sick building syndrome (SBS) is a complex phenomenon that was originally associated with physical disease symptoms in poorly performing buildings. It has since been realised that SBS is a wider phenomenon that can include recurrent complaints such as headaches, as well as more insidious feelings of discomfort and malaise that may be difficult to directly attribute to a specific aspect of the building's environment.

Among the issues assessed by BREEAM[1] are several that have an impact on the health and comfort of office workers. Because contemporary life requires us all to spend so much of our time indoors, providing environments that are healthy and comfortable is an aspect of their users' quality of life, but also contributes to the achievement of high levels of productivity in office buildings. Although the visual quality of towns and cities is an important factor, there is an obvious difficulty in rating these variables, so within BREEAM the issues addressed are only those capable of objective measurement such as comfort, humidity, noise, indoor air quality and lighting, and in offices there is a particular concern with summertime overheating. The formal assessment of an office's environment can take a considerable amount of time for monitoring and analysis. BREEAM, however, only deals with those variables that can be addressed at the design stage, and calculated by rule of thumb.

Indoor air quality issues feature high on the list of potential health risks in office buildings, whereas in domestic accommodation condensation is usually the principal concern. In offices, smoking used to be

continued ...

a difficulty though the ban imposed in 2007 has eliminated this problem. The toxins emitted by building materials particularly carpets, are problematic in office buildings, as is the presence of dust mites (though they can be removed by regular and efficient cleaning). The influence of particulates on human health is still unclear.

The goals that are rewarded within the BREEAM assessment include having windows that open, ventilation systems that take in fresh air rather than relying entirely on recirculation, and natural ventilation that achieves the same aim by the use of trickle vents. BREEAM also seeks to ensure that the intake of air to the building avoids recirculation of air exhausted from indoors, and among housekeeping issues, that an efficient cleaning regime is adopted, in conjunction with schedules of maintenance.

The occurrence of legionnaires' disease is an event when buildings are directly implicated in having a detrimental effect on human health since the majority of cases are the result of poor hot water supply systems in non-domestic buildings. Prevention is a matter of rigorous maintenance and carrying out safety checks on existing equipment. Incidence of legionnaires' disease can also be related to the design, operation and maintenance of cooling towers. The system must allow regular, complete cleaning, which greatly reduces the incidence of legionnaires' disease, and the towers have to be carefully designed to enable all the condensate to be removed. These requirements are obviously important for the promotion of good heath for the building's occupants. There may, of course, be legal ramifications where safety guidelines have not been adhered to by building owners.

Another aspect with health implications considered by BREEAM is noise. Although a high level of noise can be a nuisance, conversely, in open plan offices the lack of background noise can make acoustic privacy a problem, so a compromise needs to be reached. Thermal comfort issues in office buildings are likely to be principally concerned with the incidence of overheating in high summer. Usually, in the UK, provision of sufficient natural ventilation will overcome this problem other than in city centre locations where a noisy and polluted environment requires the installation of a mechanical system.

BREEAM also gives credit for the building having the means to locally control temperatures, and for standard techniques having been used at the design stage to assess thermal comfort, and for the building having a method of monitoring and targeting office conditions.

In terms of lighting, most people prefer daylight and a view out whilst avoiding solar gain. Artificial lighting systems need a personal level of control by occupants and a correct and maintained level of lighting. Fluorescent lighting can be responsible for headaches and eyestrain, particularly if conventional ballasts have not been replaced by high frequency ones (that also have the advantage of being energy saving).

1. Baldwin, R., Yates, A., Howard, N. and Rao, S. *BREEAM 98 for Offices*. BRE Centre for Sustainable Construction Garston 1998: www.bre.co.uk/envest

3. Resource management

3.1 Renewable energy, water conservation, recycling and waste

BREEAM assessment[9] also takes into consideration the use of resources, the extent of water conservation, the use of recycled material, and waste management aspects of office construction. The choice of A-rated building elements from the BRE *Green Guide to Specification* (as illustrated within this book) earns credits within BREEAM. The additional benefits that are cited are financial, in that ecologically friendly constructions may in fact be cheaper than alternatives particularly if they can be locally sourced. In terms of human health, the *Green Guide* is also concerned with the toxicity of materials, for the overall management and image of an organisation in being able to project a green face to the world, and in helping to establish environmental management procedures within companies.

BREEAM makes an award for the sourcing of timber from sustainable, managed forests, in line with the Forest Stewardship Certification scheme, as well as the Timber Trades Association and Forests Forever environmental policies. Among the other benefits listed are those to human health in that the preservation of tropical forests also achieves retention of the plant habitat that is the source of many of today's medicines.

The reuse and recycling of construction and demolition waste is a huge issue since the construction industry is responsible for between a quarter and a third of all the waste produced in this country each year. There are several internet-based materials information exchange systems which can help overcome the general lack of knowledge for the sourcing of recycled materials. Companies need to have management systems for waste disposal to deal with the bottles, cans and paper generated in offices, including purpose-designed storage arrangements, and a policy has to be in place for the storage and collection of office waste.

BREEAM encourages the reuse of existing buildings rather than the construction of new. Despite the fact that new buildings may be more efficient from an energy point of view compared with old ones, many buildings are demolished simply because their location is wrong rather than because they are impossible to repair or unsuited to their purpose. So, within the BREEAM assessment, the refurbishment and retention of elements from existing buildings is promoted, as is the reuse of construction and demolition materials. To achieve the aims of BREEAM, a large proportion of the existing structure and envelope of a retained building has to be reused, and recycled material should be employed.

Box 4.6 Building management systems

Originally, building management systems (BMS) were designed to control mechanical equipment. The BMS could control anything from room temperatures to security. The building energy management system (BEMS) is a type of BMS that is focused on managing the comfort conditions of the indoor environment, and can be used to monitor energy usage, and therefore control costs. Elements of a building can be controlled either manually, by opening and closing windows, adjusting blinds and so on, or automatically, by the use of timers or presence detectors (in the case of artificial lights), and a building energy management system will undertake computerised control from a central point. The BEMS relies on sensors within the building to relay information to the central controller, which sends orders to the actuators for the opening and closing of blinds and other devices. A supervisor device may be necessary to override decisions made locally by users if, for example, windows ought to be kept closed according to the strength and direction of the wind, or in case of fire.

In relation to passive strategies the BEMS can be responsible for automatically adjusting solar shading, the control of artificial lighting levels, opening and closing high-level windows for the purposes of night ventilation, and generally moderating the ventilation air flows through the building by controlling inlet vents, and high-level extracts into stacks or from roof outlets.

However, a BEMS can, if poorly designed, result in increased energy consumption where, for example night cooling is too successful resulting in the need for heaters to be turned on in the morning of the following day. So the BEMS has to be configured so that all the systems within the building work together and not in opposition. On the other hand, the building users should have the capability of overruling the BEMS, otherwise occupant dissatisfaction will undermine the system entirely, but there will have to be fallback settings for reasons of safety and to conserve energy. As with any contemporary services installation, the BEMS will have to be carefully tested and commissioned, and a maintenance manual, including operating instructions, produced by the BEMS.

Because water demand has risen so sharply over the past 30 years (by 30%)[10] and because the construction of reservoirs is expensive and environmentally damaging, UK policy is to reduce the demand for water. In office buildings, on average 43% of water is used for flushing WCs, 20% for flushing urinals, 27% for washing, 10% for kitchens and canteens. BREEAM assessment awards credit when the predicted or actual water consumption meets specified targets. A variety of technical solutions are available, such as sanitaryware needing less water, in conjunction with methods of measuring and controlling water consumption.

4. Integrated design of environment and structure

4.1 Construction: steel vs concrete

Nearly all contemporary office buildings are made from a steel or concrete frame.[11] [12] [13] [14] There is a long standing argument between the steel and concrete industries as to which performs better environmentally. The steel industry has been a leader in the promotion of life cycle assessment to evaluate these environmental impacts. The Steel Construction Institute undertook a life cycle analysis of two office buildings[15], one four storeys in height and another of a higher specification, eight storeys high, with an atrium.

The alternatives considered were:

- a concrete frame
- a precast system with hollow core planks
- a variety of steel structures employing:
  - cellular beams
  - slimfloor beams with precast slabs
  - a composite beam and permanent decking/in situ solution.

They also looked at a variety of servicing systems from natural ventilation through a number of mechanical supply and extract alternatives.

The whole lifetime analysis proceeded from:

- the origins of the materials used for building
- their manufacture into construction components
- their transportation to the building site
- the construction of the building itself
- the maintenance cycles throughout the building's life including its final demolition
- the reuse of the components and materials or their disposal.

What they found was that, based on a 60-year life, there was very little difference when considering, for example, a mechanical supply and extract option in relation to the five structural types.

This was also the case when comparison was made between their overall lifetime energy consumption, and the production of CO_2, whether resulting from the use of steel or concrete. What was also discovered was that the initial embodied energy due to the structure was a very small proportion of the overall energy consumption throughout the building's life. Comparatively, the extent of operational energy dwarfed that of embodied energy.[16]

These conclusions are advantageous if considered from the point of view of the 'steel lobby', because the production of steel is very energy intensive. The embodied energy of steel is about 20 times that of concrete. Set against this is the increasing efficiency of steel production, the amount of energy required having dropped by more than a third over the past 30 years.

Moreover, the reuse of steel is one of the most established recycling industries, and very little steel goes to waste from building sites, whereas the largest amounts wasted in terms of tonnage are concrete, aggregates, blocks and waste bricks.

This is partly due to steel structures being relatively easily demountable, so global annual steel production consists of almost 50% that is recycled from scrap; and the recycling ratio (the proportion of the actual quantity of metal in the demolished building that is salvaged and recycled, compared to the amount of usable metal from the process) is about 80%. This is a function of the limits of efficiency with which the material can be reclaimed from the site, and because the final amount of re-smelted metal produced depends on the efficiency of collection and sorting in scrap yards. Steel's embodied energy is very high but re-smelting is relatively energy efficient so as steel is repeatedly recycled the effective embodied energy drops, until after being recycled 8 or 10 times the embodied energy falls to a constant level. The same is true of the volume of emissions, carbon dioxide and oxides of sulphur and nitrogen, produced during the process.

Cement, which makes up 10–20% of its mass, is the energy intensive component of concrete. This is because of the very high temperatures required to produce the cement clinker. However, over the past 30 years, the energy used has been reduced by 35%, with accompanying reductions in CO_2 emissions, although CO_2 is actually one of the byproducts of the reduction of limestone to calcium oxide. These process emissions are very difficult to eliminate using current production methods. Steel production from ore generates about 60 times as much CO_2 as does concrete manufacture. Their relative use of water is similarly startling, a tonne of water is required to make a tonne of concrete, but 300 tonnes is needed to make a tonne of structural steel.

Steel reinforcement for concrete is almost exclusively made from recycled material, but recycling of concrete is in its infancy, the use of recycled aggregate at the BRE Environmental Building being one of the first. There are environmental concerns about the amount of dust pollution and the amount of noise involved in concrete crushing. Ideally crushing would be carried out on site to avoid demolition concrete having to be carried over long distances between recycling centres.

Disposition of thermal mass

A parallel argument has been conducted about the relative performance of steel frames and concrete frames, in terms of their thermal mass – or fabric energy storage capability, as it is sometimes called.[17] Within a passive or hybrid ventilation system the use of the building's thermal mass to control its internal climate temperature has become a central requirement. The thermal mass, principally coupled to the room spaces at the soffit of the floor slabs, is cooled at night by opening windows and purging warm air from the space.

For offices – a building type with a marked tendency to overheat in summer – the use of the building's thermal mass can reduce the discomfort felt on very hot days. Use of a heavyweight material, such as concrete, spreads the diurnal range, so that the warmest period in the day can effectively be transferred to the evening, owing to the thermal time lag within the structure. The office building will have internal gains due to lights, people and equipment, but the thermal mass can reduce the peaks of temperature by 3 or 4 degrees and defer the peak to the end of the day, the maximum temperature being delayed by up to 6 hours.

In this way, office buildings can be naturally ventilated, and the avoidance of air-conditioning can reduce the initial cost of the building by 20%; managing without suspended ceilings reduces costs by a further 5% and the height of the building shrinks as a result by 10–15%.

For fabric energy storage to work well, there should be as large as possible an area of thermal mass presented to the room, which is usually the soffit of the concrete slab. As a rule of thumb, there should be twice as much exposed area of soffit as floor area below. So corrugated forms of concrete construction are well suited to this scenario – for example troughs or coffers – but a mix of precast and in-situ concrete for slabs and columns can provide a suitable standard of visible surface.

Thermal mass and steel structures

In an attempt to counter these arguments that favour concrete construction, the steel industry has carried out tests of its own, which have suggested that the thickness of the thermal mass does not have to be as great as was formerly supposed. A concrete slab, exposed on one side, has only to be 75–100 mm thick to be effective. Indeed, slabs of greater thickness in effect have reduced admittance because of the difficulty of extracting heat from deep within the slab when using night cooling.

As a result, even relatively light steelwork construction can have adequate thermal mass. For purposes of comparison, three different structures were tested:

- a slimfloor beam system with precast units and in-situ concrete topping
- a steel frame with decking and in-situ concrete floor
- a concrete flat slab.

It was found that there was very little difference in their performance.

Box 4.7 Night cooling

Night cooling is an environmental technique common to vernacular buildings.[1] It works best in desert regions when there is a large difference between daytime and nighttime temperatures, but even in the UK, night cooling can be successful as long as the difference is not less than around 8°C.

Most usual is for high-level windows to be operated by the building energy management system so that, when they are open at night, the passage of air can be directly in contact with the soffit of the concrete slab. The thermal mass has to be coupled with the room space for adequate cooling during the day. Perforated ceilings can be effective, but they should be made of metal to form a radiant cold surface facing into the room. In this way both the air temperature and the surface temperature (the components of the dry resultant temperature, a reliable guide to comfort) can be reduced. Even when air temperatures start to rise, the presence of the cold surface of the slab within the radiant field of the room's occupants will make the room still feel comfortable.

These passive methods are adequate for many offices although the rate of heat transfer is limited, and there is little control over the extent of cooling or release of heat during the night. The dangers are that the space will feel too cold when the office is first occupied in the morning leading to the heat being turned on, or that the cooling effect will be exhausted by the early afternoon, when there will be a demand for mechanical cooling.

More successful is to use an active solution where the incoming air is channelled through, or adjacent to, the structure. This can be in the form of perforated concrete planks (the Termodeck™ system), and a number of solutions have been tested by British Steel[2] using steel ducting to confine the airflow next to the slab with grilles that provide cooled air supply at specified locations within rooms. These enable an enhanced level of control and more efficient cooling of the concrete slab.

1. Energy Efficiency Best Practice programme *Natural Ventilation for Offices: NatVent a better way to work* BRECSU, Garston, 1999.
2. SCI, *Environmental Floor Systems*. Steel Construction Institute, Silwood Park, Ascot, UK

5 Generic construction methods

5.1 Typical UK office construction[18] [19]

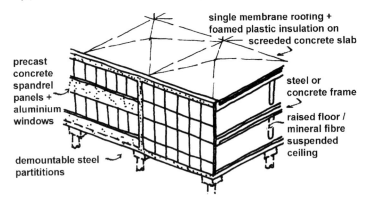

single membrane roofing +
foamed plastic insulation on
screeded concrete slab

precast
concrete
spandrel
panels +
aluminium
windows

steel or
concrete frame

raised floor /
mineral fibre
suspended
ceiling

demountable steel
partititions

Figure 4.3 Typical UK office construction

• *Steel frame with profiled decking*

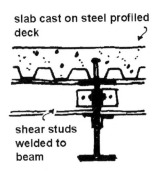

slab cast on steel profiled
deck

shear studs
welded to
beam

Figure 4.4 Steel frame composite floor construction

A steel skeleton frame with profiled decking providing permanent shuttering to an in-situ slab has become the generic 'fast track' form of construction for steel-framed office buildings. It is a moderately lightweight floor system, which explains its *Green Guide* 'B' rating compared to an in-situ reinforced concrete slab, which is rated 'C'.

Precast floors are the only type to receive an 'A' because of their ability to support equivalent floor loads with reduced self weight. Consequently a steel frame + precast concrete planks + screed would be the preferred option. The steel decking in a composite floor has the additional disadvantages of the embodied energy and water consumption involved in steel production, but with a high, but as yet unrealised, potential for recycling.

As noted above, steel production is very energy intensive with accompanying and detrimental effects on climate change and fossil fuel depletion. It is, however, highly recyclable, and the proportion of metal recycled from scrap reduces the extent of steel production's environmental impacts. These advantages are optimised if steel structures are designed to be demountable, by the use of bolted rather than welded connections.

- *Aluminium curtain walling*

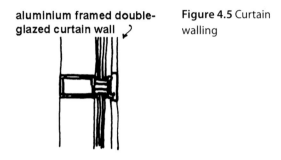

aluminium framed double-glazed curtain wall

Figure 4.5 Curtain walling

Aluminium curtain walling achieves an intermediate 'B' rating compared with timber framed glazing that alone achieves an 'A' rating, and U-PVC with its many negative environmental impacts has the lowest rating of 'C'. Despite the very considerable energy requirements of aluminium when smelted from bauxite, since 30% of UK aluminium production uses recycled metal, the overall energy requirement is substantially reduced. UK aluminium manufacture utilises off-peak electricity but hydroelectricity (as employed in Canada, for example) is the cleanest of power sources. The difficulty of sourcing aluminium from particular countries does, however, make this distinction fairly academic.

The glass within a typical double-glazed window accounts for less than 20% of its embodied energy and so the glazing specification has relatively little impact on the overall rating of the component, although it can have profound implications for the operational energy of the building throughout its life.

The ductility of aluminium enables window sections to be readily fabricated from aluminium billets. Its ease of milling to complex sections makes it well suited to accommodate opening lights for night cooling, and the wireways required for BEMS systems. The future of aluminium curtain walling might seem assured from these points of view, except that the conductivity of the metal is so high that the heat loss from the assembly tends to be very unfavourable. The thermal breaks within the sections usually guard against condensation but do not guarantee better thermal performance. Manufacturers' figures should be obtained for U-values through the framing as well as the U-value at the centre of the glazing, and for the assembly as a whole.

- *Single-ply roofing*

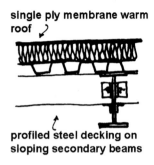

single ply membrane warm roof

profiled steel decking on sloping secondary beams

Figure 4.6 Profiled deck roof plus single-ply waterproofing

Single-ply roofing is regarded as having a life of only 15 years, so the frequent intervals at which it has to be replaced explains the 'C' rating that the construction achieves.

Many of the materials used for the manufacture of single-ply membranes are derived from oil-based hydrocarbons that have significant environmental impacts during manufacture. The mass of the concrete construction is also a factor contributing to its rating, particularly with regard to the extent of minerals extraction involved in obtaining aggregate.

- *An alternative: double-skin glazed wall*

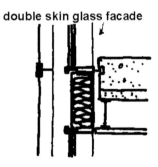

double skin glass facade

Figure 4.7 Alternative: double-skin glazed wall

It can be seen that achieving a BREEAM preferred 'A' rating is relatively easy with lightweight steel frame and curtain walling technology, whereas concrete construction with heavy cladding performs badly.

Double-skin glazed walls have become increasingly commonplace in recent office construction in a variety of different configurations; the cavity between the walls being used as a services duct in mechanically ventilated buildings, or as a system of horizontal or vertical plenums for use as a solar chimney in naturally ventilated or hybrid systems. The considerable extra expenditure required can be justified on environmental grounds particularly if the site is noisy. The usual specification is for an aluminium double-glazed curtain wall to form the inner skin, and for a single pane structurally glazed to form the outer weatherproof layer. The assembly can give enhanced thermal performance, and the use of the air space to accommodate solar shading has made the use of clear glass, rather than tinted, the chosen option, with accompanying advantages for maximising the use of daylight.

As noted above, the relatively low impact of the glass means that the lifetime energy advantages can be achieved whilst incurring relatively little additional embodied energy.

- *Floors: concrete slab*

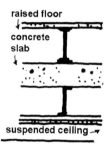

Figure 4.8 Concrete: concrete flat slab floor

Being a high mass element, this floor system achieves only a 'C' rating, though lighter weight alternatives, such as ribbed slabs or waffles, do better with a 'B'. Flat slab construction does particularly badly in relation to the volume of mineral extraction it requires, because the quarrying of aggregates has a considerable impact on its local environment. Recycled aggregate has advantages from this point of view, and its use is increasing. However, from the point of view of energy, the crushing, sorting and transport of recycled aggregates is likely to be comparable to the virgin material, and there may be quality control issues requiring additional cement content in the mix thus undermining the environmental benefits.

• *Cladding*

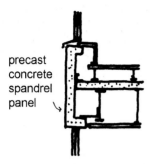

Figure 4.9 Precast concrete spandrel panels

precast concrete spandrel panel

Precast concrete, because of its high mass, receives a 'B' rating across a number of alternative specifications. When used as the inner skin to marble cladding panels its rating drops to 'C' because of the stone's high mass and the extensive support system required.

Composite windows with an aluminium rainscreen outer surface to an inner timber frame achieve a 'B' rating similar to aluminium windows but with improved ratings across most categories of the analysis compared to aluminium, for example in relation to both CO_2 emissions and climate change.

• *Roofs: inverted warm roof*

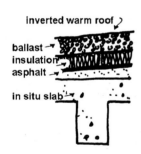

inverted warm roof

ballast
insulation
asphalt

in situ slab

Figure 4.10 Inverted flat warm roof

A galvanised steel profiled deck with an asphalt inverted warm roof, and insulation weighted down by paving slabs, achieves an 'A' rating comparable with timber joisted roof constructions. This rather surprising result is due to the relatively light weight of this alternative, but the rating reduces to a 'C' if a steel deck is used in combination with a warm roof built off a concrete slab. Inverted roof construction has the advantage of providing a protective environment for the waterproofing which lengthens its serviceable life between replacement intervals. In the *Green Guide*, this is given the rather conservative estimate of 30 years for an asphalt roof. The waterproof layer is the roof component with highest environmental impact on the rating for the roof as a whole.

Table 4.2 Ecopoints evaluation of generic constructions for offices, using BRE's Envest tool

		Generic office type: 30m × 15m (450 m² per floor); total 2250 m²; no. storeys: 5; storey height: 3m; % cellular: 10%; location: S.E. England; soil type: firm clay .		
			Ecopoints	**%**
Ground floor	150 mm precast concrete slabs + 50 mm topping		717	4.9
Upper floor	Steel deck + 150 mm in-situ concrete slab		2969	20.2
External walls	Precast spandrel panels + 20 mm granite cladding, inner leaf of block		3063	20.8
Internal partitions	Aluminium demountable partitions		908	6.2
Windows	Aluminium double glazed		571	3.9
Roof	Asphalt + paving, 100 mm foamglass insulation on 200 mm precast concrete slab		1389	9.4
Floors	10% 2 mm vinyl sheet		237	1.6
	90% wool/nylon + sponge rubber underlay		1404	9.5
		Sub-total	1642	11.1
Wall finishes	5% 6.5 mm ceramic tiles		92	0.6
	95% 2 coat render + emulsion		400	2.7
		Sub-total	492	3.3
Ceiling	Mineral fibre suspended ceiling		319	2.2
Sub-structure	Piled foundations		788	5.3
Super-structure	Steel frame		1023	7.0
Total embodied including material replacements over 60-year lifespan			14726	
Total embodied per sq m of floor area			6.6	

Source: based on Anderson, J., Shiers, D.E., Sinclair, M., *Green Guide to Specification*, (3rd Edition), BRE, Watford, 2002.

Commentary: As might be expected for a building with heavyweight cladding consisting of a stone facing to concrete spandrel panels, the external elevations account for a high proportion of the total. The extensive use of carpet, a short life component with high embodied energy, also makes a significant contribution to the embodied energy per m² of floor area. The overall figure is, however, moderate compared with other building types, as a result of the compact building form.

6. Generic office environments

6.1 Daylighting

To optimise the use of daylight requires the careful design of glazing, in order to achieve a balance between heat loss, daylight admission and solar gain. For passive solar purposes in temperate climates such as ours, a south-facing orientation is preferable, but whether the solar heat gain will be useful depends on the internal heat loads, in particular the number of machines being employed. Skylights are an efficient way of admitting daylight to the central core areas of office buildings on upper floors, though in terms of outside awareness their usefulness is limited.

The first metre or so above the floor provides little daylight for a useful depth into the room, but will admit solar gain. A view of the sky is necessary to bring unobstructed light into the space, and tall windows for that reason provide light deeper into a room, but bright patches of sky can also be the cause of glare.

6.2 Artificial lighting

To limit emissions due to lighting, the use of energy-efficient lamps in conjunction with automated controls is effective, but it is best to make maximum use of available daylight by, for example, ensuring that internal finishes are light in colour. The optimum is to provide artificial lighting only in relation to the ambient conditions being provided by natural light, through the use of controls and lights with dimming capability.

Providing a low level of general lighting, supplemented by local task lighting using compact fluorescent tubes, is an energy saving strategy. In existing offices old 38 mm tubes should be replaced with 26 mm (T8) tubes with high frequency electronic ballasts that can achieve 30% savings in power usage.

Luminaire efficiency is dependent on the design and reflectivity of the materials used; in many offices anti-glare low brightness fittings will be required to eliminate reflections from VDU screens.

6.3 Natural ventilation

Adequate ventilation in summer is a function of the size and type of window openings and the depth and relationship of rooms. These rules are well established and have long been available as software (e.g. BRE's BREEZE). There are limitations[20] to the depth of rooms that can be ventilated on one side only, and natural ventilation will be a lot more successful if a through draught can be arranged. Rooms that are in depth more than two and a half times the height of the room will have difficulties from this point of view. Whereas a cross-ventilated space can be up to 5 times the height of the room in depth, effectively this limits the overall dimension from side to side, or side to atrium, to 15 metres. Floor to ceiling heights should best be around 3 metres, to give sufficient height for buoyancy airflow through the space.

6.4 Mechanical ventilation

Mechanically assisted natural ventilation is a low energy option where local conditions are not able to support the operation of an entirely passive option throughout the year. A simple hybrid system such as extract fans contained in extract chimneys can be designed to operate only at times when supplementary pressure is required.

Because the efficiency of air as a medium for heat transfer is so low compared to water, HVAC systems use a large volume of air and entail large amounts of electric fan power. Minimising the fan power used for HVAC is an effective approach to reducing energy since fans typically use more energy than chillers. Air recirculation, although frequently used to save electricity, will pose health problems by spreading indoor pollutants around the building.

A number of efficient alternatives to conventional HVAC are now established technologies:

- River water or ground cooling: either by drawing water from a bore hole or river, or by casting water circulation pipes in piles, a source of free cooling can be connected into the building services via a heat exchanger.
- Evaporative cooling: the expenditure of latent energy that is made during the phase change of water to vapour is used to cool the air, and up to 10% cooling energy reductions can be achieved by the use of indirect evaporative coolers.
- Thermal wheel: a rotating wheel made from ceramic tubes is used to extract heat from the exhausted indoor air and by rotation of the wheel into the path of the air supply from outdoors, the energy is reused for pre-heating. Pre-cooling can be achieved in summer by passing the outgoing air through an evaporative cooler before it enters the thermal wheel.
- Absorption heat pump: this is a heat-operated refrigeration machine that operates at lower efficiency than ordinary chillers but which can be

a worthwhile option where there is a supply of waste heat, from a CHP plant for example.

6.5 Space heating and cooling, and water heating

Although space heating is a major use of energy in office buildings, in terms of primary energy, even in naturally lit and ventilated buildings, space heating is unlikely to be the largest use of energy. Even so, heating requirements can be reduced by the use of well-sealed and insulated construction, and the best use of energy in combination with careful disposition of openings within the building envelope.

Hot water supply in offices can be very wasteful if supplied from a central boiler and if long pipe runs are required. Local calorifiers sited close to points of use may be an economic alternative. Water saving devices such as spray taps and low volume WCs will also help reduce energy usage.

7 Case studies

7.1 New Street Square – a commercial development in the City of London

This case study was supplied by courtesy of Bennetts Associates.

Client: Land Securities
Architect: Bennetts Associates
Contractor: Sir Robert McAlpine
Structures: Pell Frischmann
Size: 102,200 m²
Design: 2003–4
Completion: Spring 2008

Background

It has long been accepted that design innovation in the office sector is most likely to come from the owner-occupiers. Organisations such as Powergen and Wessex Water see radical change in the workplace as part of an overall, long-term plan and make corporate decisions tailored to their operational needs.

By contrast, the sector that deals in offices for rent is notoriously conservative. Short-termism and the need to avoid buildings that are aimed too specifically at one user or another dominate trading patterns.

This is graphically illustrated in the UK by their typologies:

- owner-occupied office buildings have (at least since the late 1990s) tended to follow the north-European pattern, with narrower plan forms and more benign environmental systems
- commercial developers have steadfastly adhered to the American, air-conditioned model regardless of local conditions.

Architects, and many others interested in sustainability, have known for years that the commercial office sector would be among the last to embrace the changes needed for the pursuit of sustainability. The reasons for this conservatism are worth exploring further, to set the New Street Square scheme in its economic context:

1. Office developments are often bought, sold and let like any other commodity. It is unlikely that the initiating entrepreneur/developer will get a return from any additional investment which benefits the occupiers such as, for example, installing sun shading.

2. Anything considered novel (such as an exposed structure or air supplied from the floor) would be certain to attract unwelcome questions about future performance from potential purchasers such as the investing institutions, who buy property to bolster the nation's pension funds.

3. Rented office buildings must appeal to the broadest range of tenants if they are not to run the risk of being un-let for extended periods. This generally rules out inflexible plan shapes or technical solutions such as natural ventilation.

4. Advisors and agents are generally paid on results, so an innovative design will be resisted for reasons of vested interest unless they confer a market advantage.

5. The structure of property transactions in the UK is closely linked to that of the USA, one byproduct of which is the standardisation of technical specifications to suit global occupiers. In this respect, the City of London office market is perhaps the most conservative of all, as it is dominated by large, fast-changing occupiers in the worldwide banking and legal sector. The sheer scale and speed of property transactions in the City makes the introduction of innovation especially hazardous; it is a highly specialised market that often seems resistant to ideas from outside.

Planning, form and construction

The site

The 2-hectare site lies on New Fetter Lane, mid-way between Fleet Street and Holborn Circus. To the immediate south, the Fleet Street conservation area comprises a series of charming courts and alleys, culminating in Dr Johnson's House facing the site boundary. The site itself, and the land to the north, is the creation of post-war reconstruction, with little to commend it in terms of townscape and streetlife.

The brief and design rationale

In statistical terms the brief was for an enormous development – 100,000m² of accommodation – which made it the latest in an small group of 'campus' type City developments that have faced issues of large-scale urbanism as well as the conventional pressures of market acceptability. Learning the lessons of its own development on the site 40 years before, Land Securities was particularly keen to create a sense of place and a destination for the immediate area, to replace the existing group of bland 1960s slabs that had reached the end of their natural life.

Land Securities is not only the UK's largest property company, but it is also one of the few to retain its office developments as long-term investments, rather than trade them for a short-term profit after the initial letting. Whilst the company's brief for New Street Square conformed to industry norms in many respects, their retention policy meant that they were prepared to take a view about operational issues for their tenants who would be more likely to renew their leases at premium rents if the landlord's service was good. In other words, they did see market advantage in lower running costs and a degree of resilience against potential energy taxes that might hit the tenant market at some time in the future. Most significantly, the new generation of senior management at Land Securities saw sustainability as an important corporate responsibility and, alone among major developers, the company had begun to measure and understand the environmental performance of its current building stock.

Design – site masterplan

In social terms, the design concept attempts to stitch back together the spirit and vitality of the historic street pattern, avoiding the plazas, changes of level and wide, formal routes that characterise the existing development. To do this, a new, public square is located at the centre of the site, completely surrounded by new buildings (Figure 4.11). The square replicates the approximate size, name and position of a historic square that disappeared from maps around 1680. It is of a scale and intensity that should distinguish it from its recent antecedants at Paternoster Square and Broadgate.

Connecting the development with the network of surrounding spaces and streets are four points of pedestrian access, radiating like a pinwheel from the square, thereby creating an informal series of routes that impose a degree of

Figure 4.11 Overall View: building A is to the rear of the site, buildings B and D (medium rise) in front of building A and the low-rise block (building C) and the management pavilion (building E) to the front of the square. Lower buildings are to the South of the site.

Source: Bennetts Associates Architects

discovery on the users. Each serves a different audience: the east-west route provides a desire-line for pedestrians who are presently obliged to walk around the area, whereas the north-south route creates a direct, canopied connection to Holborn Circus at one end and an entrance to the small scale of Pemberton Row at the other. All of these new connections are lined with shops or restaurants and the wider spaces are animated by meeting places, public art and places for performance, so as to create life and public activity at street level.

The conjunction of a regular pattern of spaces or routes with an irregular site boundary generates four plots around the square for major buildings of various sizes and plan forms with the intention of ensuring a degree of economic flexibility in a constantly changing market – one high-rise tower (Building A), two medium-rise, atrium buildings (Buildings B and D) and one low-rise block (Building C). In addition, there is a small pavilion (Building E) that serves as a management suite and access to the basement car/cycle park. Quite apart from townscape considerations, the varying height of the buildings ensures the maximum level of sunlight penetration into the square, with the tallest to the north and the lowest to the south.

Scale and materiality are also used to establish appropriate relationships between the scheme and its surroundings. Buildings B and E defer to the adjacent residential block and Dr Johnson's House, whereas Buildings B and D are intended to perform a neutral, background role. Building A, by contrast, is relatively assertive, its sharply pointed corner signalling the development from Holborn Circus.

By City standards, the New Street Square development is, therefore, unusually versatile and site specific but it also brings together several existing strands of thinking that had evolved over a number of previous projects by Bennetts Associates. Sustainability provides the economic, social and environmental link between them and an invaluable 'hook' for an exceptional client and for the planning authority.

Design – individual buildings
With the existing properties on the site being demolished after only 40 years, the first principle to be established was long-term robustness. All the new buildings have simple, legible floorplates and the column grid across the site provides for a wide range of interior fitting-out layouts, with longer spans than is normal. They also follow the same formula for floor-to-floor height, with the levels aligned so that future connections between blocks are relatively straightforward. The spatial relationships between the lift/stair/toilet cores, the column grid and the perimeter are crucial in ensuring that each building can be occupied by different market sectors such as lawyers, who want cellular space, or bankers, who want open plan. The first and second floors are taller than elsewhere, to allow the possibility of trading with exceptional servicing requirements. Compared to most other City developments, the level of future adaptability is extremely high, so the probability of future waste through obsolescence is greatly reduced. The structural and services solution supports this principle and establishes the basis for operational energy efficiency.

The sustainability strategy for New Street Square extends the research from Bennetts Associates' Wessex Water project by examining embodied energy, waste, recycling and post-occupancy monitoring. The project's environmental impact assessment and its BREEAM 'excellent' rating have established further policies for transport, air quality, traffic noise, archaeology, wind and so on. All of these are being rigorously pursued through the construction process, with mandatory compliance by specialist subcontractors (from demolition onwards) supported by the main contractor and a thorough, independent audit process.

Structure

Since the widespread adoption of the American practice for steel frame construction and full air-conditioning in the early 1980s, few City buildings have been designed in concrete. The choice of concrete for the structure of New Street Square is significant, therefore, as it challenges conventional wisdom and departs from established norms for cost, speed and 'buildability' on congested sites. Thanks to pressure on steel prices caused by an overheated Chinese market, concrete in 2003–4 was competitive and, as post-tensioning meant that floor slabs with long spans could be procured without downstand beams, the resulting structure is far more adaptable than the steel equivalent. Rather than reduce the floor-to-floor heights in response to the thinner structure represented by the flat slab solution, Land Securities agreed that the additional internal height should be used to enhance flexibility by offering the prospect of several alternative servicing solutions.

Services

Thermal performance

The architects were aware that most property advisers would not accept sustainable design solutions if they were based on, say, vaulted concrete structures and natural ventilation, as they are perceived to be far too inflexible and technically inadequate for the City market. However, as long as the initial design did not prevent a conventional solution such as fan-coil air-conditioning at some time in the future, there was no reason to resist an innovative design.

Unlike steel, the dimensions of the flat concrete structure allows three possible options (Figure 4.12):

- Option 1 – fan-coil air-conditioning with a suspended ceiling
- Option 2 – a chilled ceiling combined with air supplied from the floor
- Option 3 – chilled rafts suspended from the exposed structural slab, once again with air from the floor. Bennetts Associates had already demonstrated the visual impact and technical feasibility of chilled rafts and thermal mass on one of its previous projects, so its viability was not in question.

Even though a deeper than normal raised floor is required in order to accommodate the air supply, the overall flexibility of the design means that all options can be accommodated within a conventional storey height for the life of the building. This should satisfy the agents who are interested in the first tenant as well as those who are committed to the long-term.

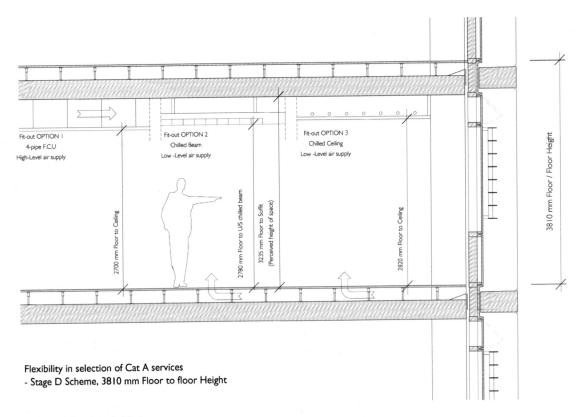

Flexibility in selection of Cat A services
- Stage D Scheme, 3810 mm Floor to floor Height

Source: Bennetts Associates Architects

The external envelope has been engineered to ensure an absolute minimum of solar gain at critical times of year, with extensive sun shading or glass treatment on all relevant elevations (Figure 4.13). The effect of this is to limit the internal heat gains only to those items directly connected with the occupier, such as lights, people and of course IT equipment.

It is expected that some tenants will have so much heat gain that it would be economically unsustainable not to offer the fan-coil solution, as it is the only one of the three with large cooling capacity. Most office occupiers, however, even in the City, do not require such high levels of cooling and there are some who are beginning to see the advantages of energy-efficient buildings with taller ceilings. The chilled raft solution, therefore, is another radical proposal in City terms but it has compelling practical, commercial and architectural advantages. For the landlord and agent, the range of alternative options means that there is no downside to the low-energy solution.

As a consequence of its extensive solar control, exposed structure, minimal cooling regime and taller interior, New Street Square has adopted many of the

Figure 4.12:
Environmental solutions

characteristics of the north European building type previously rejected by the UK property development sector. As the impact of tougher building regulations becomes apparent in the next few years, it is possible that New Street Square will become the benchmark, in just the same way that Broadgate fuelled the steel-framed, air-conditioned property boom of the 1980s.

Figure 4.13 The pavilion with medium-rise and high-rise blocks behind – note the solar shading

Source: Andrew Putler

7.2 Case Study: Arup Fitzrovia

Client: London Merchant Securities
Technical and Management Consultancy: Arup
Architect: Sheppard Robson
Social Sciences Consultant: SHM
Size: 27,770m² of open plan offices
Design: 2000
Completion: 2004

Background

In November 2000, Arup was commissioned by its landlord, London Merchant Securities (LMS), to undertake the refurbishment of the Arup head office at 13 Fitzroy Street and the adjoining building at 36 Howland Street. The project was to involve the removal of all façades and complete clearance of the interiors, back to the reinforced concrete frame and floor plates.

The intention was to provide a single high-quality building which would reflect Arup's corporate identity, both internally and externally.

Planning, form and construction

The site

The site consisted of two adjacent 1960s office blocks. The underlying structure, frame and floor plates, was of reinforced concrete. Each building could operate independently, each with its own stair and lift core.

Figure 4.14 Interior of the 'hub'. These areas are positioned adjacent to the main vertical core and provide informal meeting, breakout and quiet spaces on each floor.

Source: © Morley von Sternberg

The brief and design rationale

Aspirations for the project included:

- to provide an exciting and inspirational workplace that would encourage creativity, innovation and interaction
- to be an exemplar for sustainable design, within the constraints of the existing buildings
- to create flexible (i.e. generic) space for future adaptation and change
- to maximise the asset value within the requirements of the agreement for lease.

The project objectives that were developed and agreed by the client, the project design and management team and Arup's London Accommodation Committee (representing building users) included:

- to reflect, and exceed where possible, best practice in environmental and sustainability matters in building design, construction and operation
- to create a building that will act as an exemplar for environmental and sustainability solutions for projects of this nature.

Arup's SPeAR™ (Sustainable Project Appraisal Routine), introduced in Chapter 1, was used as the basis for the sustainability appraisals and is considered in detail at the end of the case study.

Design

The new building delivered 27,770m² of modern, open-plan office space with floor-to-ceiling external glazing and comfort cooling. The amount of office accommodation was increased, relative to the existing buildings, by adding a four-storey, steel-framed extension.

A range of studies and measures, contributing to various aspects of sustainability, were incorporated into the design process, including:

- a detailed study of the aspirations and preferences of future building users, as commissioned from SHM, during design development
- a Building Research Establishment SMART survey, commissioned to determine what materials from the existing buildings could be recycled
- a requirement in the construction tender documents to ensure that contractors operated an Environment System.

The building was planned to reflect aspirations that emerged from early staff surveys for more flexible spaces and a high quality environment with a sense of presence. Important elements of the architectural response to these desires are:

- the 'hubs' (Figures 4.14 and 4.15), which were designed to encourage the sharing of space for social interaction and information exchange
- the large interior atrium
- the spacious entrance foyer.

Arup views the 'hub' as integral to the use of the new building, but it is also forms an important part of the environmental servicing strategy. Air supply ducts bring air from plant on the roof and radiate from the green body of the hub – reading rather like legs for a giant green invertebrate – before reaching the floor plenums. In comparison, the ducts on the Fitzroy Street façade seem very much more conservative, being in a rectilinear arrangement (Figure 4.16).

Another important design decision was to reorganise vertical circulation. The lifts and stairs to the original two buildings would not have linked up when the buildings were combined so a new core was added adjacent to the building's entrance.

Figure 4.15 Howland Street façade. The hub areas are visible on the outside of the building

Figure 4.16: Fitzroy Street façade, showing the vertical (green) intake ducts

Table 4.3 Different environmental strategies for the building façades

	Fitzroy Street	**Howland Street**	**Rear**
Orientation	north-east	south-east	south-west
Light (solar gain and glare)	external louvres	louvres within double façade	automated solar blinds
Heat	double-glazed windows	double façade	
Air	manually operated windows as air quality here is acceptable	air quality is poor, so air is supplied mechanically, rather than through windows to the street	
Noise	noise levels acceptable, so no noise reduction other than double glazing	sealed double façade acts as a buffer for noise from busy Howland Street	

Services

Thermal performance

A key problem with the refurbishment was the development of a heating and ventilation system that would meet the twin objectives of cost-efficiency and sustainability. The low floor-to-ceiling height of the 1960s buildings ruled out ceiling ducts. To overcome this problem, fresh air is drawn via a roof-mounted plant down the façade into floor plenum chambers. A computer-controlled Building Management System (BMS) controls the heating and ventilation systems.

The expression of the ventilation ducts is not the only way in which the building's façades differ (compare Figure 4.15 and Figure 4.16). They all respond to their orientations and to the street onto which they face, see Table 4.3.

Light

Generous glazing maximises daylight in the building, within the constraints of the existing low floor-to-ceiling heights. A new atrium also brings daylight into the heart of the building.

Artificial lights are always going to be needed when natural light is insufficient; these are controlled by daylight sensors.

Water

Showers have been installed, along with cycle parking, to discourage car use.

Communications

The building includes fully equipped server and communications rooms, key elements of Arup's resilient systems programme, designed to ensure that communications can be maintained and data protected during extreme events and emergencies. These are connected via high-speed fibre optic links to two other server rooms in nearby Arup offices to provide a high degree of resilience.

Designing with SPeAR™

Sustainability was a major goal for the building design, so Arup Environmental assembled a sustainability team to advise the design team. Skills in the sustainability team included materials science, mechanical and electrical engineering, public health engineering and environmental sciences.

SPeAR™ appraisals were used at each of the main RIBA design stages: preliminary, Stage C and Stage D design. (See Box 1.4, where SPeAR is discussed in more detail.) However, a baseline appraisal was carried out first, on the existing office buildings, to understand their strengths and weaknesses compared with contemporary building standards and to give an awareness of limitations imposed by the site and city centre location – see left of Figure 4.17.

Prior to setting up the project delivery team, six months work had been spent developing the preliminary design, which became formalised through the agreement to lease. This was the basis of the 'preliminary' SPeAR™ appraisal – see right of Figure 4.17. Results of the baseline and preliminary appraisals indicated that the emerging design was a vast improvement on the existing buildings, but also highlighted areas where improvements should be sought.

Setting design targets

It was recognised that there was a need to set specific, more detailed sustainability targets in order to address areas which were priorities for improvement and in order to 'balance' the diagram. (As was seen in Chapter 1, a project is most sustainable when all four considerations – 'environment', 'natural resources', 'economics' and 'societal' – are optimised. For the same overall result, with all sectors were averaged, it is less desirable to have one very poor rating than two ratings that are less poor.) Minimum targets were set as follows:

- Match or exceed a 'median' (good practice) score on the SPeAR™ diagram for all segments
- Improve upon the Baseline SPeAR™ score for all segments.

A detailed set of 'primary targets' was then developed from the SPeAR™ spreadsheets, drawing on expertise from the sustainability team. These were developed

Figure 4.17 The baseline SPeAR™ diagram (left) and preliminary design diagram (right)

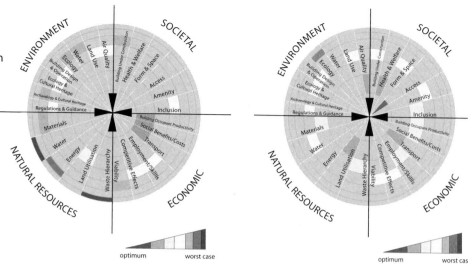

Table 4.4 Primary targets developed for one indicator – 'conservation of water resources'

• Use low water appliances and intelligent water/control flushing	
• Use treated potable water to meet all potable demands (drinking, kitchens, showers) and good maintenance.	
• Use borehole water for flushing toilets	
• Use filtered tap water rather than bottled. Fit a water meter to mains supply. Adequate maintenance (stop dripping taps etc.)	
• Direct rainwater runoff onto gardens in localised areas where appropriate	
• Collect, treat, store and distribute harvested rainwater for toilet flushing	
• No harvesting	
• Borehole water to meet all potable, flushing, cooling water demands. Heat exchangers for cooling water and hot water systems. Push button taps. Low water use and intelligent controls	Ideal (Score 3)
• Borehole for toilet flushing. Mains for potable. Low use appliances/intelligent controls.	Good (Score 2)
• Low use appliances/intelligent controls.	Acceptable (Score 1)

Source: Arup

with the aim of providing site-specific design solutions. Table 4.4 illustrates primary targets for one indicator from the spreadsheet, 'conservation of water resources'.

During the concept design and scheme design stages, the primary targets were used on a day-to-day basis as a mechanism for iteratively appraising and refining the design process.

Assessing the scheme against the cost plan

Towards the end of the scheme design, extensive clarification was undertaken to establish which components of the scheme were allowed for by the project's cost plan and those which were 'design aspirations'. What transpired was that, although various design elements – such as including PVs within the atria roofs or the provision of gardens – had been developed, there was no cost allocation for them within the budget. As a result, the overall appraisal for the scheme design showed few improvements when compared to the concept design.

That the scheme design did not improve on the project design was largely a result of the constraints of the project's budget. Despite not meeting all of the sustainability objectives set at the beginning, the scheme shows a significant improvement in comparison with the former buildings on the site.

The process that the Fitzrovia design team used can be seen as not unrepresentative of how the process of 'sustainable' design works in many cases. To achieve progress towards sustainability Thoreau-esque high targets need to be set. In this case, the commercial property requirements placed real-world constraints on the achievability of initial aims.

Conclusions

Tackling the broad concept of sustainability using SPeAR™ on the Fitzrovia Project has helped to identify some critical areas, which are fundamental to the success of any efforts aimed at enhancing the sustainability of a scheme:

- bringing in sustainability considerations at the earliest possible point, before preliminary designs are outlined;
- pitching any sustainability advice at the correct level of detail depending on the design stage: increasing levels of detail are required as designs progress towards a full scheme;
- in a commercial context, detailed business case studies may be required to evaluate some sustainable design options at scheme stage; and
- the importance of identifying key interfaces between the Design and Sustainability teams, e.g. social scientists involved in spatial layout – or energy efficiency advice incorporated into façade design.

Using SPeAR™ on this project demonstrated the complexity involved in appraising the sustainability of a design project at this level and the need for detailed specialist input in a wide range of technical areas. Above all, the project demonstrated the value of using this type of mechanism for engaging the whole project team in the pursuit of sustainability and in developing understanding of the complex issues and interactions. This is regarded as a highly worthwhile achievement, even though in a commercial environment it may not be possible to deliver all of the sustainable development objectives set.

8. Notes

1. The Movement for Innovation Sustainability Working Group Report, *Environmental Performance Indicators for Sustainable Construction*. The Movement for Innovation, www.constructingexcellence.co.uk, 2001, p.17.

2. Carbon Trust, *Energy Consumption Guide 19 – Energy use in offices*, 2003 edition, Action Energy/The Carbon Trust, www.thecarbontrust.co.uk, 2003.

3. Energy Efficiency Best Practice programme, *Good Practice Guide 274 Environmentally smart buildings: A quantity surveyor's guide to the cost-effectiveness of energy-efficient offices*. BRECSU, Garston, 1999.

4. BRE IP9/02 Part 1 *Refurbishment or Redevelopment of Office Buildings? Sustainability comparisons*, BRE, Garston, www.bre.co.uk, 2001

5. Grigg, P.F. BRE Digest 457 *The Carbon Performance Rating for Offices*, BRE, Garston, www.bre.co.uk, 2001.

6. Burton, B. and Stoker, C. 'Hidden Costs', *Architecture Today 34*, p45.

7. Pank, W., Girardet, H. and Cox, G., *Tall Buildings and Sustainability*. The Corporation of London, February 2002 (unpublished).

8. DEGW, *Automation of America's Offices: 1985–2000*, (the Orbit report), DIANE Publishing, Pennsylvania USA, 1985.

9. Baldwin, R., Yates, A., Howard, N. and Rao, S. *BREEAM 98 for Offices*. BRE, Garston www.bre.co.uk/envest, 1998.

10. ibid.

11. British Steel, *Ecobuild in Steel*. Scunthorpe. Marketing Dept. Redcar.

12. Clarke, M. and Somerville, G. 'Concrete in the Environment'. *Concrete Quarterly*, winter 1992.

13. Edwards, B. and Hyett, P., *Rough Guide to Sustainability*. RIBA, London, 2002.

14. Stevenson, J. and Spooner, D., Concrete and the Environment. *Concrete Quarterly*, autumn 1992.

15. Eaton, K.J. and Amata, A., *A Comparative Environmental Life Cycle Assessment of Modern Office Buildings*. Steel Construction Institute, Ascot, 1988.

16. Corus., *Environmental Designs in Steel: Life cycle assessment in steel construction*. Scunthorpe: www.corusconstruction.com

17. Reinforced Concrete Council, *Fabric Energy Storage: Using concrete structures for enhanced energy efficiency*. Crowthorne, www.rcc-info.org.uk, 2001.

18. Brookes, A. *Cladding of Buildings*. Spon, London, 1998.

19. Energy Efficiency Best Practice programme, *Report 30: A Performance Specification for the Energy Efficient Office of the Future*. BRECSU, Garston, 1999.

20. Awbi, H.B., *Ventilation of Buildings*, Spon Press, 2003.

5   Schools: a Changing Curriculum

1 Discussion

The school system in the UK is a very large organisation both in terms of its scale – there are 8 million children in full-time education attending 25,000 schools around the country – and in accounting for a cost of £20 billion a year, or over 5% of the government's total expenditure[1]. The process of education in schools is dependent on the mobilisation of large quantities of material and resources, for example books and paper, furniture, school meals and the energy used in their preparation, in addition to the components and energy used in the construction and operation of buildings. The national energy bill for schools exceeds £100 million per year.

All of these various aspects of resource deployment impact on the wider environment. Most definitions of sustainability, including the one most often quoted, as propounded by the Brundtland Commission[2], make reference to the ecological legacy we are bequeathing to our children, and what must be done for the benefit of future generations to reduce the impact that human activities have on the natural environment. There are, as a consequence, two aspects to the drive for sustainability in the use of energy and materials in schools. The first is to make school consumption patterns more efficient, and the second is to educate children to understand the importance of these issues so in future better-educated attitudes can be brought to bear on the achievement of a more sustainable world.

1.1 Energy consumption profile of schools

Schools vary in their pattern of energy consumption depending on their type of fuel supply. Most schools rely on fossil fuel, that is gas, oil, coal or liquid petroleum gas (LPG), for heating, hot water and the operation of some kitchen appliances. A minority of schools are exclusively dependent on electricity, or use it to a greater extent, for example to heat rooms and for cooking purposes. More generally, electricity is the power source for artificial lighting, fans and pumps, and some kitchen equipment. The energy consumption profile for a typical school in the UK anticipates that nearly 80% of the total goes towards space heating and the supply of hot water, less than 10% each are given over to the next largest uses, which are lighting and catering. Powering computers is a growing energy cost but, at the time of the ECOnstruct research, it was still only in the region of 2% of the total.[3]

In order to save money, therefore, the achievement of greater efficiency of heating systems is an obvious focus for attention. However, since electricity is often six times as expensive as fossil fuel in terms of delivered kWh, the actual cost of the fossil fuel used in schools may, in effect, only represent less than 45% of the total expenditure, despite fossil fuel energy being responsible for the vast majority of overall consumption. In cost terms, the relative proportions attributable to different areas throughout a school are rather different as a result. The percentage used to heat spaces and water is reduced to only just over 50%, and lighting becomes a lot more significant at 24%.

Consequently, achieving reductions in the amount of electricity used in schools is a priority for the reduction of costs. In addition, of course, electricity production has a major impact on the volume of CO_2 that finds it way into the atmosphere, because of the inefficiencies involved in the generation of electricity, and the losses inherent in distribution via the National Grid.

CO_2 generated by schools

A series of benchmarks have been derived from a survey of 2000 schools in England, which recorded their energy consumption data in 1999–2000[4].

The median benchmark derived from the data is the value at which 50% of the schools surveyed will have recorded a higher figure and 50% lower – typically, primary schools had relatively more fossil fuel consumption per m² per annum than secondary schools, and electricity consumption was shown to slightly increase with the age of the student. A secondary school with a swimming pool did, however, have a higher consumption in terms of both fossil fuel and electricity. The ratio of fossil fuel to electricity use was, in all cases, 4 or 5 to 1, but since the CO_2 emissions per annual kWh attributable to electricity use is 2.5 times that of natural gas, electricity-dependent uses such as lighting emerge as a significant concern in terms of the limitation of CO_2 emissions.

The growing use of IT equipment is also of interest, particularly since the heat generated by computers increases the likelihood of classrooms overheating in summer. The consequent demand for installation of mechanical cooling or air-conditioning has implications for the quantity of CO_2 that will be produced by schools in future. To avoid overheating without air-conditioning requires a balance between internal loads and solar gain in relation to the available rate of ventilation, and competing requirements of daylight and winter heat loss. Completely avoiding mechanical ventilation may prove difficult but the combination of thermal mass with night ventilation can provide useful pre-cooling and should be combined with shading to block the admission of solar gain. It might then be possible to install an extract-only system, or at most supply and extract, but avoiding the use of artificial cooling.

The more widespread introduction into schools of air-conditioning systems would be not only be detrimental to aspirations for increasing sustainability in schools, but also for the health of school children. Most current HVAC systems have only 15% fresh air intake, with the rest of the supply being re-circulated to reduce energy costs[5]. The filters used remove particles down to 5 angstroms, leaving a high concentration of fine particles; this can be removed with electrostatic filters but at added cost.

Contemporary HVAC systems can occupy a considerable percentage of the internal volume of a building, and their operating costs can outweigh other main items of day-to-day expenditure; so they are a trend that needs to be strongly resisted.

Instead, the inbuilt energy-saving devices now standard in electrical equipment can help alleviate the problem, in combination with energy management strategies. The stand-by energy consumed by PCs is 50–75% of that when in operation. Turning machines in schools off when not in use can reduce overall energy consumption to 10% of what would be the case if they were left on all the time. Other equipment such as printers and photocopiers are very significant energy users. Photocopiers can have up to 25 times the wattage of a PC, and since they are also responsible for the propagation of compounds that are a concern for human health, their location in the building and provision for local ventilation is a design problem.

1.2 Measuring environmental impact

One way of evaluating the environmental impact of an average school is to measure the mass flow of materials and energy that passes through the school during a year.

For the purposes of this analysis, goods that enter the school but have an extended life, such as furniture or the construction elements of the building, have their mass averaged over their expected lifespan. Energy in kWh is converted to mass (in kg) by reference to the raw material, gas, oil or coal that was used for space heating or hot water, or for electricity generation at the power station. Per pupil, the energy used for the journey to and from school is found to be more than one-third of the energy used for heating and lighting the spaces the pupils occupy within the school. In terms of mass, by far the greatest input to the school is its water supply, and the mass of inert material is approximately six times the amount of food consumed.[6]

1.3 Embodied energy vs operational energy for schools

The inert materials that are consumed by the school[7] are in the form of:

- large appliances
- fixtures and fittings
- the buildings themselves.

Large appliances mainly refers to computers which, by the end of the 20th Century were found in primary schools at a level of provision of one machine per thirteen pupils; in secondary schools the ratio was one per nine. Taking account of the numbers of printers and photocopiers, this means that on average there could be one large appliance per 10 students in UK schools, with an assumed composition of 50% inert and 50% plastic, and a five-year lifespan.

Fixtures and fittings are principally furniture, which the analysis assumes are made from an equal mixture of inert material, plastics and wood.

The third category is the structure and constructional elements of the school buildings.

School buildings fall into a number of constructional types. The most recognisably obvious of these are the brick-built Board schools from the Victorian era, many examples of which are still serviceable and in use, and the steel and panel prefabricated system schools from the 1960s. The vast majority of the school building stock (80%) was built after the Second World War and, of these, 50% are of steel or concrete frame construction. A study in New Zealand[8] has shown that the CO_2 emissions from the building materials used for both concrete and steel frame construction is comparable to the equivalent forms of construction used for office buildings which, based on a 50-year lifespan, is approximately 9 $kgCO_2/m^3$ per year.

To determine the outputs in terms of mass flow, generally liquids and solids remain liquids and solids as they pass through the school. The exception is energy, since fossil fuels, once burnt to produce heat and electricity, produce gaseous waste in quantities that can then be converted to a mass of CO_2, or a mass of carbon, emitted in relation to one pupil per year. Energy is by far the largest of these at over 50% of the total. The CO_2 emissions due to the admission of inert material, including the schools construction materials, is 10% – comparable to that attributable to other categories of material such as paper, plastics and packaging and chemicals. Food constitutes 3% of the total, and the CO_2 impact of the mass of water supply is minimal.

Clearly, the operational energy of a school is the significant factor in any strategy aimed at reducing its environmental impact and increasing its sustainability. Of equal importance will be the environmental management of the building, and its environmental design. Management decisions can aim to make reductions at each of the three stages of the lifecycle of the inputs to the building. The first is reducing the supply required, either by changing to a supply that produces less CO_2, such as reducing electricity use in favour of fossil fuel, or better still by converting to renewables. Second, the environmental impact of the school can be ameliorated by improving the efficiency of the heating system, for instance by installing condensing boilers. Finally, the outputs from the school can be reduced by the introduction of recycling strategies. The educational benefits from engagement with management approaches are self-evident. For example, aluminium cans dispensed from the schools vending machines may impact badly on the success of the strategy – unless, of course, the aluminium has been recycled rather than smelted from ore, a study that can be made by the children themselves.

2. Environmental issues – the problem of air quality

2.1 Ventilation vs heat loss vs draughts

Most schools in the UK are naturally ventilated using windows, or with passive stacks and vents admitting air from the outside. There is, however, an increasing degree of interest in mechanical systems, as well as passive and hybrid methods, because of the increasing concerns about the quality of the indoor environment in schools.

To achieve an engineered level of ventilation requires an accommodation between the competing parameters of ventilation rate, pollutant concentration, and the energy load that is a result of drawing fresh air in from outdoors. The concentration of pollutant will fall as the ventilation rate increases, and, at a given level, it will no longer constitute a risk to indoor air quality. The rate of heat loss will also increase as the ventilation rate rises, so the design level for the ventilation system should be sufficient to maintain air quality, but not be too great.

As insulation standards have risen, ventilation heat loss has constituted a larger proportion of heat loss from buildings. As with other building types the necessity to seal the construction to guard against air infiltration and heat loss is a contemporary requirement for school buildings. This has been a long-standing requirement in the cold climates of Scandinavia, but now even Mediterranean countries such as Italy have introduced regulations stipulating the need for airtight school construction.[9]

This is principally in order to reduce heat loss at times when the building is unoccupied, during night time in winter, and at weekends. At these times the temperature difference between inside and outside increases the rate of heat loss, which is exacerbated by air infiltration through the fabric. Ideally the ventilation system, whether natural or mechanical, should be designed for the maximum occupancy and, at times when the building is empty, the background level should be enough to provide a residual level of freshness.

The government guideline requirement is that all school working areas and halls should be capable of ventilation at a rate of 8 l/s of fresh air per person. At a minimum there should be provision of 3 l/s per person throughout the year, but this figure is very low by international standards. In addition, most countries now specify a satisfactory CO_2 concentration of between 1000 and 1500 ppm, which corresponds to an air change rate of between 7 and 9 l/s per person. That the concentration of CO_2 should be used as a measure of indoor air quality was first proposed by Professor Pettenkofer, from the University of Munich in 1858. He suggested that this could, by inference, be a measure of other pollutants influencing indoor air quality that at the time were impossible to measure.

2.2 Measurement of air quality in schools

Classrooms are often densely occupied, so the metabolic aspects of ventilation tend to be uppermost in importance, in which case measuring the concentration of CO_2 in the air should give a good indication of its freshness. The amount of CO_2 that is exhaled increases with metabolic exertion so its concentration gives a measure of the adequacy of the room's ventilation rate. At the levels usually found during the monitoring of rooms, CO_2 does not cause a hazard to health, but such measurements have shown that classrooms are prone to very low levels of ventilation, and pollution levels can rise very rapidly as a result. Drowsy children lacking attention and lacklustre teaching may be the direct result.

Perhaps not surprisingly, there is little agreement about the best way of measuring the quality of indoor air in schools. While at school, children are exposed to microbes, toxins and allergenic substances. Arguably, CO_2 concentrations give inadequate guidance for the design of ventilation systems to control these more insidious components of indoor environment. A survey of schools in Denmark[10] has shown that even though 70% of the schools had CO_2 concentrations in excess of 1000 ppm there was no positive correlation with Sick Building Syndrome (SBS) symptoms. However, there was a close relationship between CO_2 levels and measured concentrations of particles and mould spores. Children are more susceptible to air pollution than adults because they breathe a larger volume of air proportional to their size.

Experimental evidence suggests that the symptoms of SBS increase in frequency if spaces have a low rate of ventilation. Below a ventilation rate of 8–10 l/s per person the risk of SBS increases markedly. Relating this to metabolic rates for the production of CO_2 gives a satisfactory steady state concentration of between 800 and 1000 ppm (or about 600 ppm above outdoor levels). A study of schools in Sweden in 1996 suggested, however, that achieving a recommended CO_2 concentration of 1000 ppm did not entirely dispel the symptoms of SBS. Similar studies in Swedish schools, and in Plymouth in the UK, showed that ventilation systems, designed to meet a maximum CO_2 concentration of 1000 ppm, failed to dispel the build-up of coarse particles in the air. In the Plymouth survey of two nursery schools, health problems (6–8% recorded illnesses) were still in evidence despite meeting the 1000 ppm CO_2 stipulation, and the concentrations of coarse particles were shown to be related to indoor activities. To complicate the issue, CO_2 and coarse particles in excess of PM2.5, can be dispelled by the air movement induced when windows are opened, whereas fine particle concentrations can actually increase since they are principally the product of traffic fumes, and other combustion processes

Box 5.2 Measurement of indoor air quality

Indoor air quality is a particular problem in schools. The true cause of health problems in relation to indoor environments is as yet little understood, despite much research, particularly in Scandinavia. A variety of illnesses are thought to relate to problems of indoor air quality and exposure to pollutants within buildings; the phenomenon often referred to as Sick Building Syndrome (SBS).

This is a problem exclusively found in artificially ventilated buildings. It has come about, as the general population increasingly has to live and work in artificially ventilated environments. The UK population now spends more than 80% of its time indoors. During the 19 hours a day that we spend, on average, inside buildings, we breathe approximately 17,000 litres of unfiltered air.

The problem is particularly acute in school environments. From the ages of 5 to 18 years children spend approximately 15,000 hours at school, at an age when they are particularly susceptible to problems of indoor air quality because their immune systems and lung capacities are as yet undeveloped. Although there is much ongoing research in this area, there is little firm proof linking indoor air quality characteristics with specific illnesses.

taking place out of doors. Particulates include a wide variety of pollutants such as pollen, mould, bacteria, insect faeces, asbestos and tobacco smoke, with a range of health implications, so this debate is far from over.

Designing for good indoor air quality

The provision of oxygen for breathing and the dilution of metabolic products (CO_2, water vapour and odour) is, as a consequence, far from being the sole function of a ventilation system. Ventilation may also be required for cooling, as well as being needed to dissipate concentrations of other pollutants within the space. The control of pollutants that would otherwise enter the building from outside is a particular problem that is most extreme in urban locations. Despite the mass of legislation designed to limit emissions damaging to outdoor air quality, there are still times when air pollution exceeds legal health and safety limits, and so buildings in problematic locations need to present a robust barrier to the admission of poor quality air from outdoors.

A variety of measures are available from this point of view. Although a building's location is least amenable to design control, the locations at which air is admitted to a building can help avoid local sources of pollution (such as car parks). Buildings also have to be airtight to ensure that the air change rate is not dominated by uncontrolled infiltration of air, and this is particularly important if the admission of pollutants from outside is to be avoided. In some cases, outdoor pollution is transient, where for example there are peaks at times of rush hour traffic. It may be possible to close windows and vents and use the volume of air within the building to give sufficient ventilation while this short-term condition continues. For a building like a school, having a high occupant density, the length of time for which this might be feasible may, however, be as little as twenty minutes.

Clearly, activities such as laboratories should have localised control using fume hoods, or that part of the building should be maintained at a negative pressure relative to the rest.

Ventilation flow patterns through the school will depend on a number of factors such as the disposition of windows, doors and partitions. Buoyancy-driven flows within the internal spaces, and particularly within the shafts created by accommodation staircases between floors, and the pattern of wind speed and direction around the building, will influence the extent and direction of flow.

The conjunction of trickle vents within windows for the admission of air in conjunction with passive stack vents, requires that unobstructed cross-ventilation is maintained between intake and supply, while allowing sufficient flexibility for the reconfiguration of the teaching spaces. Passive stacks have to extend to the highest point of the roof, a ridge terminal being required at the apex of a pitched roof. In this way the stack will not only work by buoyancy, but will also benefit from wind-induced extract irrespective of the wind's direction. Tile terminals do not work well from this point of view (and because they entail a reduced height of stack).

The top floor of a school beneath a pitched roof will have a stack height at least to the apex and achieve adequate flow, but achieving sufficient stack height beneath a flat roof may prove problematic. Tests on passive stack systems[11] have shown that their operation is increasingly driven by the wind once wind speeds have increased over 4 m/s. Wind speeds are higher in winter, as is the temperature difference between indoors and ambient, so passive stacks in conjunction with trickle vents work well in wintertime. For summertime ventilation, supplementary mechanical extract may be required if the throughput of the stacks is to be increased for use in conjunction with opening windows.

Fan pressurisation tests can be carried out to check that the completed building is not excessively leaky; government guidelines recommend an achievable level of 0.3 air changes per hour. Tighter restrictions seem likely to be introduced in future revisions of the Building Regulations.

The relationship between airtightness, the achievement of indoor air quality requirements and energy goals is closely related to the choice of construction system. Composite constructions made from materials with different movement characteristics are likely to be particularly problematic from this point of view. Lightweight prefabricated frame and panel constructions, for example, are likely to combine timber panels that are particularly susceptible to movement according to the moisture content of the atmosphere, with a steel structure having a high coefficient of thermal expansion. Schools of this sort are likely to have to rely on the flexibility of (short-life) mastic sealants to achieve ongoing airtightness.

Heat loss due to infiltration is particularly likely in schools at the perimeter of doors and windows. Windows need to be adequately sealed into their structural openings. Window types that permit the use of compression seals are able to achieve better airtightness. Sliding windows and doors are a problem from this point of view. Many older schools are likely to be equipped with ageing, and probably corroded, aluminium sliding windows that will provide a poor seal. Replacement windows that close positively onto compression seals (such as tilt-turn windows), rather than relying on the sliding brush seals used in sliding windows, have the added advantages of opening safely, and can be cleaned from within the building.

Doors need to be weather-stripped and equipped with door closers; draught lobbies being required at entrances. Little is achieved, however, if external doors are left wedged open, so adequate specification needs to be accompanied by analysis of the school's circulation patterns and how they can be controlled. The concept of intermediate zones between different environments within the school can help control energy consumption and define areas having different indoor air quality requirements.

2.3 Daylighting: providing an adequate environment

It has long been recognised that the visual quality provided by daylight is particularly important for teaching and learning environments. The tall windows characteristic of the Victorian Board schools were able to project light to the back of rooms, and their high ceilings helped guard against overheating. Window sills were some way above floor level, which left a large amount of wall that could be used for display purposes, but made for an introspective and repressive environment. Post-war UK schools, on the other hand, were heavily glazed to admit the maximum daylight, and to allow a view out, but were also very uncomfortable in summer owing to excessive solar gain, and in wintertime were too cold because of large single-glazed windows. These problems were exaggerated by the lightweight system constructions characteristic of the period. They had minimal insulation and thermal mass so that the buildings had little inherent capability to even out temperature peaks.

Primary schools are particularly suited to the creative use of daylight because they are generally occupied during daylight hours, and are often single storey so that roof lights can be used to illuminate inner spaces, and thereby enable relatively deep plan buildings. Since rooflights provide the most efficient method of daylighting (because they face towards the unobstructed sky, and can be equally useful for ventilation purposes), they are an intrinsic component of this type of school.

The eternal problem in daylight design is less to do with the average and minimum daylight factors achieved within a room, than the underlying difficulty of the uneven distribution of daylight provided by vertical windows on one side of the room. The excess of light at the front of the room only serves to exaggerate the relative lack of light at the back. The horizontal bands of windows common within contemporary schools can often result in the wall beneath window sills appearing relatively dark, and a potential source of glare. Even under the generally overcast skies of the UK, light shelves can be useful in providing a more even distribution of light within classrooms while avoiding excessive heat gain and glare. Although a classroom with a single window wall is the convention, light scoops, rooflights, light tubes and clerestory windows have all been used in recent schools to overcome the problem, as well as transforming school spaces by the creative use of light.

Electricity for artificial lighting is a significant running cost, with considerable implications for the extent of CO_2 emissions. In an environmentally aware school community, it is of course relatively easy to control the use of artificial lighting by appointing light monitors to switch off lights that have been left on in unoccupied areas. The school caretaker also has to be drawn into the school's energy strategy since old, flickering and dirty light fittings operate at a greatly reduced degree of efficiency. Day-to-day maintenance can also be the opportunity for replacing tungsten bulbs with compact fluorescents (CFLs) which, although more expensive initially, have a far greater lighting efficacy and a longer life. Old and inefficient fluorescent tubes can also be substituted for the more efficient types that are now available, the old 38mm diameter tubes having now been superseded by 26 mm tubes.

Energy-saving lighting controls that are straightforward and respond to daylight levels should be employed; so, for example, it should be possible to operate the lights farthest from the windows separately from those at the perimeter. [12] [13]

Box 5.3 Lighting and heating controls

A range of simple and cheap heating and lighting controls are available that have the advantages of being user friendly and more reliable, providing enhanced comfort, and saving energy. In general, simple controls for local use are likely to be more successful than complex and centralised systems.

a. Room thermostats

Electronic thermostats can operate to fine tolerances (down to 1°C). Controls incorporating the traditional bi-metallic strip operate over a range of about 3°C, a difference in temperature that is very evident to those using the building, and which can result in the thermostat being set higher than necessary with consequent waste of energy. A system installed in schools in Hertfordshire achieved a remarkably low payback time of 6 months and was very reliable in use.

b. Key-operated lighting switches

A system in use in Bedfordshire schools allows anyone to alter the levels of the background lighting, but for a more intense light, only the class teacher can operate the controls with the aid of a swipe card. The switches have a timer to reduce light levels back to a minimum after a set period, and can also be used to control electric heaters and fan-assisted gas convectors.

c. Time-delayed light switches

These are particularly useful in store cupboards where lights may be left unused over an extended period of time. Pneumatic switches of this type are commonly used on stairwells and circulation, but have the disadvantage that they can readily be manually overridden. At about twice the price, electronic switches are more secure from abuse, and still have a payback time of only two years.

d. Occupancy sensor lighting controls

School halls and gymnasiums are well suited to this approach since they can remain unoccupied for extended periods throughout the school day. Occupancy sensor controls are sensitive to the movements of people in a space; if no movement is detected, after a set period of time the controller will switch off the lights. The devices are only suitable for larger spaces because they are not economically viable for use in smaller rooms.

2.4 Solar utilisation

Schools are particularly suited to the application of passive solar design principles.[13] [14] The occupied period for schools is at the same time of day when the sun is likely to be able to contribute to requirements for heating and lighting. Primary schools are most likely to be single storey, so they can be lit from rooflights as well as from the perimeter so that a deep plan form of building punctuated by courtyards or atria may be possible, the large area of roof having the potential to be heavily insulated.

The high illuminance levels required in school classrooms, coupled with the necessity to maintain good air quality, does however make for a challenging brief in relation to the passage of the sun. The exposure of thermal mass within the building, and solar shading outside, will help make best use of solar energy while avoiding overheating in summer. The benefits of solar heating are likely to be greatest in the spring and autumn, when sunshine can be quite intense even though air temperatures are still cold, and the angle of inclination of the sun is still quite low.

Because daylight levels on overcast days in winter can be barely sufficient, a roof overhang or other shading device fixed above windows, although useful to prevent overheating in summer, will significantly reduce light levels at the back of rooms since it will also cut off the view of the sky. It might seem preferable for the shading to be adjustable from within the building, but in a school environment the complex operation and lack of robustness of retractable shading systems usually results in them being inappropriate.

Box 5.4 Solar pre-heat sunspaces

Atria and conservatories can be particularly useful in schools. Not only are they relatively cheap spaces to provide but they can also have the environmental advantages of buffering internal rooms from ambient temperatures in winter, utilising solar energy, providing high illuminance levels by daylighting, and pre-heated ventilation.

Sunspaces can, however, be extremely wasteful of energy and cause overheating in adjacent rooms unless they are carefully designed to function without heating and to optimise the utilisation of daylight. Light levels at the floor of a multi-storey atrium will be a fraction of that outdoors, and large windows or glazed doors may be required to adequately light adjoining rooms. At higher levels where a clear view of the sky can be seen through the atrium roof, light shelves can aid the distribution of light and equalise light levels across rooms.

Adapted from: Baker, N., and Steamers, K., *Energy and Environment in Architecture: A Technical Design Guide*, Routledge, 1999.

3. Construction: robustness vs energy efficiency

School designs have to be robust in at least two senses, both of which address issues of sustainability. On the one hand, schools are subject to heavy use and require an approach to the use of materials which envisages a fairly basic level of maintenance. On the other, the design needs to be robust in relation to the changing needs of teachers and the curriculum, to act as a backdrop rather than an impediment to the future life of the school. It is evident that some previously acclaimed models failed to live up to this ideal. The SCSD (Southern California School Development) system for example[15], attracted a lot of interest in the UK, but its intention of producing a future flexible environment was at odds with its unsustainable reliance on artificial servicing.

To develop a design that enables the use of natural lighting and ventilation without mechanical cooling, and the least environmentally damaging use of resources, requires close coordination between the form of construction and the environmental strategy, in particular, the disposition of glazing and heavy-weight elements of the construction in plan and section. For a humane and environmentally sensitive approach to the making of school environments, the history of school design in Hampshire over the last 30 years is of great interest.

Box 5.5 The cardboard club

An innovative approach to school construction has been the outcome of a project funded by the EPSRC.[1] Cardboard is almost entirely manufactured from recycled material. To test its sustainability when used for construction, it has been used for the loadbearing, insulating and waterproofing elements of a cardboard school clubroom at Westcliff-on-Sea, designed by Cottrell and Vermeulen. Their intention was to construct the after-school club using 90% recycled materials, and with the future goal of making the building 90% recyclable at demolition. Cardboard tubes were used for structural columns and to make the end palisade walls of the building. To give stiffness, the shape of the walls and roof are folded forms using the same principle as origami. The parts of the building where cardboard have not been used are mostly made from other recycled building products. The architects established the form of the building by making a series of folded paper models. The process has been used as an educational tool. The school has made use of the project as an educational vehicle, the children were involved in the design development, collected card for recycling, and took part in a BBC radio live broadcast about the project.

1. RIBA Awards 2002, The Cardboard Building, Westcliff-on-Sea, Essex, *Architects Journal*, 7/10/02, www.ajplus.co.uk

Box 5.6 Schools Environmental Assessment Method (SEAM)

SEAM[1] is an adaptation of the BREEAM methodology for the assessment of school environments. Its aims are not only to make schools more sustainable in their construction and use, but also by improvement of school environments to make students aware of issues which are increasingly finding their way into the school curriculum.

SEAM addresses 23 separate environmental factors in relation to which schools have an impact, and makes recommendations for implementation by head teachers and school governors. Using the same methodology as BREEAM, points are awarded according to the relative importance assigned to individual topics. Some of these are of note for building construction generally, such as site selection, sources of hardwoods and softwoods, and use of recycled materials in new buildings whereas others are very specific to school environments, school grounds and school environmental policy.

Not surprisingly, the largest number of points is given for limiting energy consumption and CO_2 emissions. The measures anticipated are divided between those concerned with the buildings themselves and also those relying on environmental management. The allocation of points favours old schools, which are assumed to be operating at a disadvantage. So existing buildings can achieve the highest (band A) rating of 11 points compared with the maximum of 7 given to new buildings. Common problems within old schools include, within the fabric, poor insulation, but mostly they are concerned with inadequacies of the building services, particularly lack of sophisticated controls, and outdated boiler plant and distribution systems for heat and hot water.

The rating of newly designed schools (through bands A to F) is carried out by a method of calculation that relates fabric and ventilation heat losses to the characteristics of the building such as the U-values of its components and the density of occupation, also taking into account its dimensions in relation to the school's orientation, volume and glazing ratio. Solar gains are calculated by use of a solar utilisation factor multiplied by an orientation factor and adjusted according to the glazing specification. Cases that, at the first attempt, achieve only poor performance, can be recalculated to incorporate adjustments to the form of construction such as improved windows and higher performance boilers.

The method of calculation for existing buildings uses recorded annual energy consumption figures for gas and electricity, multiplied by their respective CO_2 conversion factors. The energy consumption of swimming pools and kitchens is not included in the calculations; they have to be estimated if there are not specific energy readings for them. The heating consumption is corrected according to the number of degree days in that geographical area to give a simple steady-state evaluation for the building. This is expressed in CO_2 emissions per square metre of floor area in relation to size, the assumption being that smaller schools (of less than 4000 m² in area) will inevitably have higher relative levels of energy consumption and correspondingly greater emissions.

1.   BRE, *Building Bulletin 83: School Environment Assessment Method (SEAM)*. BRE, Garston, 1996.

3.1 Integrated design of environment and structure

Most current school construction is what might be termed medium in weight. This has not always been the case since Victorian schools, many of which are still in use, which were multi-storey buildings with thick load-bearing brick walls.

The school 'systems' that were invented to overcome the school buildings shortage of the post-war era. Most famously the one developed in the architects' department of Hertfordshire County Council[16], swung in the opposite direction, towards lightweight steel-framed construction.

Some of the more long-lasting of these, such as CLASP (Consortium of Local Authorities Special Programme), later incorporated heavier-weight masonry cladding. Essentially these system-built schools were lightweight framed constructions that had very different environmental characteristics from their Victorian predecessors. With extensive areas of glazing in a continuous band across the width of the classroom, and relatively low ceiling heights, they tended to grossly overheat in summer while having draught problems caused by the cold surface of the windows in winter.

Contemporary construction favours the use of a steel or concrete frame allowing a flexible plan form. For economy, much use has been made of external rendered blockwork permitting stimulating colour schemes, but with the implied detriment to the environment that repainting is required throughout the building's lifespan. Timber, particularly cedar cladding, has also been a popular choice in recent years, the dimensional stability of the wood and its relatively small maintenance requirements being clear advantages, although sources of cedar are now being depleted at a rate which is unsustainable.

4. Generic construction methods

4.1 Typical UK school construction

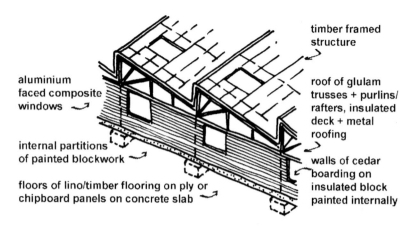

aluminium faced composite windows

timber framed structure

roof of glulam trusses + purlins/ rafters, insulated deck + metal roofing

internal partitions of painted blockwork

walls of cedar boarding on insulated block painted internally

floors of lino/timber flooring on ply or chipboard panels on concrete slab

Figure 5.1 Typical UK schools construction

Structure

- *Timber frame with external walls of rendered block, or loadbearing insulated block, plastered internally and clad with cedar boarding*

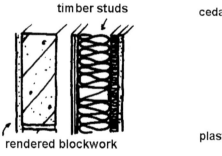

timber studs

rendered blockwork

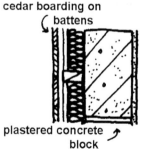

cedar boarding on battens

plastered concrete block

Figure 5.2 Timber stud + insulation/ cavity + rendered blockwork

Figure 5.3 Blockwork + insulation/cedar boarding external cladding

The low-energy characteristics of timber framing result in this alternative receiving an 'A' rating.[17] Its anticipated life matches the 60 years assumed for the building as a whole. Although limited recycling of timber is carried out at present there is potential for recycling with positive implications for energy savings.

Roof

- *Glulam trusses + purlins/rafters, insulated deck + metal roofing*

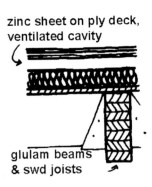

zinc sheet on ply deck, ventilated cavity

glulam beams & swd joists

Figure 5.4 Glulam beams and columns, sw joists + sw boarding, zinc sheet waterproofing

Schools are usually low-rise buildings, so the construction of the roof can be expected to have quite a large impact compared with other elements of the construction.

Perhaps surprisingly, low pitched roofs perform almost as well within the *Green Guide* ratings as does traditional clay tiled pitched roofing, even when built off a steel structure, on account of their low mass and lightweight construction.

Zinc sheet roofing has become more efficient in recent years owing to the introduction of long strip metal sheet, which has reduced the amount of cutting and waste and the number of joints required across the fall of the roof.

Zinc is generally considered to have a relatively short life expectancy compared to other sheet metals, particularly compared with lead which has been the traditional choice in the UK. However, zinc alloy, which is the contemporary 'zinc', has relatively enhanced life expectancy.

As with other metal roofing materials, zinc can be recycled, with the expenditure of far less energy compared with the production of virgin metal from ore.

Floors

- *Lino/timber flooring on ply or chipboard panels on concrete slab*

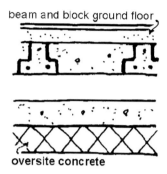

Figure 5.5 Ground and upper floors: Screed over beam/ block suspended floor

As in the case of roofing, the ground floor in a low-rise school can be expected to have a relatively large effect on the overall environmental impact because of its large area.

Although timber structure would be the preferred option, the use of beam and block flooring is lighter in weight and therefore has less impact than a comparable solid concrete slab. Beam and block has the additional advantage of being speedy to assemble on site, having easier quality control and being less susceptible to the effects of ground movement. A beam and block floor with screed covering achieves an 'A' rating.[18]

The amount of insulation in everyday construction is a small proportion of the overall mass of the floor and so makes little difference to the rating, unless a type of insulation is chosen that entails the use of ozone-depleting agents (see Chapter 2). It can be seen that achieving a BREEAM preferred 'A' rating is relatively easy with lightweight steel frame and curtain walling technology, whereas by comparison concrete construction and heavy cladding performs badly.

Poured-in-place concrete floors, on the other hand, achieve a 'C' rating because of their relatively greater mass. Power-floating does, however, remove the necessity for the use of dense and heavy sand/cement screed, which is an advantage.

Environmental impact can be further improved by the use of PFA (pulverised fuel ash) or GGBS (ground granulated blast furnace slag) aggregate which are by-products of electricity and steel production and consequently have limited impact.

Glazing

Aluminium-faced composite windows

Composite windows with an aluminium rain screen outer surface to an inner timber frame achieve a 'B' rating similar to aluminium windows but with improved ratings across most categories of the analysis compared to aluminium, for example in relation to both CO_2 emissions and climate change.

So despite having reduced climate change impact (particularly compared with aluminium framed glazing such as curtain walling), the proportion of timber in their make-up reduces the extent of recycled material used in their manufacture.

Because the impact of the glass is less than 20% of the embodied energy content of the window, the specification of the glass and whatever coatings are employed has little effect on the overall environmental impact, despite the improvement that extra panes and coatings might have on the glazing unit's thermal performance.

Partitions

Painted blockwork or brickwork

Brickwork used for internal partitions can achieve the best ratings if it is fair-faced rather than plastered, receiving an 'A', as does aerated block even if it is finished with plasterboard (on dabs) and painted. The aggregates used for the production of lightweight block have to travel a long way whereas the materials for heavyweight block are relatively close to hand for UK construction. Therefore and perhaps surprisingly, dense block finished with plasterboard and paint also receives the best rating, and aerated block uses less raw material but has limited potential for recycling.

Table 5.1 Ecopoints evaluation of generic constructions for schools, using BRE's Envest tool

	Generic school type: 50m × 18m (900 sq m ground floor); no. storeys: 1; storey height: 4.5m; % cellular: 60%; location: S.E. England; soil type: firm clay.		
		Ecopoints	%
Ground floor	150 mm beam and block suspended floor + 50 mm topping and 80 mm rockwool insulation	1434	24.4
Upper floor	none	0	0
External walls	Timber stud inner leaf and outer skin of reconstituted stone	869	14.8

Internal partitions	140 mm dense blockwork	420	7.1
Windows	Steel windows double glazed	258	4.4
Roof	Timber roof + purlins 1.4 m c/c, rafters, insulated deck + metal (copper) roofing, 150 mm rockwool insulation	1385	23.5
Floors	90% 3.2 mm lino on concrete slab	103	1.8
	10% 12.5 mm quarry tile	139	2.4
	Sub-total	242	4.1
Wall finishes	Gloss paint	200	3.4
Ceiling	none	0	0
Sub-structure	Trench fill foundation	721	12.3
Super-structure	None – built off load-bearing walls	0	0
Total embodied including material replacements over 60 year lifespan		5881	
Total embodied per sq m of floor area		6.5	

Source: based on Anderson, J., Shiers, D.E., Sinclair, M., *Green Guide to Specification*, (3rd Edition), BRE, Watford, 2002.

Commentary: Given the single-storey model used for this analysis, the predominant role of the ground floor and roof is not surprising. The floor construction is heavy in weight and has a high embodied energy, but because of the energy used in the extraction and manufacture of the metal roofing the Ecopoint rating for the roof is nearly equivalent to that of the floor. Although the elevations form a lesser part of the overall area, the same argument applies to the figures relating to the materials used for the walling and metal windows.

5. Generic school environments

5.1 Daylighting

Windows can provide daylight that will be adequate for 6–7 metres into rooms, but light-coloured wall and floor surfaces should be used to maximise the internally reflected component of the daylight factor.

Light surfaces adjacent to windows will also help to reduce the incidence of glare, particularly if the window frames and reveal sections are designed to create areas of intermediate brightness adjacent to the glazing.

The provision of adequate wall display area can discourage the practice of sticking student work to windows. Walls to be used for display need to be specifically designed for the purpose, flat and without projections such as surface conduit.

Box 5.7 Comfort in primary schools

By Peter Williams, while at the Martin Centre for Architectural and Urban Studies,
University of Cambridge

At a time when the design of schools is being championed by the government, with designs emerging which are embellished with 'sustainable motifs' such as the ubiquitous green roof and glazed atria, it is perhaps imperative that we stand back and examine how the classroom itself and the environment of the primary school – manifest in its architecture and landscape – interacts with the practice of teaching and learning at its most fundamental level.

Children develop the foundations of their knowledge during their primary school years, and it is important that they are exposed to a stimulating environment in which, and from which, to learn. The primary schools of the Hampshire County Architects Department (HCAD) have, over the past 25 years, led the way in the design of learning environments for children. Their schools have been significantly different from all others in that they have always sought to push the maximum environmental standards of their schools beyond those set by the regulatory bodies. However, this is always carried out through a challenging analysis of the relevant standards, which is part of an iterative process between the architect and the client, in defining the kind of environment which will suit the pedagogy and needs of the child.

To examine the design of the primary school classroom environment, three distinctly different HCAD schools were chosen and examined in some detail: Queen's Enclosure First School, Great Binfields Primary and Knightwood Primary. The studies consisted of tangible analyses in the form of on-site temperature, humidity and light measurements, as well as intangible analyses in the form of questionnaires, group talks with pupils, and a week of on-site study and behavioural analysis. From these studies, a profile was constructed for each school, allowing an analysis of how the buildings physically perform against how their users perceive the success of the school's environment, or its failures.

The results from the studies were at times unexpected. Central to the findings was that the teachers and the students valued the possibility of adaptability of their environments. An example of this is in the use of daylighting and the issues of heat gain. The Queen's Enclosure First School suffered high heat gains, with internal daily ambient temperatures varying from 18°C to 33°C, but excellent levels and quality of light throughout the spaces, which did not need to be supplemented by artificial lighting. While Great Binfields did not suffer the problems of heat gain, it too benefited from very high levels and quality of daylighting. The classrooms in both schools were similar in their design, linking directly, physically as well as visually, with the surrounding landscape.

Both schools were compared with Knightwood, which had a more traditional cellular plan of individual classrooms, rather than the open plan of both Queen's Enclosure and Great Binfields. At Knightwood the reverse was found, with optimum temperature and humidity results conforming to the latest bench-marking for environmental standards. However, the minimum internal lighting levels could only be

continued ...

achieved through the use of artificial lighting. Through talking with the staff and pupils it was clear that, owing to their ability to control their thermal environment, by drinking a cool drink, or opening or closing a window, that thermal extremes were not of great concern, unlike the quality and amount of daylight which, within the fixed envelope of a building, is much more difficult to increase.

Knightwood did not benefit from the direct visual and physical landscape around it, unlike the other two schools. In talking to the staff and pupils at all schools, it seemed that the buildings which responded environmentally to the seasons and their site as well as creating an open 'internal landscape' with the use of light and temperature to create a thermally and visually dynamic environment, provide the most stimulating of learning and teaching environments with the most positive user feedback.

Those who are involved in the design of primary schools therefore must challenge the guidelines which they are presented with, which require maximum and minimum temperature, humidity, acoustic and lighting levels, as these are not what result in successful design; rather it is the interpretation of these and a response to the client in providing a dynamic and stimulating environment.

The findings of the study, and a reason for HCAD's success in the design of their school buildings, can be summed up in the words of Nev Churcher, an architect with the HCAD who has been responsible for some of their most notable and successful schools:

"The ancient adage from Vitruvius, 'commodity, firmness and delight', is still just as relevant today, and underpins our design aims, to which we now add sustainability, energy and access criteria. Most important is the need to produce a sense of 'place' and inevitability – and places with as rich a mix as possible – a total learning environment where natural and created elements are in harmony."

5.2 Artificial lighting

Incandescent (tungsten) lamps are cheap to install but energy-consuming and expensive to operate, so their use in schools is best avoided. Instead, the best option is to use high-frequency fluorescent tubes and high frequency ballasts in luminaires with appropriate light distribution. They will provide a uniform light distribution that can be augmented by local task lighting if required. They are suitable for the type of use encountered in schools where lights are frequently turned on and off, and where dimming is possible.

Compact fluorescents are an energy saving alternative for use in circulation spaces, storage spaces, cloakrooms and WCs. Their efficiency is much greater than tungsten lamps and they are much longer lasting.

Other kinds of lamp such as metal halide, mercury fluorescent, and high pressure sodium (SON) lamps are suitable for external spaces such as sports fields and car parking areas, and larger indoor spaces such as sports halls and school halls.

5.3 Natural ventilation

Most schools still rely principally on opening windows to provide summertime ventilation, and trickle vents, perhaps in conjunction with passive stack vents, for winter background ventilation.

When windows are closed in order to provide background ventilation, particularly in winter, trickle vents should be provided with 400 mm² opening per m² of floor area.

The depth of section of the building needs to be carefully considered when natural ventilation is the chosen solution. The Building Regulations require that window openings for ventilation should be at least 1:20 of the building's floor area and that rooms to be single side ventilated should be no more than 6 m deep. Ideally, spaces will be cross-ventilated.

Mechanical ventilation should not normally be required, but there may be some instances where natural ventilation needs to be supplemented by artificial.

The government advice is that mechanical boost may be required to achieve flow rates in excess of 8 l/s in spaces with high heat gains such as kitchens, laboratories and home economics classrooms.

This will also be true for lavatories and changing rooms where air replacement in excess of 6 ach can only be achieved by the use of mechanical extract. This may entail placing these spaces at negative pressure and drawing air from adjoining teaching areas. However, if this is likely to result in excessive air movement through classrooms, a separate air intake will be required.

5.4 Space and water heating

Although the use of renewable energy would be preferable, the currently practicable alternative to limit CO_2 emissions is for boilers to use fossil fuel rather than electricity.

The heating system should be designed to respond to the school's pattern of demand, and central plant should be located so that distribution losses can be minimised. Where a modular boiler system is being installed, the system controller should bring the boilers individually and sequentially on line to make the system most efficient.

The use of heat pumps can be an efficient option, particularly if a suitable supply of low-grade heat, such as ground water, is available.

Hot water plant should be located strategically in relation to the points of demand, in order to reduce distribution losses, and to limit lengths of pipe run. The hot water system should be separate from the space heating system. If hot water demand is limited and infrequent, the use of local hot water heaters should be considered. Where the system is centralised, and a limited amount of hot water is required, the system can prove very inefficient.

Because schools are intermittently occupied, the controls on the hot water system are important, particularly the time switching controls. Low volume taps such as spray taps, with push button or occupant sensors, should be provided.

A small school having a heating demand of less than 100 kW may be zoned to take into consideration differences in orientation and the use of its spaces. A modular boiler system may be required with manual override for out-of-hours use.

In larger schools control systems have to be more flexible. Individual zones may contain spaces with different levels of heat gain, so the location of sensors will be very important. Zones can be linked by a building energy management system which can monitor the performance of the system continuously and provide data on the overall energy performance of the school.

Where a school has a heating demand in excess of 100 kW, the system should have optimum start control, weather compensation, zoning and individual thermostats as minimum requirements.

6. Case Study

6.1 Case study: Great Binfields Primary School, Basingstoke, Hampshire

Client: Hampshire County Council
Architect: Hampshire County Council Architects' Department
Design team: Alec Gillies with Martin Hallum, Bruce Kingsley-Smith, Annie Templeton, Eilidh Gutteridge, Shaun Mildenhall, Andrew Bacon
Quantity surveyor: Neil Sheppard with Chris Hore of Selway Joyce
Mechanical engineer: Gareth Bartlett
Electrical engineer: Steve Perry
Structural engineer: Dave Williams
Landscape architect: Mike Rothery with Geoff Durk, Jonathan Howe
Contractor: Richardsons of Nyewood Ltd
Site agent: Bob Sykes
Construction: August 2000 – August 2001 (buildings), May 2002 (landscaping)

Background

Great Binfields Primary is a school for 210 pupils, with the possibility of expanding the capacity to 420. It also includes a support unit for up to 10 visually impaired children who, for the majority of the day, will be integrated into mainstream classes.

Planning, form and construction

Site

The new school has been placed on the southern edge of Great Binfields copse, an ancient woodland on the north-east outskirts of Basingstoke.

The brief and design rationale

A key aim was to create a building that would respect its natural context and establish a close relationship between its internal spaces and the surrounding landscape. It would be environmentally sensitive, maximise natural light and ventilation, and be made from low-maintenance, durable materials which weather well. A principle of overriding importance was that the school should facilitate easy access for people with physical disabilities.

Figure 5.6 The horseshoe-shaped building

Source: Hampshire County Council

Figure 5.7 The sheltered south-facing central courtyard

Source: Hampshire County Council

Design

The classrooms, roofed in cedar shingles, are arranged on the inner edge of the horseshoe-shaped plan (Figure 5.6). They look onto a sheltered south-facing courtyard occupied by sculptures inspired by the woodland (Figure 5.7). The shared teaching spaces on the outer edges of the plan open onto a natural habitat study area in the surrounding woodland.

To assist people with physical disabilities, the building incorporates extra wide doorways, three wheelchair-accessible toilets and two wheelchair-accessible showers. There is a generous drop-off area for vehicles to deliver and pick up children with special needs at the front entrance.

To assist people with visual impairment, all teaching spaces are well lit with natural light, see Figure 5.8. Artificial lighting is via dimmable high-frequency colour-corrected fluorescent fittings. All surfaces have a low reflective matt finish, and care has been taken with colour choice and contrast. All signs are in a clear simple typeface at a consistent height and incorporate Braille. To assist people with hearing impairment, there are acoustic ceilings in all of the teaching spaces and in the corridor.

Structure

The structural frame of the building is made from parallel strand lumber (PSL), shown in Figure 5.8. This is reconstituted timber made from young, fast growing small diameter trees of second or third growth. Although this material is processed, it was chosen for this project as the result of a cost–benefit analysis. Almost all of the wood on each log is used; this means that fewer logs are used for the same structural task. Although it contains some wood that is ordinarily thrown away or burned for fuel, it has structural strength superior to most timbers. Waste wood is used for energy in the plant which manufacturers PSL.

Materials

Bricks and mortar

The bricks of the external walls have been sourced locally and laid in hydraulic lime mortar which has no cement content. The use of lime mortar removed the need for mastic movement joints and will also allow the possible reuse of the bricks in the future.

Source: Hampshire County Council

Figure 5.8 The parallel strand lumber structure

All the facing bricks are from Michelmersh in Hampshire where extraction of the clay is immediately adjacent to the factory. Sourcing materials locally decreases the embodied energy of the product by reducing the amount of energy used in their transport to the site.

Materials are not the only input to the building process which was sourced locally. The contractor, including the majority of their in-house staff, is based in Petersfield, Hampshire and all members of the design team live and work in Hampshire. The artists who supplied the sculptures are based in Portsmouth, Hampshire.

Recycled materials

All of the window frames contain recycled aluminium. The damp proof membrane for the building is Visqueen™ which is made from recycled polythene. All of the pinboards are Colourboard, by Sundeala Ltd, which is made from recycled waste newsprint. The acoustic ceiling tiles contain recycled glass. The concrete block shear walls are made from blocks which contain recycled aggregate in the form of furnace bottom ash.

Recyclable and reusable materials

Service ways have been designed to be accessible and 'refittable' so that the building can accommodate change over time. The basic fabric of the building has been designed to assist its own dismantling ready to be recycled. For example, the bricks can be reused as they are laid in hydraulic lime mortar with no cement content, the PSL structure is simply pinned together and the floors are made from precast concrete beams and pots. The TPE (thermoplastic elastomer) flat roof membrane and all the polybutylene pipework for service distribution is recyclable.

Insulation

None of the insulation used in the building has been manufactured using CFCs or HCFCs.

Finishes

All varnishes and paints in the school are linseed-oil-based and made from renewable natural materials with no petrochemical-based solvents or ingredients.

The carpet is made with a high content of natural materials and has been tested for VOC emissions in accordance with German standards. Linoleum flooring has been used in preference to PVC-based material.

Services

Service ways have been designed to be accessible and 'refittable'.

The polybutylene, $[C_4H_8]_n$, pipework for all service distribution is recyclable and there is a generous provision of isolating valves to avoid draining down the systems during maintenance.

Thermal performance

High thermal mass in the solid walls and floor reduces fluctuations in temperature, and thus both summer overheating and changes in load on the heating system in winter.

Ventilation

Clerestory windows, as well as lighting the classrooms, assist natural cross-ventilation by being controlled by electronic temperature and rain sensors. This system can be overridden and operated manually by individual members of staff.

Light

The daylighting design aims to maximise natural light, while minimising discomfort from glare and overheating.

The south-facing courtyard elevation has a 1.2 m overhang over full-height windows (Figure 5.7) while high-level clerestory windows facing generally north are used throughout (Figure 5.8). Those windows facing east, exposed to the sun, use solar control glass, while those facing west are shaded by the hall. Both east and west windows are shaded to a certain extent by the surrounding trees.

All electric lighting in the teaching spaces is high-frequency high-efficiency dimmable fluorescents.

Sound

All teaching spaces and the main corridor of the school have acoustic ceilings to absorb noise within each space, thereby reducing disturbance to surrounding spaces.

Water

Percussion spray taps have been fitted, and a generous provision of isolating valves has been made to prevent the need to drain down the entire system during servicing.

Energy supply

The building has a low-temperature under-floor heating system. The high thermal mass of the floors, along with that of the walls, reduces temperature fluctuations in the space and also evens out the heat demand of the system. By reducing peak heat demand, smaller boilers could be used than with a radiator-based system; by reducing fluctuations in heat demand, the boilers can operate near to peak efficiency for a greater proportion of the day.

Source: Hampshire County Council

Figure 5.9 The school within its surrounding woodland

The boilers are fuel efficient, low NO_x, natural gas fired, condensing boilers. NO_x emissions are estimated to be only 40 mg/kWh. Natural gas contains very little sulphur, so SO_2 emissions will also be low. CO_2 emissions from the heating and hot water generation are estimated to be 75 kg/m^3. This level meets the 'good' energy targets of the government, CIBSE and BRE.

Heating system circulation is driven by energy-saving pumps with electronic speed control.

Landscape

The landscaping strategy draws heavily upon the woodland location of the new school.

Existing woodland

The Great Binfields copse is an ancient woodland and although, in the 1970s, the wood was converted to a conifer plantation, a narrow fringe of native broad-leaved trees, such as oak, ash, wych elm, field maple and crab apple has been retained. Despite the pine trees, much native woodland flora has survived with species of note including solomon's seal, dog violet, primrose and bluebell.

The management programme for the Great Binfields copse will encourage the native species present to flourish and spread while the introduced pine trees are progressively removed through felling.

Care was taken during the construction of the school to limit its adverse impact on its woodland site, with special funding being set aside to develop the adjacent woodland as an outdoor educational area for use by the school.

Although the project involved the felling of some trees, many more will continue to be planted on site. The seed-rich topsoil removed from the edge of the wood to make way for the building has been used under the newly planted tree banks to encourage woodland plants.

The subsoil taken from the foundation excavations has been used to level the playing field: off-site removal of subsoil has been minimised.

Compost used on the site will be peat-free and made from recycled garden waste.

Transport

A green travel plan has been developed for the school. The objective of this plan is to minimise the number of car journeys to and from the school to minimise pollution and encourage energy conservation as well as to reduce road traffic congestion and encourage road safety.

The modal share of journeys to primary schools in Basingstoke is 42% walking to school and 48% being taken by car. Only 1% of journeys to school are made by cycle (source: Hampshire County Council Transpol data). The target for Great Binfields Primary is 65% walking, 20% by car, 5% by cycle, and bus/taxi 10%. Wide consultation with statutory bodies, local residents, parents and staff will take place through HCC's Headstart Community Involvement Programme in order to achieve these objectives.

A path connecting the school to an existing pedestrian route to the north will be constructed. Cycle racks for 10 pupils' cycles have been included (5% of pupil numbers). A shower for staff has also been included.

7. Notes

1. DEFRA, *Foundations for Our Future. Sustainable Development Strategy June 2002*, UK Department for Environment, Food and Rural Affairs, 2002.
2. The World Commission on Environment and Development, *Our Common Future* (The Brundtland Report). Oxford University Press, 1987.

3.   Energy Efficiency Best Practice programme, *Efficiency in Schools: Some Simple Energy Conservation Measures,* GPCS101, BRESCU, 18/05/1994.

4.   Energy Efficiency Best Practice programme, Energy Consumption Guide 73 *Saving Energy on Schools – A Guide for head teachers, governors, premises managers and school energy managers* (ECON073) BRECSU, 2001.

5.   CIBSE, *Guide H: Building Control Systems.* Chartered Institution of Building Services Engineers, London, 2000.

6.   Action Energy *Building Energy Efficiency in Schools: A Guide to a Whole School Approach.* GPG343, www.carbontrust.co.uk, 01/03/2003.

7.   Southampton Environment Centre, *Greening Britain's Schools,* http://www.e4s.org.uk/biffa/, January 2001.

8.   Op. cit., Action Energy, 2003.

9.   CIBSE, *Ventilation and Indoor Air Quality in Schools.* A Symposium held at CIBSE, 12/12/2000.

10. Richardson, G. Univ. of Plymouth, Dept. of Environmental Sciences, paper at CIBSE Ventilation and Indoor Air Quality in Schools. A Symposium held at CIBSE, 12/12/2000.

11. Stephen, R.K., Parkins, C.M., Woolliscroft, M. *Passive stack ventilation systems: design and installation.* BRE Information Paper IP13/94, BRE, Garston, 1994.

12. Energy Efficiency Best Practice programme, *Energy Efficiency in Schools: Local Controls for Heating and Lighting,* Case Study 95, BRECSU, Garston, 1995.

13. Action Energy *Planning for Passive Solar Design.* ref:ADH010, www.carbontrust.co.uk, 01/01/1998.

14. Action Energy *Passive Solar Design: Netley Abbey Infant School.* GIL032, www.carbontrust.co.uk, 01/05/1999.

15. Reyner Banham. *The architecture of the well-tempered environment.* The Architectural Press, London, 1969.

16. See, for example, a recent account in Alan Powers *Britain: Modern Architecture in History*, Reaktion Books, London 2007.)

17. Anderson, J. and Shiers, D., *The Green Guide to Specification.* Blackwell Publishing, 2002.

18. *ibid.,* p. 11.

Further Reading

Energy Efficiency Best Practice programme, *Energy Efficient Refurbishment of Schools.* Good Practice Guide 233, BRECSU, Garston, September 1997.

Energy Efficiency Best Practice programme, *Energy Efficient Design of New Buildings and Extensions for Schools and Colleges.* Good Practice Guide 173, BRECSU, Garston, March 1997.

6 Supermarkets: Energy and Shopping

1. Discussion

While department stores have been closing in many city centres, supermarket chains have taken an increasing share of the UK retail market. For that reason much of this chapter is concerned with supermarkets, which are selling an increasing range of goods as well as groceries, in fact taking on the character of department stores.

Government-funded research in the early 1990s found that the annual UK cost of energy used in retail outlets was £1.8 billion[1] of which between 5% and 10%, that is £90–180 million, could be saved by better design and improved house-keeping practices.

Although this is only a small percentage of UK annual retail turnover, it is a significant percentage of retail profits, and is a large proportion of the service charges made for rented retail premises.

A basic decision in the cause of sustainability is the choice of fuel to be used for heating. Electricity is only viable for small and well-insulated premises where the additional cost involved in installing or maintaining a gas or oil boiler would be prohibitive. The prerequisites for a shop to use less energy and produce less CO_2 are that:

- it should be well insulated and use natural servicing, particularly daylighting, in conjunction with efficient forms of electric lighting incorporating energy controls;
- it should have modern and efficient appliances utilising gas as their main fuel; and
- in particular, air conditioning should be avoided.

The use of air-conditioning always implies environmentally detrimental CO_2 pollution; this is not only because of the amounts of energy required but because of the chemicals used in chiller systems, which tend to be highly ozone depleting. In the UK climate, the use of air-conditioning should not really be necessary other than in deep plan buildings. In the case of supermarkets, the loads associated with chiller cabinets pose particular problems, which have been dealt with ingeniously in the case study project included at the end of this chapter.

Among retail uses, supermarkets have the highest level of annual energy consumption, as well as the largest per m^2 figures for CO_2 emissions.[2] For buildings that only have electric heating, supermarkets are estimated to have annual electricity consumption of 750 kWh/m^2 per year, whereas supermarkets relying on a combination of fossil fuel and electricity have a higher energy use totalling 830 kWh/m^2 per year, but lower CO_2 emissions at 500 kgCO_2/m^2 per year. Less intensive energy users are buildings such as banks, building societies and post offices having a rate of energy consumption 10% less than that of super-markets, their CO_2 emissions being of the same order.

Department stores and food stores are among the most intensive energy users, but energy use, and consequential greenhouse gas emissions, is not the only environmental concern.

1.1 Location and land use

Retail development presents issues to do with location and land use, particularly on out-of-town sites where supermarkets and shopping malls entail large areas of low-rise development surrounded by a considerable amount of car parking – considerations that are incorporated by local authorities into strategic development plans. Guidance has been issued under *Planning Policy Statement 6: Planning for Town Centres* (PPS6). (This replaces *Town Centres and Retail Developments,* (Revised *PPG Note 6*) published 1996 and subsequent policy statements, published March 2005.)

PPS6 sets out the government's policy on planning for the future of town centres. It is concerned with the maintenance of the environment, and the encouragement of good design directed towards schemes based on the concept of high density and mixed use. One of the principal concerns for PPS6 is that retail premises should be accessible by different modes of transport, but with public transport the preferred option rather than relying exclusively on the use of cars. From that point of view it is recommended that if city centre sites are available they should have the highest priority for development. The least favoured alternative is building on peripheral sites.

Further guidance can be found in the government report *The impact of large food stores on market towns and district centres*,[3] which is concerned with the impact of out-of-town developments on the environment, and maintaining the viability of existing shops within the city, and the environmental quality of the city centres. From the point of view both of conserving the countryside and of maintaining the health of existing city centres, environmental policy and energy policy coincide.

Many towns have now appointed managers to champion the cause of town centres, and to ensure their continuing profitability and competitiveness. Through the process of consultation, the needs of less-mobile groups, such as the elderly and disabled and young families with children, are represented. By their involvement at the preliminary stage of design, the development can avoid loss of functionality and the risk of early obsolescence, and help achieve town centre environments that are safe and attractive. The interacting issues here are to do with access to and within the centre, crime prevention and quality of environment.

There is a complementary *Planning Policy Statement No. 7 (PPS7): Sustainable Development in Rural Areas* which also seeks to maintain viable town centres and to concentrate development on brownfield land, but also aims to promote competitive and efficient retail development that is accessible particularly by public transport, walking and cycling. PPS7 is particularly concerned with the conservation of the countryside, and its quality of environment, while safeguarding the character of rural towns and attempting to reduce dependence on the motor car. (PPS7, published in August 2004, replaces *PPG Note 7: The Countryside – Environmental Quality and Economic and Social Development*, February 1997.)

Cars and travel

The location of retail development has implications for traffic patterns and traffic volume. The growth of road transport in the UK is making the most rapidly increasing contribution to climate change, as well as producing air pollution that is the cause of thousands of deaths each year. The government's policy on transport published in 1998 – *A new deal for better transport: better for everyone* – encourages local authorities to form a strategy for dealing with road transport and its consequences for air quality, road safety and integration with public transport within their local areas.

This is in the context within which transport energy and emissions are currently rising at 4% per year, mostly due to the growing use of planes and cars, although freight transport is responsible for 10% of UK energy use. The government is committed, having first agreed to the environmental criteria set out during the

Earth Summit in Rio in 1992, to reducing motor car use, to promoting alternatives to the private car, and to encouraging development within existing centres in order to overcome the dispersal of land uses into the countryside. PPG13, the planning policy guidance note for transport, requires that residential areas are integrated with other land uses in order to reduce lengthy journeys, and that retail premises should either be located centrally, or alternatively on sites at the edges of centres. Retail premises should be close enough to be readily accessible by foot, and able to be served by a variety of transport means including public transport. It requires that local authorities take into account the amount of transport that will be generated by retail developments and indeed how travel reductions can be initiated.

This is an attempt to reverse the pattern of development since World War II and to put the emphasis back on town centres and existing areas in preference to out-of-town locations. As well as the need to reduce the energy and CO_2 emissions due to transport, the other important aims are to reduce pollution and to improve outdoor air quality. The chemicals contained within exhaust fumes can contribute to photochemical smog, and some are carcinogenic, while nitrogen and sulphur oxides cause acid rain. In addition, the noise generated by road traffic is a major reason for natural ventilation to be eschewed in favour of air-conditioning, with consequent environmental damage. Congestion makes roads dangerous for cyclists and deters bicycle riding.

The greater use of public transport and bicycles would largely overcome pollution problems, but inevitably car parking will be required at shopping centres where large and bulky purchases are being made, and for shoppers with mobility problems, or for whom public transport would be inconvenient. The reduction of vehicle pollution has implications for the location of retail development: it should be close to its intended market, employees must be encouraged to travel by public transport and bicycle, and facilities should be provided for bike parking. Shopping centres that contain a variety of types of store reduce the necessity for shoppers to visit different shopping centres to complete their purchases. Larger shopping centres should attempt to maximise the amount of shopping spend per kilometre travelled, and thereby reduce the national length of shopping journeys made per year.

1.2 Environmental aspects of supermarket design

The energy consumption profile of supermarkets is a little different from other types of retail building. Some quite basic forms of enclosure such as do-it-yourself stores have characteristics more akin to those of a warehouse than those of shops in a mall. Consequently, by far the largest proportion of their energy cost is due to electricity used for lighting, but because they tend to have high ceilings and thus a large volume to heat, fossil fuel space heating and domestic hot water are responsible for a fair proportion of the total. This proportion diminishes for other non-food shops where mechanical ventilation and possibly air-conditioning and lifts increase the relative amount of electricity that is consumed. Supermarkets, although predominantly self-service food stores, tend increasingly to include other uses such as an in-store baker, delicatessen and restaurants. In this case, it is food refrigeration that is responsible for half of the overall energy cost, air-conditioning and lighting for another quarter, and the bakery, space heating, domestic hot water and other miscellaneous electrical uses that account for the last quarter of the total.[4]

Retailers are becoming interested in the cost savings that can be made by reducing energy consumption. Sainsbury's has been a leader both in reducing energy consumption and in the development of alternative renewable sources. Its annual spending on power is around £50 million. To cut down on fuel bills, it launched a campaign within the firm called 'Save It' which is to remind employees to turn off lights and use other easily implemented energy saving ideas. Sainsbury's also introduced a programme aimed at reducing the company's energy consumption by 11% within two years, which would in turn reduce Sainsbury's carbon emissions by 10% by the year 2005. It is also looking into the use of renewable energy sources with a view to 10% of its energy bills coming from renewables in the coming years.

Another company that is very active in this area is MFI. Since 1994 the company, which in total has about 500 stores, has used a variety of measures aimed to cut its carbon emissions by 50%. A building management system, which automatically controls the stores' heating and lighting levels, was introduced at a cost of £800,000 – expenditure that was repaid by energy savings within 12 months. A typical innovation was the fitting of self-dimming lights within a 50,000 m² warehouse that paid for itself within 18 months. Having achieved rigorous control over energy bills, the company then moved on to the replacement of conventional power sources by renewable energy. Fifty outlets are being powered from renewable energy obtained from an independent supplier who sells electricity obtained from wind farms and gas from landfill.

These initiatives, although still rare, have a growing momentum. Under the UK government's Renewables Obligation every electricity supplier in the country has a requirement to provide a proportion of its production from renewable sources.

Sainsbury's approach to energy management

One of a series of case studies into methods of management to achieve energy efficiency within businesses, Good Practice Case Study 148[5] was conducted in 1994, and updated in conjunction with Sainsbury's in 1997. The company gives a high priority to environmental concerns, from packaging to recycling, and is a market leader in retail technology which is used, for example, to accurately control the temperature of products and indoor spaces. The various energy efficiency measures it has introduced are with a view to achieving the 'low energy supermarket'.

Since the inception of this programme in the 1970s Sainsbury's annual fuel bill has been reduced by approximately 19%. As well as technology, attention has been given to the managerial issues and procedures necessary for innovation to succeed. Starting after the first oil crisis in the 1970s, steps were taken to identify energy costs which had previously been lumped into overall operating expenses, the realisation has come about that, in an industry relying on high turnover with low profit margins, energy savings could be significant in achieving greater market share.

Box 6.1 Sainsbury's five-point energy policy[1]

Sainsbury's have a five-point energy policy that integrates aspects of management with technical issues:

- To consume energy in the most efficient and sustainable way and minimise waste. This concern impinges on both the design and operation of Sainsbury's buildings and equipment so that they operate at maximum efficiency.
- As much waste heat as possible is reused, and they now have a programme for the continuous monitoring and reviewing of energy performance.
- To apply to the group's operations the most recent and best of available technologies, which entails researching the most advanced building and servicing systems from sources worldwide.
- To achieve ongoing reductions in energy consumption through improved technical procedures, but also by involving staff in the drive to achieve energy efficiency.
- By the purchase of energy at the most beneficial rates, and monitoring its consumption, it becomes possible to target potential improvements. The company keeps abreast of developments within the electricity supply industry for negotiation of the most preferential deals.

Sainsbury's participates in a variety of national and international award schemes through which it aims to promote staff and customer awareness of the local and global issues relating to the efficient use of energy.

1. Sainsbury's press release: *Sainsbury's switches to Ecotricity for renewable energy*, www.j-sainsbury.co.uk.

These objectives are being achieved by a combination of strategies, one of which is an online monitoring system, RealMT, that was developed with the aid of funding from the EU Thermie scheme. RealMT has been installed at most of the company's sites including its head offices. It collects monitored information from over 4000 meters for gas, water and electricity, and 3000 sensors which log measurements for internal and external temperature and humidity, CO_2 levels and lighting intensities. These are compared with a moving target for each meter, which is dependent on weather and operating conditions, and trading patterns. An expert system is used to determine the reason for any discrepancy between target and achieved values. The system then automatically emails the store engineer describing the fault, its likely cause, and the costs involved in delay. A variety of faults can be identified including: lights being left on or switches overridden, failed passive infrared detectors, incorrect BMS settings, water leaks, poor heating or heat recovery performance, and inefficient use of refrigeration equipment.

People vs freezer cabinets

Supermarkets have a large quantity of refrigeration equipment and this is always responsible for a large proportion of the overall energy use of the building. A refrigeration system's power is mostly consumed by the compressors, which run on electricity and produce substantial amounts of heat as a by-product of the refrigeration cycle. To some extent it is possible to limit the extent of energy use by sizing the compressors to match the load, and by controlling the plant so that, if there are variations in demand, the equipment loads can respond accordingly. These problems are, however, far from solved; we have all experienced the icy conditions in aisles of freezer cabinets, and the supermarket staff wearing quilted coats to keep warm, irrespective of the prevailing outdoor temperature. Insulated covers provide insulation overnight on chest freezers, and insulated night blinds provide some degree of enclosure to freezer cabinets, but of course for these measures to be effective they have not only to be provided but actually used – which isn't always the case.

The maintenance schedule for the freezers – so that they are regularly and effectively defrosted – is important. Another significant requirement is that refrigerated store rooms aren't left with doors wide open, particularly while restocking is taking place. The waste heat from the pumps and compressors can best be utilised to heat the adjacent shop floor, a consideration that impinges on the layout of the store, because a lot of energy will be lost if the design involves moving refrigerant and cooling water for long distances around the building. However, this can be overcome to some extent by adequately lagging pipes and valves. Ideally though all refrigeration, whether for cooling or chilling, should be

Box 6.2 Sainsbury's at Beckenham[1]

This store was originally opened in 1983. It is a medium-sized supermarket, incorporating a bakery and a sizeable meat preparation area that was designed to what, at the time, was a good standard of energy efficiency. Relevant features included a heat recovery system to make the best use of waste heat from refrigeration plant, store lighting and the bakery, and to enable its reuse for the domestic hot water supply and space heating. The refrigeration plant is modular, and the units operate sequentially so that demand is matched to the operation of the plant; waste heat from the chillers is reused. Similarly, the boilers are modular and sequentially controlled for provision of heating and hot water, including supply to warm air curtains above doors (although these are only operable when the temperature falls below 15°C). Two-speed fans were used throughout so that the rate of supply could be adapted to the demand for heating or cooling.

Over the course of time, however, energy demands have increased because of the increasing length of supermarket opening hours. The building has undergone a number of modifications in order to address the problem, including some quite simple measures such as fitting insulating jackets to cover over the freezer cabinets at night. In 1992, a building energy management system was installed allowing better control of the building's services, enabling them to be operated in new and energy-saving ways. The air handling plant, controlled by the BEMS, can now operate in different modes, from full re-circulation in order to retain energy, to full fresh air to make use of free cooling from outdoors.

The store has been divided into different zones by use: main sales area, bakery, meat preparation area and staff area, each of which is separately controlled to optimise the operation of plant and lighting. The BEMS continuously monitors the indoor air quality, and if it is found to be satisfactory, the supply and extract fans are closed down. At night, temperatures are allowed to vary, the supply fans are switched to low speed, and the extract fans are turned off. Lighting levels are also controlled by the BEMS, which ensures that only security lighting operates at night (during shelf stocking periods it operates at 40%) and are only at full output when the store is open. Remote monitoring is carried out to check that set point and operating temperatures are being achieved; the BEMS periodically issues a report that pinpoints the savings to be made through improved control of the system.

The Beckenham store is not as efficient as some more recent projects, but installation of the BEMS has enabled the building's energy consumption to stay fairly constant, despite extended opening hours, and increased refrigeration and lighting loads.

1. *Introduction to Energy Efficiency in Shops and Stores.* Department of the Environment, BRESCU, March 1994.

concentrated around the same location; the waste heat is then available either for domestic hot water heating or space heating.

The refrigerants used for food storage are a problem because the large volumes of CFCs and HCFCs lost to the atmosphere through leakage, and during maintenance operations, are a major cause of ozone depletion. It is estimated that up to 80% of the refrigerant chemicals sold in the UK are lost in this way; food refrigeration plant is estimated to lose 50% of its refrigerant when the equipment is being serviced (over its lifetime), which clearly has profound implications for its detailed design. A variety of strategies can be put in place to overcome the problem. Refrigerant leakage detectors can be fitted to enclosed chillers and wired up to an alarm system, and other detection systems are available for monitoring open cabinets. The plant needs to be designed for easy maintenance, adequate space being available around all sides of the machines so that leaks of refrigerant can easily be noticed, collected, stored and returned, while the ozone depleting characteristics of the system being proposed can be determined from the initial specification of the equipment.

The relative effects of the various compounds currently in use are a function of their ozone depletion potential (ODP), which is defined as 'the total change in ozone per unit mass, when the substance has reached a steady state in the atmosphere'. CFC11 is the most damaging of these materials and, having an ODP of 1.0, is the benchmark against which the others are assessed. The first step towards elimination of the environmental damage that they cause was the Montreal Protocol that limited emissions of CFCs and halons, which was signed by many of the world's governments in 1987. The substitute materials HCFCs are, however, similarly damaging in the short term, if to a lesser extent in the long term (over a period of hundreds of years), so the intention of more recent agreements is that HCFCs should be phased out of use in the relatively near future. Chillers that employ inorganic chemicals rather than hydrocarbons are already available and have the further advantage that they can run on gas rather than electricity, but unfortunately they are a lot less efficient than the ozone depleting alternatives.

1.3 Natural ventilation – long spans and food smells

If a store is fully air-conditioned, the HVAC system can be the largest single use of energy, so air-conditioning is to be avoided whenever possible. Supermarkets are deep plan buildings, so air-conditioning may prove unavoidable, but subsidiary spaces such as the public spaces at the perimeter of the building, for circulation in and out of the store, and associated areas such as cafes may possibly be naturally ventilated. A principal reason for air-conditioning being required is the build-up of excess heat due, for example, to the amount of lighting power being used, and the heat thrown out by refrigeration equipment. Measures to reduce over-heating include making sure that any rooflights face away from the sun so as to reduce the amount of solar gain entering the space, and by limiting their area. Similarly beneficial is if shading is provided to south-facing windows by overhangs or louvres, and the use of solar control or fritted glass may also be appropriate. High volume spaces may be less of a problem from this point of view since the heat will tend to stratify at a level above head height.

In any case, it may be necessary to incorporate mechanical ventilation for smoke clearance in case of fire, then perhaps forming one component of an assisted natural ventilation system for smaller supermarkets, rather than providing full air-conditioning. In which case, appropriate measures can include designing for reduced lighting loads, specifying efficient lamps, and specifying a wider band of permissible comfort conditions when writing the design brief for the building. Unless temperatures are likely to exceed 28°C for more than a few hours a year, air-conditioning may not be required. If it proves necessary nonetheless then reducing the volume of air supplied to the minimum, and making sure that the recurrent problem of spaces being heated and cooled at the same time is avoided, will both help reduce energy consumption. Cooling the air supply to 24°C may be sufficient to achieve comfort. Given appropriate weather conditions it might be possible to use outdoor air directly for cooling; for efficiency it is important that the building is appropriately ventilated, and that good use is made of waste heat. If possible radiant cooling panels should be fitted at the point of delivery, to minimise the amount of ducting and to avoid pumping large volumes of cool air around the building.

Concern about the refrigerants used within food refrigeration equipment is also applicable to air-conditioning systems. Leak detection devices will not work when air-handling plant is out of doors, or with air-cooled condensers, which are usually located externally on a roof. In these cases, equipment should be manually checked every six months to make sure that no leaks have occurred. The chiller condenser should not be used as a holding store for the refrigerant during the shut-down process of the machine; instead a separate container needs to be incorporated within the system to store the refrigerant during the maintenance process. These 'refrigerant recovery units' incorporate a pump for the return of the refrigerant to the chiller circuit.

If on the other hand condensers are not included, particularly in older systems that employ cooling towers, the environmental problem then becomes one of avoiding legionnaire's disease. Both the cooling towers and the condensate draining from the air-conditioning plant can be a source of the bacterium which is responsible for about 300 cases a year of the infection, of which about 12% prove fatal. Consequently, the cooling towers must be properly designed, operated and maintained to allow cleaning and maintenance, and effective water treatment. A well-designed cooling system should enable the cleaning out of all the condensate and sludge and provide easily accessible drainage points at the lowest levels of the system. Of course, avoiding air-conditioning altogether also helps avoid the risk of legionnaire's disease.

1.4 Lighting strategies

Daylighting

Daylight has generally been anathema within retail buildings, with the possible exception of DIY depots, which are more closely aligned to factory or warehouse units. On the one hand, wall space is likely to be at a premium for display purposes, precluding the use of windows. On the other hand, UV light can be detrimental to the goods for sale, which tend, as a consequence, to be exhibited in artificial light despite the poorer colour rendering of artificial light when compared with natural. General use spaces, for example circulation areas such as a shopping galleria, or cafes within supermarkets may have natural light and outside awareness, but because larger shops tend to be deep span spaces, reliance on artificial services for both lighting and ventilation have become the norm. Supermarkets ought uniquely to have the potential for daylight use although the increasing length of the retail day means that a proportion of the building's use will inevitably be after dark.

Artificial lighting

Display lighting is an important aspect of merchandising. This has usually resulted in stores of all types being uniformly illuminated to a consistently high level allowing flexibility for the reorganisation of displays. Sainsbury's store at Greenwich has illustrated the potential for a return to a design paradigm closer to the 19th Century market hall, background lighting being provided by rooflights and daylight for much of the day. Display lighting can, as a consequence, be locally disposed using high intensity sources such as tungsten halogen lamps. General lighting for backup during the day and for general lighting at night is likely to be provided by fluorescent fittings or metal halide lamps, both of which have relatively favourable levels of luminous efficacy. Multi-storey shops may, of course, reduce the potential for daylighting other than on the upper retail levels as is particularly the case for larger stores with sizable floor plates.

Colour rendering of meat and vegetables

A well-designed lighting scheme is one of the prerequisites for successful retailing. In supermarkets, the quite high intensity of light, and the evenness of illumination that is required, have militated against the use of natural lighting. The amount of light provided within supermarkets makes the lighting bill one of the largest operational costs, and significant accompanying levels of CO_2 emissions. A good lighting scheme is consequently one that is energy efficient, but which also optimises the level of sales. The lighting design has to be of a high standard to achieve these goals, but also the controls and equipment have to be carefully specified, including not only the light fittings themselves, but also including stipulations for the operational management of the building.

An effective solution is one that provides the right light levels (but not too much), by the use of efficient lamps, fittings and controls, and achieves a high standard of maintenance. A good lighting scheme encourages people to enter the store, enables the shop windows to be used for display at night, and it encourages people to walk around and impulse buy. In fact, a good lighting scheme can insidiously result in shoppers remaining in the shop longer and buying more than they otherwise would as a result. To achieve the right environment for the marketing of many goods, colour rendering is an important aspect, particularly in supermarkets, where fresh food is being displayed. The lighting scheme at its best creates a distinctive image for the store.

When it comes to the specification of lamps, the same arguments apply as for other building types such as offices. Tungsten bulbs are very inefficient and can in many cases be substituted by compact fluorescent fittings. While not as efficient as contemporary tubular fluorescents, compact lamps can however be used for some types of display lighting, within downlighters for example. Because shops always require display lighting, tungsten halogen spotlights are likely to be required to some extent. Although they have a luminous efficacy greater than that of tungsten filament bulbs, they are still about three and half times as energy consuming as compact fluorescent tubes.

Replacement of the old 38 mm diameter fluorescent tubes with 26 mm triphosphor lamps achieves some improvement in efficiency, but the figure is greatly enhanced if an electronic ballast is used. The high frequency ballast has several advantages: the frequency of flickering is increased so the incidence of headaches and eye strain is reduced, or at least that is what has been found in office buildings, which presumably would also be true in supermarkets; furthermore the system can then incorporate dimming equipment. As a result, fluorescent fittings will have about the same efficiency (about eight times more efficient than tungsten filament lamps) as metal halide and high pressure sodium lamps – types that are sometimes used in uplighters, particularly in tall internal spaces such as found in do-it-yourself stores and car parks, but their colour rendering is still inadequate for more sensitive display areas.

Other measures to improve efficiency include replacing the diffusers in old luminaires with reflectors, because prismatic and opal diffusers have poorer performance. Generally, if a light installation is over 15 years old, it is worth replacing the fittings and updating the lighting controls to enable light levels to be locally controlled by the staff.

Timed controls can be installed to switch off lights in sequence across the store when the store is closing, and the sorts of controls used in offices, such as timed controls, daylight detection controls and presence controls, may also be useful in less frequently used areas such as storage rooms.

Naturally, adequate maintenance and a good operational regime are necessary to achieve efficiency. Simple measures are effective, for example appointing someone in the store to be responsible for turning lights off at the end of the day, using daylight wherever possible and keeping windows and rooflights clean, turning light levels down when the building is not open to the public but merely being used for stocking shelves, and making sure that display lighting is not used out of hours.

2. Construction

Within existing buildings, a refurbishment programme offers the opportunity for roof and wall insulation to be upgraded, and windows to be replaced with double or multiple glazing with a low-emissivity coating, or for secondary glazing to be installed alongside existing windows to improve their performance. Doors are an important source of heat loss in such heavily trafficked buildings; revolving doors perform well from this point of view, but the draught proofing of other personnel doors combined with the use of door closers, and the fitting of insulated doors to loading bays also offer energy advantages.

Shopping centres are one of the most frequently refurbished building types. The frequency of refitting is around 6–7 years for particularly popular locations but typically around 8–10 years. Over the course of the building's lifetime, the inputs of materials and energy during refurbishment programmes will be a substantial proportion of the whole lifetime energy cost. Less successful shopping centres are refurbished in order to maintain their fabric, but the more fashionable locations will be upgraded to maintain a contemporary appearance, and to retain their place in the market from the point of view of rents, their mix of tenants, and to remain competitive with other retail outlets. The importance of a recognisable image, particularly for retail chains, may place significant barriers in the way of a more ecological approach. There are, of course, exceptions such as the Body Shop where ecological responsibility has become part of the corporate ethos.

The environmental impact of refurbishment can be reduced if a policy of rational periodic renewal addresses the durability characteristics of the building's components in terms of their inherent life expectancy. Relevant factors include the tendency of retail buildings to have large areas of low-level glazing, and that particularly visible parts of the building fabric are likely to require easy replacement on account of wear and tear, and to keep a fresh appearance.

3. Generic construction methods

Retail construction encompasses a number of typologies from inner city department store to suburban DIY depot, the multi-storey mall and suburban supermarket probably being the most simply categorised of the wide range of retail construction. As for most building types in our heating-dominated climate, the provision of adequate insulation (i.e. better than the Building Regulations level of provision) is a prerequisite for energy efficiency.

3.1 Typical UK supermarket construction

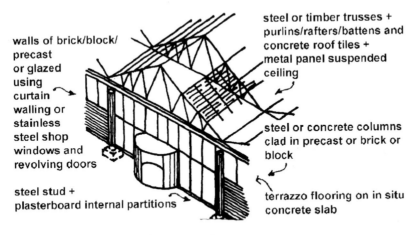

steel or timber trusses +
purlins/rafters/battens and
concrete roof tiles +
metal panel suspended
ceiling

walls of brick/block/
precast
or glazed
using
curtain
walling or
stainless
steel shop
windows and
revolving doors

steel or concrete columns
clad in precast or brick or
block

steel stud +
plasterboard internal partitions

terrazzo flooring on in situ
concrete slab

Figure 6.1 Typical UK supermarket construction

Structure

- *Steel or concrete columns clad in precast or brick or block, external block/precast cavity walls*

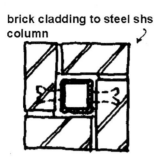

brick cladding to steel shs column

Figure 6.2 Masonry cladding to steel hollow section column

Supermarkets are essentially medium span shed buildings or frame construction, sometimes flat roofed but more usually, under planning pressures, having a structure of steel or concrete columns with welded steel trusses. The structural materials are rarely exposed but, instead, a non-loadbearing cladding of brickwork or stone aggregate precast is the visible surface. In terms of the structure, the choice of steel or concrete is likely to be of little consequence (as noted under 'offices') but the masonry cladding has considerable impact by virtue of its weight and the energy used in its production.

Roof

- *Steel or engineered timber trusses + purlins/rafters/battens and concrete tiles and metal suspended ceiling*

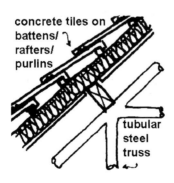

concrete tiles on battens/ rafters/ purlins

tubular steel truss

Figure 6.3 Tiled roof on rafters, purlins and exposed tubular steel trusses

Suspended ceilings are very widely used in supermarkets and form one of this building type's largest elements by area. Because they are light in weight, their impact in terms of embodied energy is limited, although proportionately their importance is greater for low-rise buildings compared with multi-storey. The best performing systems, receiving an 'A' rating, include accessible suspended ceilings with an exposed grid, which are of the type likely to be installed in a supermarket. Their life cycle impacts (as calculated for BRE's *Green Guide*[6]) are, however, predicated on the achievement of a 25-year life before replacement that may not be representative of contemporary retail construction.

Floors

- *Ceramic tiles or terrazzo flooring on in-situ slab*

tiles on screed, insulation beneath concrete slab

Figure 6.4 Tiled solid floor laid on grade

lean mix conc. on hardcore

Being a high-mass element, this concrete floor system achieves only a 'C' rating (though lighter weight alternatives such as ribbed slabs or waffles do better with a 'B'). Flat slab construction does particularly badly in relation to the volume of mineral extraction it requires, because the quarrying of aggregates has a considerable impact on its local environment. Recycled aggregate has advantages from this point of view, although it is little used at the moment. However, in terms of embodied energy, the crushing, sorting and transport of recycled aggregates is likely to be comparable to the virgin material, and there may be quality control issues requiring additional cement content in the mix thus undermining the environmental benefits.

Hard floor finishes from natural sources such as terrazzo, ceramic or quarry tiles perform well (all achieve an 'A' rating) because of the limited energy inputs to their production but also because they are hard wearing and are therefore less likely to be replaced.

Glazing

• *Curtain walling or shop windows, revolving steel doors*

stainless steel framed shop
window

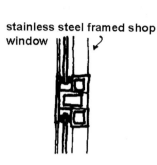

Figure 6.5 Stainless
steel shop window

Stainless steel is a favoured metal because of its ability to be recycled and because recycled material is the predominant source for worldwide stainless steel production. Although glass entails the use of major amounts of energy in its production, its overall impact is quite small. Careful specification of the glazing, with regard to the orientation of the building, and its energy characteristics, can however make a considerable difference to the overall performance of the building.

Internal partitions

Glass block walls

Although long an architectural favourite, glass blocks have adverse environmental impacts by virtue of their weight, the thickness of the material and the amount of energy used in their production.

Table 6.1 Ecopoints evaluation of generic constructions for supermarkets, using BRE's Envest tool

		Ecopoints	%
Generic supermarket type: 100m × 20m; (ground floor 2000 sq m); no. storeys: 1; storey height: 5.0 m; % cellular: 10%; location: S.E. England; soil type: firm clay			
Ground floor	200 mm in situ reinforced concrete slab + 80 mm rockwool insulation	4690	32.1
Upper floor	none	0	0
External walls	50% non-loadbearing cavity brickwork + 60 mm rockwool insulation	774	5.3
	50% double glazed curtain wall 1250 × 1000 grid	996	6.8
	Sub-total	1770	12.1
Internal partitions	Glass block	514	3.5
Windows	Aluminium double glazed non-opening	413	2.8
Roof	Steel trusses + purlins 1.4 m c/c /rafters/battens, 0.75 kN/m² loading	466	3.2
	Concrete tiles + 150 mm rockwool	3786	25.9
Floors	terrazzo	197	1.3
Wall finishes	10% 6.5 mm ceramic tiles	171	1.2
	90% 2 coat render + emulsion	304	2.1
	Sub-total	474	3.2
Ceiling	Metal suspended ceiling	222	1.5
Sub-structure	1200 × 450 Column base foundation	383	2.6
Super-structure	Concrete columns	1059	7.3
Total embodied including material replacements over 60 year lifespan		14618	
Total embodied per sq m of floor area		7.3	

Source: based on Anderson, J., Shiers, D.E., Sinclair, M., *Green Guide to Specification*, (3rd Edition), BRE, Watford, 2002.

Commentary: The extensive use of high embodied energy materials for both structure and finishes explains the quite high overall figure for the total embodied energy per sq. m. The long span roof and large volume enclosed might give a different impression if considered in terms of embodied energy per cu. m. But the other damaging characteristics of this building type – in terms of travel, food miles and operating energy – result in embodied energy being a relatively minor consideration.

4. Case study

4.1 Sainsbury's store at Greenwich, London

Client: Sainsbury's plc
Architects: Chetwood Associates

Background

Although highly atypical of general UK supermarket construction, the Sainsbury's store on Greenwich Peninsula, close to the Millennium Dome, represents the first of a new approach to a more sustainable standard for supermarkets.

The site

The store is located at the end of the Greenwich peninsula next to the (former) Millennium Dome, the site has been planned to accommodate a bus lane, designed to accommodate a future London Transport Transit link. Behind the supermarket is a lake and planted meadow that are to be a wildlife reserve used as a retaining area for surface water running from the car parks, selected indigenous plant species being used for landscaping. The external illuminated shop signs are powered entirely by wind and solar energy, excess electricity being stored in batteries for use at night. The masts onto which the advertising panels are mounted also provide support for a wind turbine and photovoltaic array. By generating electricity on site CO_2 emissions are reduced.

Two 75-mm deep boreholes were sunk into the aquifer beneath the site to provide water at a constant temperature, the water is used to cool the building through a system of underfloor piping; it also supplies water to the refrigeration system. In turn, heat from the refrigeration system is discharged to the boreholes as an alternative to air-cooling, which, with the relative variability of air temperature compared with ground water, makes for a more efficient system.

The form of the building is completely integrated with its site, which is banked up to the roof, the outline of which has been designed as an integral aspect of the overall form. Earth is mounded against the building on two sides, which forms a smooth profile, reducing wind turbulence that would otherwise increase winter heat loss. Air is drawn into the store under the surrounding earth banks through the suspended sales floor and supplied to the sales areas using natural buoyancy.

Other aspects of the site layout include landscaping with indigenous and drought-tolerant plants, the inclusion of a Woodland Trust reserve, sheltered cycle racks with access to a system of footpaths and cycleways across the Greenwich Peninsula.

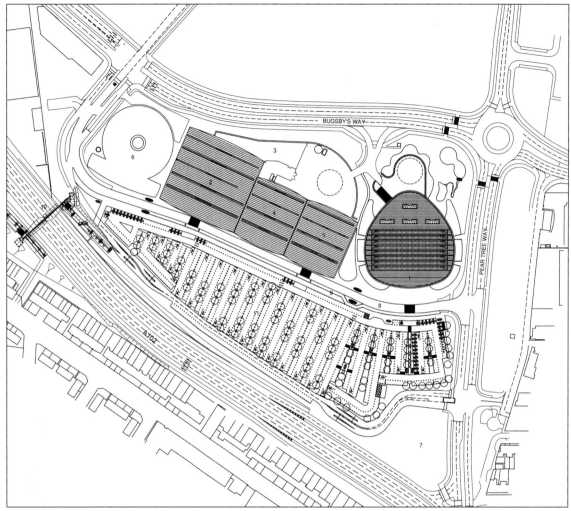

Source: Chetwood Associates Architects

The brief and design rationale

Figure 6.6 Masterplan

Sainsbury's Greenwich is the principal, if not the only, example of green super-market design in the UK[7]. A competition was launched, the brief being to achieve a 'green' design compatible with the environmental aspirations of its neighbour, the Millennium Village. This design was the winner, beating another major supermarket chain.

The ecological aspects of the project are not merely additions to an otherwise conventional building. Instead, the process of development of the scheme has been to investigate the possibility of transforming the nature of supermarket buildings, to make them more sustainable. These considerations were central to decisions made about the environmental engineering of the building, and the selection and use of materials; for example the roof is made from mill-finished

Figure 6.7 Building Plan

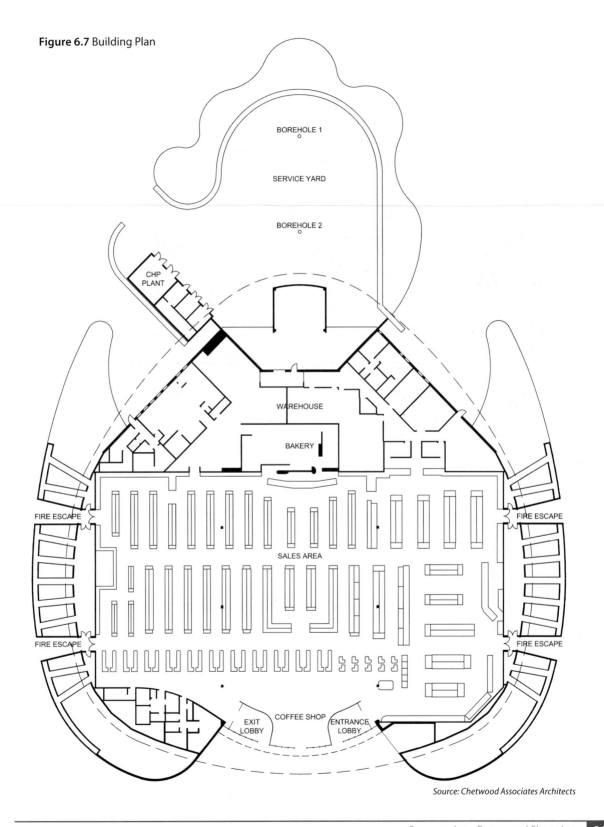

BOREHOLE 1

SERVICE YARD

BOREHOLE 2

CHP PLANT

WAREHOUSE

BAKERY

FIRE ESCAPE

FIRE ESCAPE

SALES AREA

FIRE ESCAPE

FIRE ESCAPE

EXIT LOBBY

COFFEE SHOP

ENTRANCE LOBBY

Source: Chetwood Associates Architects

Figure 6.8 Roof view

Source: Chetwood Associates Architects

aluminium, the walls flanking the earth mounds to either side of the entrance are clad with untreated oak boards with Forestry Stewardship Council certification. The internal environment of the building explores the possibility of reducing electricity consumption by the use of daylight to as large an extent as possible, and the use of natural rather than mechanical ventilation.

Design

As with any long-span shed type building, the design of the roof is a major consideration, particularly so in this case since the roof is the main lighting mechanism for the building and it also plays a part in the ventilation system. The overall form of the roof is a northlight factory profile, but the angle of the glazing is somewhat less than 90 degrees to make the shape more aerodynamic since it was decided that the sharp angles characteristic of traditional northlights

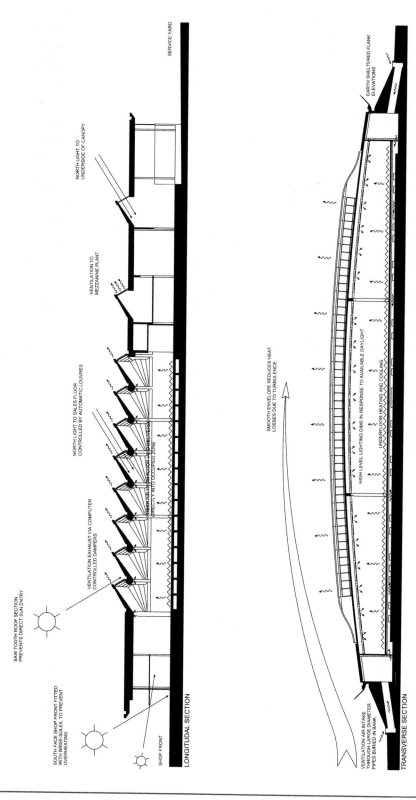

SAW TOOTH ROOF SECTION
PREVENTS DIRECT SUN ENTRY

SOUTH FACE SHOP FRONT FITTED
WITH BRISE-SOLEIL TO PREVENT
OVERHEATING

SHOP FRONT

VENTILATION EXHAUST VIA COMPUTER
CONTROLLED DAMPERS

FRESH AIR PLENUM FLOOR AIR DELIVERED
DIRECTLY INTO OCCUPIED ZONE

NORTH LIGHT TO SALES FLOOR
CONTROLLED BY AUTOMATIC LOUVRES

VENTILATION TO
MEZZANINE PLANT

NORTH LIGHT TO
UNDERSIDE OF CANOPY

SERVICE YARD

LONGITUDAL SECTION

SMOOTH ENVELOPE REDUCES HEAT
LOSSES DUE TO TURBULENCE

HIGH LEVEL LIGHTING DIMS IN RESPONSE TO AVAILABLE DAYLIGHT

UNDERFLOOR HEATING AND COOLING

EARTH SHELTERED FLANK
ELEVATIONS

VENTILATION AIR INTAKE
THROUGH LARGE DIAMETER
PIPES BURIED IN BANK

TRANSVERSE SECTION

Source: Chetwood Associates Architects

Figure 6.9 Building section

Source: Chetwood Associates Architects

generate turbulence, and the resulting suction pressure increases heat loss from the roof. The choice of roof covering was between the mill-finished standing-seam aluminium that was eventually used, and a PVC-based membrane. The latter was rejected because of the controversy that broke out when it was used for the Millennium Dome, and because the metal roof that was chosen resulted in a more distinctive design.

That the choice was between two less than ideal alternatives illustrates the difficulty of constructing sustainable flat roofs, or roofs with little slope. Mill-finished aluminium does at least obviate the need for the VOCs used to make the plastic coating to profiled roof sheeting. Also, standing-seam strip roofing relies on its method of jointing to achieve watertightness rather than being effectively glued together with mastic, the short-life hydrocarbon sealant required by other low-slope systems.

The insulation used was Rockwool™ which, rather than one of the foamed plastic alternatives, is free from CFCs and HCFCs, and is 10% thicker than required by the then current Building Regulations. The roof panels were profiled on site in standard module widths of 400 mm. The rolling plant was located adjacent to the building so the motive force of the machine could provide enough impetus to project the lengths of metal strip up onto the roof. Fabrication of some complex forms was required. The combination of a barrel vault with the inclined surfaces of the sawtooth rooflights resulted in an S-shaped profile at the junction, but it was found that this could be made without using tapered sheet as was

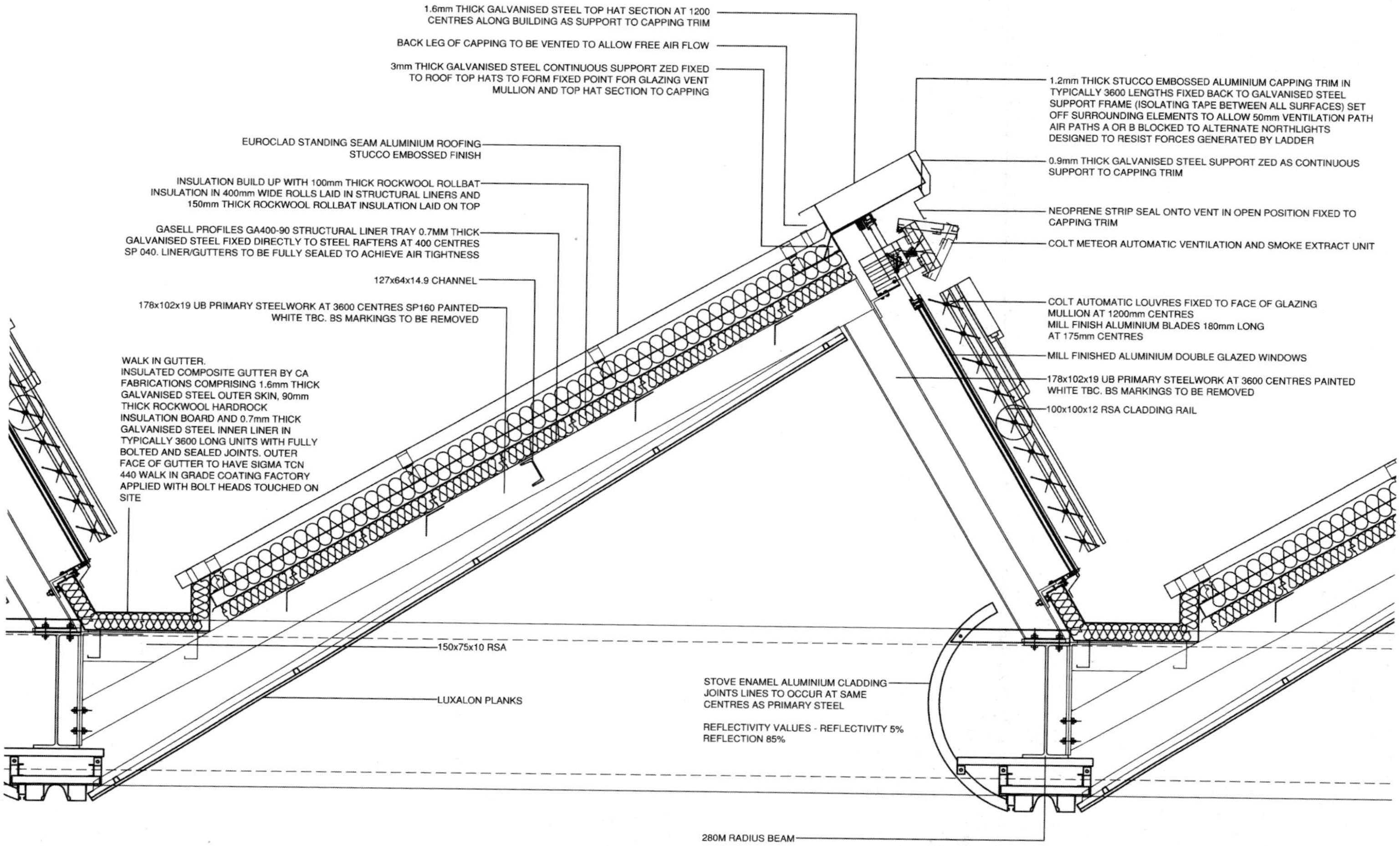
1.6mm THICK GALVANISED STEEL TOP HAT SECTION AT 1200 CENTRES ALONG BUILDING AS SUPPORT TO CAPPING TRIM
BACK LEG OF CAPPING TO BE VENTED TO ALLOW FREE AIR FLOW
3mm THICK GALVANISED STEEL CONTINUOUS SUPPORT ZED FIXED TO ROOF TOP HATS TO FORM FIXED POINT FOR GLAZING VENT MULLION AND TOP HAT SECTION TO CAPPING
EUROCLAD STANDING SEAM ALUMINIUM ROOFING STUCCO EMBOSSED FINISH
INSULATION BUILD UP WITH 100mm THICK ROCKWOOL ROLLBAT INSULATION IN 400mm WIDE ROLLS LAID IN STRUCTURAL LINERS AND 150mm THICK ROCKWOOL ROLLBAT INSULATION LAID ON TOP
GASELL PROFILES GA400-90 STRUCTURAL LINER TRAY 0.7MM THICK GALVANISED STEEL FIXED DIRECTLY TO STEEL RAFTERS AT 400 CENTRES SP 040. LINER/GUTTERS TO BE FULLY SEALED TO ACHIEVE AIR TIGHTNESS
127x64x14.9 CHANNEL
178x102x19 UB PRIMARY STEELWORK AT 3600 CENTRES SP160 PAINTED WHITE TBC. BS MARKINGS TO BE REMOVED
WALK IN GUTTER. INSULATED COMPOSITE GUTTER BY CA FABRICATIONS COMPRISING 1.6mm THICK GALVANISED STEEL OUTER SKIN, 90mm THICK ROCKWOOL HARDROCK INSULATION BOARD AND 0.7mm THICK GALVANISED STEEL INNER LINER IN TYPICALLY 3600 LONG UNITS WITH FULLY BOLTED AND SEALED JOINTS. OUTER FACE OF GUTTER TO HAVE SIGMA TCN 440 WALK IN GRADE COATING FACTORY APPLIED WITH BOLT HEADS TOUCHED ON SITE
1.2mm THICK STUCCO EMBOSSED ALUMINIUM CAPPING TRIM IN TYPICALLY 3600 LENGTHS FIXED BACK TO GALVANISED STEEL SUPPORT FRAME (ISOLATING TAPE BETWEEN ALL SURFACES) SET OFF SURROUNDING ELEMENTS TO ALLOW 50mm VENTILATION PATH AIR PATHS A OR B BLOCKED TO ALTERNATE NORTHLIGHTS DESIGNED TO RESIST FORCES GENERATED BY LADDER
0.9mm THICK GALVANISED STEEL SUPPORT ZED AS CONTINUOUS SUPPORT TO CAPPING TRIM
NEOPRENE STRIP SEAL ONTO VENT IN OPEN POSITION FIXED TO CAPPING TRIM
COLT METEOR AUTOMATIC VENTILATION AND SMOKE EXTRACT UNIT
COLT AUTOMATIC LOUVRES FIXED TO FACE OF GLAZING MULLION AT 1200mm CENTRES MILL FINISH ALUMINIUM BLADES 180mm LONG AT 175mm CENTRES
MILL FINISHED ALUMINIUM DOUBLE GLAZED WINDOWS
178x102x19 UB PRIMARY STEELWORK AT 3600 CENTRES PAINTED WHITE TBC. BS MARKINGS TO BE REMOVED
100x100x12 RSA CLADDING RAIL
150x75x10 RSA
LUXALON PLANKS
STOVE ENAMEL ALUMINIUM CLADDING JOINTS LINES TO OCCUR AT SAME CENTRES AS PRIMARY STEEL
REFLECTIVITY VALUES - REFLECTIVITY 5% REFLECTION 85%
280M RADIUS BEAM

Figure 6.10 Northlight details

Source: Chetwood Associates Architects

originally thought necessary; studies carried out with scale models showed that the material had enough flexibility to make the shape from standard sheet, with favourable implications for the amount of off-cut waste that was discarded.

The glazed sections are about 1800 mm high and total in length about half a kilometre of glazing, which is either high-performance double glazing, or incorporates automated louvres to control the direction and quantity of light entering the building. The structure of the roof is a series of steel beams intersected by curving secondary beams beneath each of the sawtooth sections. The insulated profiled metal roofing is supported off steel frames fixed alternately to the bottom and top of the secondary steelwork to create a location for an insulated steel double skin gutter that forms a walking surface between the sloping glazing and profiled roofing. The glazed sections have, at the apex of the sawtooth, automated ventilation and smoke extract dampers. As far as possible, recycled material has been used throughout the building. It is, of course, one of the advantages of aluminium that a large proportion comes from recycled sources although the virgin metal is very energy intensive to produce.

The lightweight steel frame was quite fast to erect so the roof construction could begin before completion of the mass concrete surrounding walls, which provide thermal mass to the building and help to reduce temperature fluctuations.

Other examples of the use of recycled materials in the building include the rubber flooring to the entrance area, which was made from recycled bus and aeroplane tyres. Walls within the landscaped areas that obscure the service yard are made from gabions containing crushed concrete reclaimed from the site and are planted with creepers. Internally, linoleum flooring is used on account of its relatively benign environmental characteristics compared with plastic flooring, and partitions within the customer toilets are made from recycled plastic bottles.

Services

The design makes a concerted effort to deal with the more intransigent aspects of energy consumption within this kind of structure. Whereas artificial lighting and ventilation are the norm for supermarkets, here the principal background lighting is provided through the rooflights assisted by the light-coloured floor and ceiling that make the best of available daylight. Artificial lighting is used only to directly illuminate the merchandise on display, rather than providing general lighting. The sales floor background lighting is turned off during the day, with display lighting maintained at the level required for local illumination. The light fittings themselves have been chosen for low energy operation. The exception to that is the sparing use of tungsten halogen lamps for the lighting of higher value products, the luminaires being attached to display shelving for flexibility, and independent of the lighting to the adjoining aisles.

The controls that make this possible are similar to those that would normally be found in an art gallery. Sensors operate banks of louvres within the rooflights, to reduce the direct admission of sunlight, but also to maintain a constant level of illumination while preventing night time light pollution.

The floor finish is white-flecked terrazzo, which provides a reflective surface to bounce light back onto the metal ceiling, preventing the incidence of glare but also rendering the interior bright and airy.

The ventilation system is similarly innovative. Air is tempered by passing through a concrete undercroft, having been drawn in from outdoors, before entering the space at the base of the display cabinets. Hot water coils within the undercroft make it possible to preheat the air if necessary. The resulting displacement method is energy efficient since the air only needs to be cooled to one or two degrees below comfort temperature, consequently only low-grade heating and cooling sources are required, as provided by the on-site CHP plant and borehole water cooling. The system is also healthy since used air and germs are expelled at the high point of the roof, where mechanical dampers at the head of the glazing exhaust air directly to the outside.

The disadvantage is that, whereas cold air spilling onto the floor from refrigerator cabinets would, in a conventional installation, become mixed with the room air, because of high velocity supply air entering above head height, in this instance the cool air isn't so readily dispelled. In order to overcome this problem, and to prevent the chiller cabinets having to be continually defrosted, they have extract grilles beneath them to take air back into the undercroft and thereby to recycle some of the cool, and consequently dry, air. The refrigeration packs are ozone benign and propane-based, a glycol solution being used within the under-floor pipework which supplies the sales floor cabinets and freezers.

As is usual in supermarkets, because of the presence of the chiller cabinets within the sales space, some heating is required for the majority of the year. The CHP unit is not only able to provide 85% of the annual electrical load, but also to provide enough heat energy for background space heating of the store. Effectively, therefore, the heating is provided without any CO_2 being generated, but because the available heat is more than sufficient to meet the supermarket's needs, an economic case could not be established for reclaiming heat from the exhaust ventilation. Delivery into the space is by an underfloor piped low pressure hot water system so the sales floor acts as a giant radiator. Heat is supplied by the CHP plant via a plate heat exchanger, or alternatively, when cooling is required, by use of borehole cooling water, which is at a constant temperature of 10–12°C.

This is an incisive and radical solution to making supermarkets more sustainable, and the building's performance has been monitored in use. Discomfort adjacent to the chiller cabinets proved a problem during the initial period of operation: air temperatures in the vicinity were still too cold, requiring some adjustment to the system. In terms of the life cycle performance of the building, it will be interesting to see whether the fresh air system can deal with the expected growth of car traffic adjacent to the building, and whether the undercroft can be kept free from the mould growth that is very usual in such spaces. A major criticism of the scheme generally is, of course, the size of the adjacent car park, an unsustainable but unfortunately inevitable concomitant of this building type.

5. Notes

1. Energy Efficiency Best Practice programme, *Introduction to Energy Efficiency in Shops and Stores*, Department of the Environment, UK, 1994.

2. Prior, Josephine J., *Sustainable Retail Premises: An Environmental Guide to Design, Refurbishment and Management of Retail Premises.* BRE, 1999.

3. DETR, *The Impact of Large Foodstores on Market Towns and District Centres.* HMSO, September 1998.

4. *ibid.,* p.1.

5. Energy Efficiency Best Practice programme, *Energy Management – J Sainsbury plc. Good Practice Case Study 148* Department of the Environment, March 1997.

6. Anderson, J. and Shiers, D., *The Green Guide to Specification.* Blackwell Publishing, 2002.

7. 'Retail Therapy' *RIBA Journal*, November 1999. p. 42.

7 Factories: the Industrial Agenda

1. Discussion

Since the 1970s, the pattern of new industrial building in the UK has followed the direction of the country's economy, resulting in a marked reduction in heavy industry, and a shift towards light engineering and services, which have very different requirements in terms of space[1]. At the same time, the increasing need for energy saving has led to a closer control of construction standards; consequently comfort conditions have improved, with positive benefits for productivity within the workplace. The general environment in these new and improved factories may, as a result, not be very much different from that found in contemporary office buildings.

1.1 Site planning

During initial strategic planning, the extent of heat loss from factory buildings can be controlled by careful site layout. For example, heat loss will be reduced if loading doors are designed to face away from the prevailing wind, and particularly if the doors allow easy operation so that they are likely to be kept open for shorter lengths of time. Factory buildings can be grouped together to reduce the extent of heat loss (if perhaps at the expense of future flexibility for expansion), and of course uninsulated party walls between units will lose heat if the factory next door is unheated. Shelter belts of trees, or moving earth to form mounds around the site, can reduce wind speeds and thereby the rate of heat loss, since infiltration from the building will be generally dependent on the ambient wind speed and direction. The elevation of the roof is important because a shallow slope will enclose a smaller volume needing heat, provided that a higher roof isn't required either by the production process, or the need for tall storage racking.

General issues

It has been estimated that half of the readily achievable energy savings in UK factories are related to a relatively small number of factors: the extent of the building's insulation and air leakage, inadequacies in the heating system and losses in distributing heat around the building, lack of controls, wrongly set thermostats, lack of maintenance, and inefficient lighting installations.[2] Since the early 1990s, the government's Energy Efficiency Best Practice programme has taken steps to improve the energy performance of all sectors of industry by providing information and guidance (e.g. through site visits) to help factory owners and tenants introduce energy management – not just to control their buildings, but the processes too.[3]

1.2 Pollution

Undoubtedly, energy savings are possible in most types of industrial building, with benefits not only in terms of energy consumption and cost, but also in relation to CO_2 emissions, and the increased profitability and competitiveness that accompanies this reduction in overheads. These savings can be significant since energy-efficient factories can consume 30–50% less energy than those of average performance. The refitting of some older buildings has achieved a 50% reduction in heating and lighting costs without detriment to comfort conditions or quality of product.

The amount of energy used varies widely across the industrial sector depending on the type of building, the processes that it is to enclose, and the nature of the site and its location. To determine the amount of energy use is quite difficult since it depends not only on the type of fuel being consumed, but also on the proportion that is devoted to heating, lighting and ventilating the building, as opposed to the energy required for the production process. This can sometimes be difficult to determine; for instance a ventilation system in a factory may be an essential aspect of the production process as well as providing a satisfactory internal environment.

1.3 Processes

Energy consumption varies widely across industrial sectors. The largest users are the paper industry and factories producing cooked foods, which have an average fuel consumption of between 800–1000 kWh/m^2 of gross floor area per year, as compared with the relative frugality of cold food production units where the median for the sector is just short of 200 kWh/m^2.[4] Across all industries, the top 10% have been found to be consuming 50% more than the average for their sector. Some of this may be due to variations in production processes, but it indicates the potential for the reduction of energy use in factories.

Despite the wide range of manufacturing processes, very few use more energy to service the building than does the process taking place within it, when considered on a kWh/m^2 per year basis.

Different industrial processes use different types of fuel; the older heavy industries tend to consume fossil fuel, while light manufacturing makes greater use of electricity. Similarly, most building heating will be supplied using fossil fuel as the delivered form of energy, but because electricity is that much more costly per m^2 of floor area, the electricity costs roughly match those of fossil fuel across most types of process. Since the extent of CO_2 emissions varies more or less in proportion with the unit cost of fuel, the relative costs also give an indication of the relative production of greenhouse gas between sectors; laboratories and chemical production plants being the worst polluters, and light manufacturing and engineering are among the least polluting of industrial uses.

It is also worth noting the trend towards a change in use for 'traditional' shed-type factory buildings. For example, where steel manufacturing factories once covered acres on the fringe of an industrial town, we now see similar acreage covered with massive distribution centres or shed-type buildings used as quasi-offices for the ubiquitous call centre.

Box 7.1 Adnams' brewery

Adnams' brewery near Southwold in Suffolk was winner of the 2007 Carbon Trust Innovation award.

Adnams have taken an holistic view of their environmental policy from introducing new processes to the invention of a lightweight beer bottle which not only means the use of less glass, but also represents a decrease in fuel required for distribution. The company estimates that the new bottle design will save 415 tons of CO_2 per annum, the equivalent of taking 138 cars off the road.

Its new distribution building has lime and hemp walls, rainwater harvesting, solar thermal panels and a sedum roof. The company estimates that, by comparison with its former warehouse, it will use 30% less gas and 55% less electricity per m^2.

The new brewery is one of the most energy efficient in Europe. The steam that was previously discarded is now being used to provide 90% of the heat needed for brewing.

1.4 Typology

Government-funded research dating back to the 1990s classified factory buildings into four types[5]:

- Buildings for storage and distribution – Typically these are warehouses with a clear height of 7.5 metres, suitable for pallet racking, naturally ventilated and heated to around 16°C, lighting being provided by high pressure sodium lamps achieving 150 lux (but with higher levels of provision in dispatch and office spaces). Rooflights occupy approximately 10% of the roof area. Refrigerated warehousing is, however, excluded from this category having much higher energy consumption.

- Factories for light manufacturing – Light industrial factories require approximately 5 metres internal clear height, to offices spaces and storage and dispatch areas. They are usually naturally ventilated but with the possibility of some mechanical extract, and with heating provided by warm air or radiant heaters to achieve 16°C or 18°C. A light level of 300 lux at the work surface is usually supplied by fluorescent or high pressure sodium fittings. Once again, about 10% of the roof area would be given over to rooflights. This is a building type that might be used for light engineering or the assembly of electronic equipment.

- Factory/office buildings – Being closer to our usual expectation of office space rather than industrial, factory/office buildings have office, production and storage areas that are all provided with the same level of environment. Typically, they have a clear internal height of 4 metres, but with office spaces having reduced height underneath suspended ceilings. Fluorescent lighting is used to achieve 500 lux at the work surface, windows are double glazed, with a ducted warm air system for the internal spaces, and perimeter heating provided by radiators to achieve 20°C throughout. There may also be local areas of mechanical ventilation or air-conditioning.

- General manufacturing buildings – The norm for general manufacturing buildings is a clear height of 8 metres, possibly with gantry cranes and storage racking, and tall equipment. High pressure sodium, metal halide or fluorescent fittings are used to achieve 200 lux; there may be clerestory windows or rooflights but, in this sort of building, they are likely to be dirty and heavily obscured. There may be mezzanines in parts of the building, heating to 16°C being provided by warm air, radiant heaters or steam heating. High level natural ventilation or mechanical extract may be used to exhaust the excess heat produced by the manufacturing process.

1.5 BREEAM for industry

BREEAM5[6] was introduced in 1993 to extend the BREEAM methodology to industrial buildings, which was previously only applicable to offices, supermarkets and homes. An added complication for this building type is that factories are constructed either as bespoke buildings for particular enterprises or as speculative units that are built only as shells. Environmental aspects of particular relevance to factory construction – such as ventilation heat loss through doors, and infiltration through cladding – are included in the BREEAM5 assessment, encouraging the execution of thermographic surveys and pressure testing of the building on completion.

In terms of site planning, the rating system awards BREEAM credits for a reduction in the overshadowing of neighbours, for reclamation or reuse of derelict sites and minimising ecological damage, for controlling noise in relation to neighbours, and for providing delivery vehicle space and storage for skips and pallets.

In relation to indoor climate conditions credits are awarded for achieving specific ventilation rates and a good standard of natural lighting in offices, and for the provision of a view from operational areas of the building.

1.6 Benchmarking

Surveys carried out on industrial buildings during the 1990s were used by the government's Energy Efficiency Best Practice programme to build a software tool that rates factories against benchmarks for their design and operation.[7] The surveys were of a wide range of industrial buildings of different sizes and ages, with a wide range of performance in a proportion of one to eight from the least to the most energy consuming. The main contributory factors to poor performance were aspects of the operational management of the building such as loading doors that were left open, and poorly controlled heating and lighting systems. Interestingly, it was shown that buildings could be refurbished to a standard equivalent to new buildings, suggesting that there is a lot of potential for enhanced environmental performance within the industrial sector.

The benchmarks, now published as Energy Consumption Guide 81 (ECON 81), are site-specific, and can be used to identify and prioritise areas where savings can be made. The benchmarks were developed in relation to a level of performance better than that required by the Building Regulations at the time, but anticipating the future direction of the Regulations. The most recent version of the benchmarks includes two different performance measures, because it was thought that refurbishing older buildings to current requirements is unlikely to be cost effective. So, for pre-1995 buildings, a benchmark has been defined relative to the Building Regulations Part L 1991, and for post-1995 buildings relative to the 2002 revision. Similarly, because smaller buildings are more difficult to make thermally efficient than larger ones, there are separate benchmarks for buildings under 5000 m^2 in area, and for those over 5000 m^2.

The benchmarking process establishes a performance indicator, which users of the software tool can then compare with the benchmark for the actual building in order to identify energy saving measures, consideration being given to the extent to which process energy contributes to the overall heating needs of the building. The input data includes information on the factory's lighting systems.

The outputs from the program are based on a comparison of the heating energy used by the building with a base case which incorporates correction factors that recognise the working hours regime of the building, and its height and volume (since these aspects have an impact on the ventilation loads, in relation to the degree days of the locality).

Common opportunities for savings – the recommendations provided by the program – include better time and temperature control of the heating system, measures to make the building more airtight to reduce ventilation heat loss, replacement lamps to make the lighting installation more efficient, and improved lighting controls.

2. Construction issues – reducing environmental impact

2.1 Air tightness and infiltration

Excessive air infiltration is a problem in most UK factories, whether old or new, and this leakage can more than double the heating costs of a building. Air infiltration rates are often related to external wind speed, so on exposed sites the rate of heat loss can be further exaggerated.

Doors, particularly large doors, are a problem, although they can readily be replaced by contemporary insulated doors, which are designed to form a good seal when closed. Well-sealed doors have been shown to reduce an average small (250 m^2) factory's rate of heat loss by around 40% compared with buildings with older roller shutter doors. Roller shutters may in any case be a problem because when they are closed many designs leave a gap at the top to allow for the increased diameter of the roller when the door is open. The heat load involved in restoring comfort temperatures after doors have been left open can be a major proportion of a factory's overall heat loss, which can be exacerbated if doors face towards the prevailing wind – so an orientation 90 degrees to the prevailing wind direction is the most favourable. Well-sealed and insulated doors that are easy to operate, perhaps by their being operable by electric motor, offer the best solution to these problems. Plastic curtains or air curtains can be beneficial for room comfort and can have energy advantages if doors are often left open; on the other hand they can result in excessive periods of door opening during milder winter weather because people do not bother to close the doors!

As with other building types, increasing levels of insulation result in ventilation heat loss becoming the predominant issue; fabric losses having been reduced in recently constructed factories. Adequately sealing to eliminate infiltration in winter is an increasingly important and difficult issue given the lightweight cladding usual for factories. The extent of leakage depends primarily on wind speed, if it is in excess of 2 m/s, but during calm conditions it will be driven mainly by the air buoyancy within the building induced by the difference between inside and ambient temperatures. Because wind speeds vary considerably, the rate of infiltration in winter is also likely to vary: for a typical 1000 m² factory the rate varies between 0.1 and 0.8 ach, with an average of 0.25 ach. Smaller buildings, having a larger surface to volume ratio, are likely to have a yet larger rate of leakage, typically averaging 0.5 ach for a 250 m² building.

Junctions between elements of the construction are the most usual cause of leakage, requiring both careful detailing and attention to workmanship on site. Leakage often occurs at junctions between the roof and walls at lower level where lightweight wall cladding abuts lower-level brickwork, and around doors and roof vents. Surveys have shown that filler blocks sealing the ends of profiled sheet cladding are often omitted. Similarly the eaves junction, or where lightweight cladding abuts a masonry plinth wall, and also the corners of factory buildings, have been found to be common causes of leaks.

2.2 Ventilation implications

Inadequacies of the ventilation system, such as a lack of controls on ventilators, or if ventilators are not properly used, also leads to excessive ventilation heat loss. A well-sealed factory still has to provide sufficient ventilation for the health of the occupants throughout the heating season. A system of controllable ventilation is required, preferably by a combination of roof-top louvres, and roof-mounted fans, which can be operated separately from one another to accommodate both winter and summer conditions. In a well-sealed building, ingress of air to compensate for that which has been extracted requires controlled operation of fans, although it has been shown that fans supposedly designed for 4 ach in actuality only achieve 2 ach unless doors are left open. Unless this is anticipated, air can be drawn in through the heating system's flue. If fans for summer operation are being used in winter, and high levels of air extract are required, the heating system has to be designed accordingly. Extract will especially be required if the production process is polluting, for example local to welding booths and soldering baths.

Natural ventilation is usually only suitable for industrial buildings that do not have excessive heat gains due to the processes involved or to the level of occupancy, and not where pollutant concentrations are high, or where a very controlled environment is needed for the production process.

2.3 Volume heating

Heating systems in existing factories may be very inefficient because of their age and lack of maintenance, inappropriate operation or lack of insulation. Often, replacing old plant is cost effective, particularly if it is required for both the heating of spaces and the manufacturing process, and if the plant is to be in use over long running hours. Condensing boilers, in conjunction with a low-temperature hot water distribution system, may be appropriate as an efficient method of upgrading an existing system.

For many types of factory, industrial heating systems that use warm air or radiant heat will provide adequate levels of comfort and relatively low energy consumption, to form one component of an energy-efficient design. They are best suited to matching the reduced heat loss found within an adequately insulated building; to be responsive to variations in the amount of heat used or contributed by the manufacturing process; and to compensate for heat loss during periods when doors are open or where there are greater demands during the warming-up period at the beginning of the day.

Warm-air heating

Warm-air heating systems come in a variety of types either using fuel such as gas directly, or indirect systems employing piped steam or hot water fed from a central boiler. Air is directed by a single-speed fan over the heat source and delivered into the space through adjustable louvres at about 60°C, cooling to about 40°C within a metre of leaving the unit. At higher temperatures, air has too great a buoyancy, stratifying at high level rather than mixing with the air within the room. If the heated air is supplied at a lower temperature, occupants are likely to complain about draughts. Warm air heaters are available for floor or wall mounting; and condensing, indirect gas heaters are now available that function at about 90% efficiency.

Radiant heaters

Radiant heaters come in different forms that operate at different temperatures. Gas-fired types and electric quartz units heat to about 800°C; direct gas-fired radiant tubes to 400°C; and lower-temperature medium-pressure hot-water heaters are fed from a central boiler plant at 110°C. The higher the temperature, the greater the extent to which they work by the radiation of heat to bodies and objects within the space, while at lower temperatures heat is transferred into the room mostly by convection currents established by the contact of moving air with the surface of the heater.

Choice of system

In older buildings that are likely to be poorly insulated and have higher ventilation rates, a high proportion of convected heat will be lost through the fabric, so a radiative type of heater would be more efficient, although high temperature radiators are more likely to lead to overheating. In more contemporary, well-insulated and sealed factories, convection will lead to a general raising of air temperatures that will be contained within the building envelope, contributing to a feeling of comfort, but in large volume buildings with high ceilings, radiant heaters may be preferable because they can efficiently heat people and surfaces without having to heat all the air within the building.

The problem with warm air systems is that hot air tends to collect beneath the roof, resulting in: higher conduction heat losses through the fabric and higher ventilation heat loss; higher average room temperatures; and, in spaces beneath lower ceilings, overheating. In order to improve the distribution of air, ducted systems are preferable to the use of unit heaters. In high or poorly insulated spaces ceiling-mounted fans can help to produce beneficial air movement and will guard against stratification by mixing the air; this can be particularly useful during hot summer periods. However, the mixing achieved increases the overall air velocity, which may be the cause of discomfort in lower rooms or where sedentary work is being performed. Fans should not be necessary in modern, well-insulated spaces, for a factory with its eaves at a height around 5 to 6 metres, if a temperature gradient of less than 4°C can be achieved.

In light industrial factories, where work can be mostly sedentary, a heating system that dominates the environment such as high-velocity air heaters, or high-intensity radiant heaters, may be less appropriate than a method providing overall heating from a low velocity warm air system or a low temperature radiant system. This is contrary to the traditional pattern of heating systems for industrial buildings which provide a heat source and a defined volume of heat distribution, outside the limits of which one would not necessarily feel comfortable. In contemporary, well-insulated buildings a more uniform, less 'emitter dominated' environment is likely to be preferred.

Often spaces are heated even though some areas of the building are not occupied, in which case a suitable system would have an overall background level of heating that is augmented locally. Radiant heaters can be suitable for this purpose, whereas for spaces that are to be continuously heated, there may be a less marked difference in the energy consumption characteristics of radiant and warm air systems.

Heating system controls

Heating installations that are oversized are difficult to control, and result in inefficient space heating. Dynamic effects such as loading doors being opened and closed may, however, require the heating system – in an otherwise well-insulated building – to be 100% oversized. The heating system will then be operating at less than full capacity for much of the time, particularly if the manufacturing process is contributing to the heating requirements of the space.

Under these circumstances a simple on/off thermostat will be insufficient, and some form of modulating control will be required, for example in the case of warm-air heaters, by varying the number of burners in operation or by the use of multi-speed fans, or both. However, if constant fan speed is used in conjunction with the operation of a reduced number of burners, occupants may complain about the resulting draught.

Modulating control can be provided in different ways according to the type of system. Gas radiant tubes can have a variable number of burners in operation, combined with a variable supply of combustion air. Modulated control is less usual for radiant devices, although radiant panels fed by medium-pressure low-temperature hot water are readily controlled in this way and provide good comfort conditions; however, their initial cost is high since they are fed from a central boiler.

2.4 Lighting strategies

Artificial light versus daylighting

At the design stage, factory units rarely have a clearly defined set of requirements, so the energy consumed by lights in industrial buildings has often been assumed to be outside the remit of low-energy design. A greater reliance on daylighting can, however, result in significant savings, although keeping rooflights and windows clean in factories is a persistent problem. The provision of rooflighting to achieve a 5% daylight factor can achieve a level of lighting suitable for a wide range of factory processes, combined with readily accessible user-operated switches for the artificial lighting. Lights are often left on for no other reason than the difficulty of turning them off, so switches need to be well located and marked, but appropriate staff attitudes and training are also important.

Box 7.2 Recommended lighting levels

Lighting level recommendations depend on the level of detail involved in the tasks to be performed. For general tasks, without discrimination of detail being required, a general lighting level of 300 lux is recommended as adequate, entailing a benchmark electrical power provision of 5–6 W/m², but where detailed tasks are necessary the recommended level is 500 lux or 8–10 W/m². It is rarely economic to light whole areas to a light level in excess of 500 lux, local task lighting being used instead. The variables affecting electricity consumption are consequently the size and type of lamp selected, and the height at which they are mounted above the working plane, in order to obtain uniform light levels while avoiding glare.

One special condition is lighting for the aisles between storage racks where 150 lux is often an adequate provision, or 300 lux where greater detailed acuity is required. As a result, the lighting layout and the operating energy consumed depends on the width of the aisles and the height at which the lamps are mounted, considerations that can double the anticipated power density up to 17 W/m² (for an aisle width of 3.0 metres and a mounting height of 8 metres, if 300 lux is to be achieved).

Accommodating a daylighting strategy

Daylighting design for factories has attracted little attention in recent years, mostly because operational costs for artificial lighting are a small proportion of overall costs for industrial organisations. The development of roof forms for daylighting, which defined the form of pre-war factories (most notably those designed by Albert Kahn for the car industry in the US), have ceded to the economic advantages of the double-pitch portal frame. Northlight roofs that were so characteristic of that period had the advantage of reducing solar gain and glare, but gave a directional light with heavy shadows that could be dangerous for some industrial processes. Furthermore, northlights can admit sunshine early during the day and on summer evenings, and even a small deviation from due north will result in the admission of more sunlight. The 'monitor roof' was invented to overcome these problems by introducing smaller rooflights facing south to even-out the distribution of light, and overcome the problem of shadows, but with potential for overheating.

Double-pitch shed roofs or flat roofs are suitable for daylighting, provided that vertical surfaces are light and reflective to even out the appearance of brightness in the space, and as long as there are sufficient rooflights to provide adequate daylight levels. An even pattern of rooflights covering about 10% of the roof will achieve a daylight factor of approximately 5% and adequate visual rendering of the space. Multiple bay shed roofs have a number of detailing problems such as lengthy valley gutters, plus the difficulty of integrating luminaires and ducting within the roof shape, so rooflights have to be designed with these considerations in mind.

Integrated solutions

A good case can, however, be made for a better standard of construction for factories, as is required anyway for better thermal performance, so that roof lighting can provide an overall level of background lighting with local tasks being performed with the aid of artificial task lighting. Although it has been popularly assumed that, to reduce heat loss, you require smaller windows and rooflights, an adequate provision of daylight can offset the requirement for artificial lighting to be extensively used, and thereby enable both savings of primary electrical energy and the consequent high levels of CO_2 emissions.[8] This strategy is dependent on adequate controls that are easy and convenient to use being an intrinsic element of the design.

Controls can then enable general artificial lighting to be in operation only when daylight levels are inadequate, in which case, total annual primary energy consumption is minimised if the area of rooflight is between 15 and 20% of the floor area of the building, so although heating energy rises with increasing rooflight area it is more than offset by savings in artificial lighting. This is, however, contrary to the advice given in the CIBSE guide[9] which suggests that, in speculative factories that are predominantly daylit during working hours, lighting control systems will not be economic. Furthermore, there are recorded cases of factory units designed to be daylit, where the control system has been disabled and artificial lighting used all the time. However, where the building is being designed for a specific enterprise, the greater use of daylight and control systems may be justified as part as an overall energy strategy, and factory units having 10% area of the roof as rooflight, imparting approximately 5% daylight factor, represent a good baseline for the achievement of contemporary energy-saving criteria.

Fluorescent lighting

Where electric lighting is required to be used for extended periods of time, use of the most efficient lamps for their purpose militates in favour of 26 mm diameter fluorescent tubes replacing older 36 mm tubes, provided that the existing control gear is 'switchstart'. Similarly, long-life compact fluorescents should have replaced tungsten GLS lamps in all service areas and corridors. It can be worth replacing lighting installations as little as five years old, since contemporary systems can be twice as efficient if high-intensity discharge lamps are used, or slightly less if using efficient fluorescent fittings with high-frequency electronic ballasts. Of all the main energy efficiency measures that can be implemented in factories, improved lighting has the lowest payback period, a mere 1.5 years.

Choice of lamp

The usual choice of lamp in factories is between fluorescent and high-pressure sodium, although metal halide lamps are sometimes used where a better standard of colour rendering is required, but the resulting power consumption is likely to be greater. The choice between sodium and fluorescent fittings, from the point of view of operating energy, is not significant provided that high efficacy types are used and contained within luminaires having a high light output ratio. Better colour rendering can be obtained with fluorescent lamps, but where they are to be mounted at heights in excess of 4.5 metres, installation costs are likely to favour sodium.

Lighting controls

In areas such as storage rooms, which are intermittently used, or if the building's users cannot readily operate light switches, e.g. in a warehouse occupied by forklift truck drivers, presence sensors may be an appropriate solution. More complex control strategies such as completely integrated building energy management systems (BEMS) are usually implemented on larger sites. They do not necessarily result in efficiencies; in fact, control regimes are often too lax, resulting in lights being left on for longer than necessary. So controls need to be combined with a strong management strategy promoting automatic reversion to 'lights off' and clearly indicating when lights around the building are, and are not, in operation.

2.5 Process heat

Although, in theory, the heat produced by manufacturing processes could be reclaimed for use within the building, this rarely happens[10], and the contribution of process heat to the building is equally rare, heat usually being provided by boilers to make up for process air that is lost to the atmosphere. However, the reclamation of heat within production processes, for return to the process, is beneficial, with an anticipated payback period of 1.8 years, although the overall savings to be made are small compared with those due to other heating-related factors such as the efficiency of the building's boilers.

Box 7.3 Passive solar factories

In the early 1990s the UK government's passive solar design studies programme[1] was responsible for a number of sketch schemes for factories being produced by different architects for a variety of clients. The point of departure was the belief that there would be a financial advantage to introducing daylight if more rigorous insulation standards were going to allow closer control of a building's heating energy requirements (resulting in lighting costs becoming the major energy use). The disadvantages of daylighting are the attendant problems of heat loss, glare and summer overheating implied by an increase in the proportion of glazing, and that energy savings are likely to be very small per m² compared with building's capital cost.

The buildings were designed to different briefs for different clients and were notable for the different patterns of rooflight that were proposed. Computer simulations were used to compare the schemes with conventional base case designs. In each case, beneficial use of daylight was demonstrated while reducing the potential for winter heat loss and summer overheating. These advantages would, of course, only be realised if operation of the buildings precluded the continuous – or poorly controlled – use of artificial lighting. The computer simulations were unable to predict the likelihood of glare, making it impossible to foretell the possibility of extra shading being installed by users.

Sensitivity analysis showed that the designs were all reasonably robust compared to the reference buildings under a series of conditions:

- if the building's orientation was changed by 45 degrees
- if heat gains from people or equipment was doubled
- if a different shift pattern was introduced
- if the ventilation rate determined by the production process was altered.

Overall costs were comparable with the base case, although a higher proportion was being spent on the roof, rooflights, frame and lighting of the passive solar factories. (Having said that, it has to be conceded that lighting controls do add to factory construction costs.)

Since the schemes succeeded in producing energy savings, the project was considered to point the way ahead for low-energy factory construction.

1. Jestico + Whiles, Ryder Nicklin, ECD Partnership, for the 'Design Studies Programme', *Architects' Journal*, 31 January 1990, pp59–65.

2.6 Construction – 'vernacular' factories

Although the typical form of building for factory use is the medium-span 'shed', in recent years the change in the nature of the UK's shrinking industrial base, and the introduction of more stringent requirements for energy efficient design within the Building Regulations, have impacted on standards of construction.[11] The use of a steel or precast concrete frame and lightweight cladding remains the norm. For lower cost installations, the use of a three-layer construction, consisting of an inner liner panel, insulation (either in quilt form or higher density batts) being loose-laid between it and the outer plastic-coated profiled sheet, is the vernacular solution. The largest range of profiles is available when using steel cladding, which became possible after the introduction during the 1960s of plastisol-coated galvanised steel sheet. The material is available in a wide variety of colours which vary in their colour fastness, but some can escape re-painting for an extended period of up to about 15 years. Steel profiled sheet can be obtained in both trapezoidal and sinusoidal sections, whereas aluminium is usually sinusoidal in shape, as is fibre cement sheet, the contemporary substitute for asbestos cladding, which is manufactured in a limited number of colours and depths.

Thermal performance

A high proportion of both the steel and aluminium used in construction comes from recycled material. Nevertheless, both are materials with high embodied energy in their manufacture, impacts that are amplified by the plastic-coated finishing process. They also require the use of thousands of self-tapping screws which join the cladding back to the purlins in the roof, and cladding rails in the walls. The large number of fixings form cold bridges, and the standard of workmanship is critical because misalignment can cause localised buckling of the outer panel and potential leaks. In addition, if inadequate care is taken when fixing the insulation, misalignment can largely negate its value, an effect that has been demonstrated by the use of thermographic cameras.

A common cause of reduced performance is compression of low-density quilt insulation, often as a result of the thickness of the insulation being greater than the spacers between the inner and outer sheets. If end laps are inadequately sealed, the resulting air movement through the air gaps within the panels will similarly reduce their U-value by inducing cooling convection currents around the insulation. A variety of other workmanship-related faults have been shown to result in increased heat loss – gaps left between abutting sheets, missing areas of insulation around roof openings and rooflights, insufficiently fixed and sagging insulation within walls, and whole areas of insulation missing as a result of poor site supervision.

The form of construction itself exacerbates some of these problems: for example, quilt insulation is difficult to install in walls on windy sites, and the lack of dimensional coordination between insulation and other components in many site-assembled three-layer walls and roofs, results in excessive trimming to size and poor performance. A three-layer insulation should, however, be capable of good thermal performance if these practical difficulties are avoided.

Box 7.4 Summertime condensation

Summertime condensation is a particular problem for three-layer cladding systems. At night in summer, following hot and humid days, the air temperature under clear skies can drop considerably. The outer metal surface of the cladding radiates its heat to the night sky and may drop in temperature to below ambient. The moisture-laden air trapped within the corrugated outer sheet may then condense out at the back of the cold outer cladding. The resulting condensation can soak the insulation, reducing its effectiveness, and causing it to rust through the sheeting, particularly at the vulnerable drilled fixing holes.

Avoiding the problem of summertime condensation is difficult. Ideally, the rate of air movement within the construction should be made as low as possible by eliminating air gaps. In a three-layer construction, a breather membrane should be located to the outside of the insulation allowing moisture from within the building to escape, while repelling water that has condensed at the purlins or other relatively cold parts of the structure, and draining it away from a roof to a gutter, or to the outside of a wall. Uninsulated parts of the structure have been shown to be responsible for localised U-values being 20–50% lower than those achieved by the construction generally. Spacers are required to make sure that the ventilation air path is uninterrupted, but the air flow rate should not be excessive otherwise heat will be drawn from the building and further moisture-bearing air will be introduced into the roof.

A solution, manufactured by some companies as a system, is to incorporate rigid insulation pre-formed to the shape of the inner and outer sheets; all internal air gaps are eliminated and the potential for summertime condensation is reduced, but the problem of the large number of fixings remains. However, these systems are sold as dimensionally coordinated components avoiding many of the problems outlined above.

- *Secret-fixed panels* – Alternative systems that secret-fix the cladding sheets have been introduced to overcome reliance upon self-tapping screws. Long strip panels that are push-fitted onto brackets mounted on the roof purlins have fewer lap joints within their length and do not make use of external fixings. These systems are available in both steel and aluminium.

- *Composite panels* – The most sophisticated of these lightweight cladding types are composite or sandwich panels that are fabricated as steel or aluminium boxes and then, in an online process, are filled with liquid-foamed plastic insulation. The resulting panels have a notable standard of insulation for their thickness, can be internally fixed to eliminate cold bridging, and their inner surface acts as a vapour control layer. These environmental benefits are, however, achieved at the cost to the environment of the polyiscyanurate and polyurethane foam insulants that are used, even though restrictions on the use of the gases used as foaming agents were introduced some years ago.

- *Thermal mass within lightweight enclosures* – The resulting lightweight enclosure may be suited to most forms of workshop manufacture, occupancy being intermediate and corresponding to a pattern of shifts. For continuous manufacturing processes the advantages of thermal mass can only be achieved by coupling of the mass of the floor slab to the volume of the building. The nature of shed type factories is that, relative to their floor area, they have a large volume to heat and ventilate, which will be affected (in ways sometimes difficult to predict) by internal air movements within their high spaces, and by the effects of outdoor temperature and wind conditions on the leakage characteristics of the cladding.

3. Energy efficiency in 'advanced' factory units

During the 1990s, the government's Energy Efficiency Best Practice programme devoted several case studies to 'advanced' factory units. This section draws out some of the key points from these studies.

3.1 Warehouse/offices in Milton Keynes

Case Study 106[12] investigated a warehouse and offices in Milton Keynes, occupied at the time by Barclays Bank plc, and used principally for storage of promotional leaflets.

The building is of conventional construction comprising roof and wall panels of profiled steel cladding with quilt insulation and, at ground level, a 2.5 metre high plinth wall of cavity construction. Only 3% of the roof area was given over to site-assembled double-glazed rooflights. The warehouse has two large insulated and electrically operated delivery doors. The small area of offices at the north end of the building is fully glazed with single glazed windows and insulated spandrel panels.

The offices were originally equipped with a boiler and low-temperature hot water system providing heating and hot water. The warehouse was subsequently fitted out with an indirect gas-fired ducted warm air system, controlled by temperature sensors incorporating a locally controlled branch adjacent to the doors that was designed to compensate for periods when they are standing open. Extract fans providing 4 ach were located in the roof for summertime ventilation. Fluorescent lamps in reflective luminaires were used throughout to give a light level of 300 lux in production areas and 150 lux in the warehouse, where movement detectors switch individual aisles between storage racks.

Thermographic photographs illustrated some missing areas of insulation and sheeting rails forming cold bridges; also, inadequate sealing at the junction between the profiled cladding and the plinth showed up in the photographs as air leakage. Even so, the rate of infiltration annually was 0.3–0.45 ach, favourable in comparison with the CIBSE guideline of 0.5 ach.[13]

The energy consumption statistics indicated that the energy consumption of the building, at 192 kWh/m², was within the 'good' performance band, because the environment throughout was more typical of a factory rather than a warehouse. Gas consumption for space heating was the major energy use at 86%, although only constituting 58% of the total cost. Lighting energy use was low, although artificial lighting was in constant use in the north-facing offices, despite their considerable area of glazing, a source of thermal discomfort that led to the installation of extra radiators. Overall, the case study's appraisal highlighted the problems associated with quilt insulation but applauded the positive contribution to energy saving made by the movement sensors in the warehouse.

3.2 Printworks in Colchester

Case study 144[14] looked into the operation of a newspaper print works at Colchester operated by Reed Southern Print Ltd, incorporating a linear printing press at the centre of the building, with paper storage to one side and racking and plate-making areas to the other. A two-storey sales office area occupies the northernmost bay of the building. The cladding was site-assembled with an outer face of profiled steel and fibreglass insulation achieving a U-value of 0.43 W/m²K. The roof incorporates 10% of its area as double-glazed rooflights, and the building has two large sectional overhead doors that are electrically operated. The offices are clad with curtain walling, having double-glazed units with anti-sun glass, and insulated spandrel panels that also have a U-value of 0.43 W/m²K. The occupier was involved in the later stages of design development, and concerns about the possibility of overheating led to a doubling of the number of opening windows in the offices. Even so, and despite the glazed wall being north-facing, the offices did overheat in the summer of 1990, although this was thought to be due to the amount of electrical equipment in use rather than solar gain.

A gas-fired boiler supplies the radiator system, with thermostatic radiator valves, heating the offices and plate-making area. Hot water is produced local to points of use by electric water heaters.

Unit air-conditioners have been installed in the plate-making room and rooms housing computer equipment. In the factory areas, heat is provided by six gas-fired warm air heaters hung from the roof that are controlled by thermostats and time clocks. These spaces also have de-stratification fans and roof extract fans that can provide ventilation, extraction and re-circulation as required by the varying heat loads in the building, according to the operation of the printing press.

In the offices, high efficiency fluorescent and compact fluorescent fixtures are used with metal halide lamps, for good colour rendering, illuminating the production areas and designed to give 300 lux at the work surface. Locally, this is raised to 500 lux by the addition of fluorescent lighting.

Thermographic photographs confirmed that the building that was generally well installed, achieving the intended design values, although the photographs revealed one area where the insulation had either slipped or had not been installed at all. Pressurisation tests in the offices indicated a rate of leakage of 0.31 ach compared with the CIBSE guideline of 1.0 ach suggesting that the curtain walling was well sealed.

The building is in operation seven days a week throughout the year, and has high process energy consumption, which also contributes to the space heating requirement for the building. Although 84% of the electricity used was for the printing press, making the building overall energy intensive, the building itself was found to be within the 'good' rating band. This was due to the high-efficiency lighting and hot water systems, and because the cladding was shown to be providing the overall level of thermal enclosure that had been intended. Generally, the appraisal was good; comfort conditions having largely been achieved – despite the variable heat output of the printing press – by the use of appropriate energy-efficient equipment and straightforward controls.

4. Generic construction methods

4.1 Typical UK factory construction

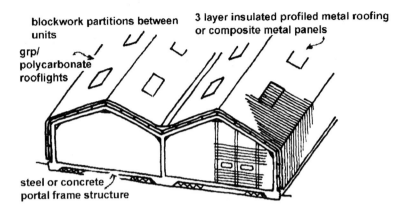

blockwork partitions between units

grp/ polycarbonate rooflights

3 layer insulated profiled metal roofing or composite metal panels

steel or concrete portal frame structure

Figure 7.1 Typical UK factory construction

Structure

- *Steel or concrete portal frame, external walls of three-layer insulated profiled metal or composite metal panels/brick cavity walling at plinth*

The choice of steel or concrete is likely to be of little consequence (as explained in Chapter 6, 'Offices').

Roof

- *Three-layer insulated metal roof or composite metal panels*

3 layer insulated profiled sheet outer panels and internal liner panels

Figure 7.2 Three-layer construction

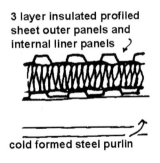

cold formed steel purlin

Lightweight cladding systems all achieve an 'A' rating[15] if they are of three-layer construction having an inner metal liner panel with insulation sandwiched between the liner panel and the outer profiled sheet. This is true for both steel and aluminium systems but most particularly if stainless steel is employed because of its ability to be recycled and because a large proportion of the alloy is already returned to use as a result of recycling. Systems with a drywall lining on galvanised cold-formed steel framing (rather less common nowadays) are rated less highly.

Floors

- *Cast-in-place slab, insulated beneath, grano or similar wearing surface*

grano finished concrete slab with insulation on lean mix over hardcore

Figure 7.3 In-situ concrete slab laid on grade

The mass of concrete required, along with the large amount of mineral extraction, explains the 'C' rating[16] of this flooring. However, the use of recycled aggregate (provided it is sourced relatively locally) can improve things somewhat.

The mass of the concrete, which is undesirable in terms of transport energy, can improve the internal environment of the completed building, and in industrial buildings this may be the only available thermal mass. Compared to traditional masonry construction, where thermal mass is exposed, the lightweight materials usual for cladding contemporary factories has relatively little thermal mass. If the factory is in nearly continuous occupancy (if the production process is 24-hour) the concrete floor can provide valuable thermal mass, as long as it is effectively coupled to the space, i.e. without any floor covering.

Glazing

- *Glass reinforced plastic (GRP)/polycarbonate rooflights, patent glazed clerestories*

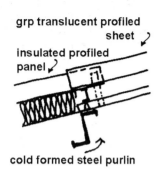

grp translucent profiled
sheet

insulated profiled
panel

cold formed steel purlin

Figure 7.4 Translucent GRP profiled sheeting

GRP is a lightweight material, and the area of the external envelope of an industrial building is unlikely to be significant compared with other elements of the building. Of itself though, the material is not favoured owing to the polluting and energy-consuming characteristics of its production, and the limited extent and capability that it has for recycling.

Internal partitions

- *Blockwork between units*

As noted in Chapter 3, (Housing), blockwork, whether aerated or dense, performs well under analysis (for the *Green Guide*). Some manufacturers produce blocks that are suitable for fair-faced construction, only requiring a coat of paint, which, if it is of appropriate specification, will result in an environmentally favourable specification.

Table 7.1. Ecopoints evaluation of generic constructions for factories, using BRE's Envest tool

120m × 80m diagram	Generic factory type: 120m × 80m; (ground floor 9600 sq m); no. storeys: 1; storey height: 7 m; % cellular 20%; location: S.E. England; soil type: firm clay		
		Ecopoints	%
Ground floor	200 mm reinforced concrete floor slav + 80 mm rockwool insulation	22510	49.0
Upper floor	none	0	
External walls	Plastisol-coated 80 mm thick galvanised steel sandwich panel + polyurethane insulation	3331	7.3
Internal partitions	190 mm dense blockwork	3774	8.2
Windows	Patent glazed/ single glazed clerestorys	1275	2.8
Roof	Steel trusses +	1292	2.8
	galvanised steel sheet and 150 mm rockwool insulation	3145	6.9
Floors	25 mm granolithic finish	1265	2.8
Wall finishes	Gloss paint	1248	2.7
Ceiling	none	0	0
Sub-structure	Raft foundation	439	1.0
Super-structure	Steel frame	5768	12.6
Total embodied including material replacements over 60 year lifespan		45885	
Total embodied per sq m of floor area		4.8	

Source: based on Anderson, J., Shiers, D.E., Sinclair, M., *Green Guide to Specification*, (3rd Edition), BRE, Watford, 2002.

Commentary: For a fairly minimal type of construction that is generally light in weight the ground floor construction is a major contributor in terms of overall embodied energy impact. The generally poor performance of the building type in terms of operational energy consumption, which is commonly without heat reclaim, will however be a larger concern for lifetime energy evaluation.

5. Case studies

5.1 Production facility, Cummins Power Generation, Manston, Kent

Client: Cummins Engine Co.
Architects: Bennetts Associates
Structural engineer: WhitbyBird
Services engineer: Ernest Griffiths and Son
Cost consultant: Gardiner and Theobald
Main contractor: Tarmac

Figure 7.5 Floor plan

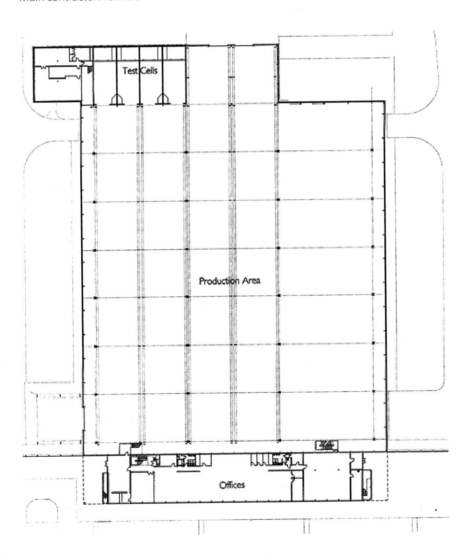

Test Cells

Production Area

Offices

Source: Bennetts Associates Architects

Background

For many engineering companies, the 1990s were uncertain times. In East Kent, where the local coalfields had been closed and the port of Ramsgate was in decline, this was especially true.

One engineering firm had been manufacturing diesel generators in the region since the 1930s but, after a period of decline, its future was secured when it was acquired by the American corporation Cummins.

The Cummins Engine Company has a long history of architectural patronage. In the USA, the company's home town of Columbus, Indiana, features a diversity of buildings by distinguished modern architects from Saarinen to Meier and, in the UK, plants were designed by Kevin Roche in the 1960s and ABK in the 1970s. The company ethos supported the design of high-quality workplaces for all employees and, with this, a responsible attitude to long-term flexibility and adaptability.

Planning, form and construction

For the new Manston generator factory, the appointment of architects was led by the US parent company. They approached RIBA and visited a shortlist of architects before appointing Bennetts Associates in June 1996. At that time, the practice was mainly known for its work with end-user clients on headquarters buildings for PowerGen and John Menzies, and for its approach to low-energy, flexible workplaces. The Cummins facility was to present opportunities to develop both these themes on a larger scale.

Site

By 1996, East Kent had been allocated European regeneration funding. A new business park was proposed on land around the former RAF base at Manston, and a private consortium took over the airfield itself with a view to developing its commercial potential. The generator manufacturer acquired by Cummins was located in nearby Sandwich, on a site constrained by a legacy of inflexible post-war buildings. The prospect of a purpose-built factory on the new business park at Manston was the catalyst for the company's decision to relocate, and a plot was purchased in 1996.

The brief

The new plant was to be used for the manufacture of generator sets ranging from small portable units to containerised stand-alone sets with outputs of over 2 MW. The production process involves assembling each generator from chassis, engine, alternator and controls (all sourced from other Cummins plants). The scale of the largest units requires craneage of up to 60 t with a hook height of

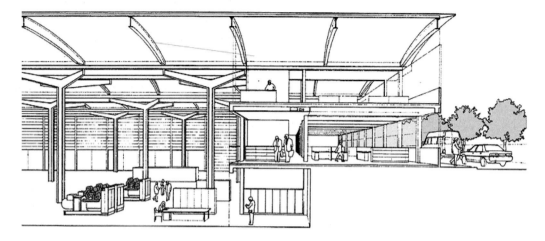

Source: Bennetts Associates Architects

8 m above the finished floor. The completed sets are then subjected to a testing regime prior to shipping. The testing process involves continuous running of sets under load for up to 24 hours and necessitates total acoustic enclosure. Engine exhaust is vented, and cooling air supplied. This process takes place in large, highly serviced enclosures known as test cells.

Figure 7.6 Cutaway section

The 8 ha site purchased by Cummins was large enough to allow for the construction of an initial 15,000 m² of accommodation with space for future expansion by up to 100%.

Design

Initially Cummins prepared a diagram of the production process in which the test cells were located at the sides of the production lines; this layout resulted in a long rectangular plan with test cells at the three-quarter point in the process. Although ideally suited to the current production process, this layout would have severely constrained future flexibility.

Bennetts Associates' response was to propose that the process of testing take place outside the main production hall, and that the test cells and a despatch bay be housed in a series of 'plug-in' units attached to the rear of a main production space. In this way, the main production hall could be constructed on a uniform grid and height, in a more flexible square plan without the constraints introduced by the 'abnormal' activities. The resulting uniform cross-section was designed to integrate daylighting, natural ventilation, heating and services routes within a single structural idea.

The building users range from the fitters, planners and production staff, closely tied to the factory floor, to the office-based sales and support team. The plant is also visited by customers both prior to orders being placed and for the witnessing of tests at the end of the production process. For this reason, the building has to be both a high-quality workplace and a showcase for the company.

Corporate standards of the multinational parent company dictated that all the building users should share the same front door, and the internal planning of the building was configured to both emphasise the connection between factory and offices, and to give customers a dramatic view of the production work in progress from the main reception.

Offices and entrance are housed in a strip across the entire eastern face of the production hall. The three storeys of accommodation are contained beneath an extension of the main factory roof which oversails to provide entrance canopies at either end of the offices. A level change across the site of about 3 m results in the lowest floor of the offices forming an undercroft at production-floor level while a retaining wall across the site allows the main building entrance to occur at the middle office level. From here, there are dramatic views across the production floor through a fully glazed firewall.

Like many of Bennetts Associates', buildings, the design of the Cummins factory emerged through consciously developing a series of opportunities. From the

Figure 7.7 Interior view

initial analysis of the process, selected key ideas were refined in order to create drama on a large scale. This was achieved within an extremely limited budget and a total project timescale of 18 months.

Structure

The steel-framed roof of the main production hall is divided into three linear bays supported on structural columns at 28.8 × 14.4 m centres. Travelling cranes are provided to two of the three bays. The cranes sit on their own supporting structure on a square grid of 14.4 m. This structure is independent of the factory roof enabling other crane configurations and orientations to be adopted for

Figure 7.8 Interior view

Source: Peter Cook/VIEW

future production processes. The initial three bays are located across the site such that, in the future, the grid could be continued and the building extended by a further three bays.

Each roof column is cruciform in plan and, once above the height of the craneage, divides into four tapering arms. These arms support the edges of a 7.2 m-wide flat roof strip which delineate the three main structural bays of the roof. Between these flat roof strips, curved beams span the remaining 21.6 m, forming a distinctive arched cross-section. At the apex of each of the three bays, a linear rooflight provides uniform daylighting and opens for ventilation. Pipework and cabling runs are concentrated in the flat-roof sections above the column grids. This leaves the main curved spans virtually free of services.

Services

The office strip is 14.4 m deep and is divided into an open plan area and a highly serviced strip. The production area and offices are naturally ventilated via openable windows, and 'hotspots' requiring mechanical ventilation, such as meeting rooms, equipment rooms and cellular offices, are placed along the glazed wall between factory and offices.

The production area is predominantly day-lit, and the effect of this lighting is emphasised by a white concrete floor throughout. Glazing proportions and rooflight positions were modelled prior to the design being finalised. The resulting strip windows at the base, clerestory and apex of the factory serve to accentuate the component parts of the building and maintain views and even daylighting while maintaining relatively modest glazed areas.

Heating of the production space is by radiant panels which ensure that, in such a large volume, the heat is delivered where it is needed. The openable high-level rooflights operate in tandem with continuous horizontal strip-windows at low-level. Opening lights within these lower strips provide natural ventilation to the production area with air exiting at high level. The large expanse of concrete floor also plays an important part in the stabilisation of the internal factory environment by providing valuable thermal mass not present in the relatively lightweight superstructure.

One of the main by-products of the testing regime is waste electricity. Early in the project it was agreed to make provision for the possible export of this waste power to the national grid. At the time, there was little interest in take-up from the grid and, regrettably, the export provision was not carried out. Provision was, however, made for future export in the configuration of the main electricity terminations for connection to the grid.

The end result is a building of simplicity, economy, flexibility and dramatic spatial quality. Glazed areas are limited but daylight and natural ventilation are carefully controlled, resulting in good thermal performance. The long-term environmental benefits of this approach are appreciated both in the day-to-day use of the building and as the inevitable changes in the production process are made.

5.2 Gateway Development production unit at Baglan Energy Park, Neath Port Talbot, South Wales

Background

Architects: Neath Port Talbot County Borough Council – Directorate of Property and Procurement
Developer: Neath Port Talbot County Borough Council
Environmental Design: Welsh School of Architecture
Managing contractor: Tilbury Douglas Construction

The Gateway Development at Baglan Energy Park was designed as a landmark industrial development with sustainable credentials. It consists of 3400 m² of factory production space, and over 500 m² of offices, forming the entrance to Baglan Energy Park, which is being developed on a 250 ha brownfield site at Port

Figure 7.9 Exterior view

Source: Neath Port Talbot County Borough Council (copyright: Peter Knowles Photography)

Talbot that was formerly a BP chemicals production plant. A proposed CCGT power station will service the site and the Gateway Building; this will enable the Energy Park tenants to benefit from competitively priced electricity. The park is situated between J41 and J42 of the M4 Motorway. The Gateway Development is Phase 1 of the scheme.

Planning, form and construction

The brief and design rationale

The brief for the project was to provide an architectural statement, illustrating energy efficiency and sustainable design. The building contains 3400 m^2 of production space and 514 m^2 of offices. The Port Talbot Partnership Challenge – a joint venture between Neath Port Talbot County Borough Council, the Welsh Development Agency and BP Amoco – initiated the project, which was launched in 1996. The scheme aims to promote the physical and economic regeneration of Port Talbot.

Figure 7.10
View at night

Source: Neath Port Talbot County Borough Council (copyright: Peter S. Jones)

Because of the speculative nature of the project at the inception stage, it was decided to design in sufficient flexibility to allow the production space to be let by multiple tenants, working on the principle that the internal space could be divided equally. This resulted in an idea to form 'pop-ups' and 'pop-outs'. The enlarged spaces inform the service design, by providing a means of daylighting, ventilation and services containment and access; predominantly they provide a means of sub-dividing the production area.

The building has been let to an automotive cable system company who chose the Gateway Building as the location for its European manufacturing operation because of the building's innovative sustainable design approach, which they believe reflects the image they wish to promote. Since occupation, the tenant has taken advantage of the adaptable design and has expanded its office accommodation into the second floor level. Further plans are in hand to expand the production area by 100%.

Figure 7.11 Elevation including photovoltaic panels

Source: Neath Port Talbot County Borough Council (copyright: Andrew Southall)

Construction

The basic structure of the building is a repeated portal frame with blue-coated composite cladding, thin film amorphous photovoltaic panels marking the entrance to the reception and production areas at the south façade. Windows to the office areas are shaded by 45-degree-angled awnings onto which are mounted crystalline photovoltaic cells which, it is estimated, will have the capacity to provide more than double the electricity required for the external lighting scheme. This was used as justification for the external lighting that spectacularly renders the building fluorescent blue when illuminated at night.

Materials

The cladding appears to change colour with the weather, while in the evening the external lighting imparts a 'fluorescent blue glow'.

The building was designed to satisfy the requirements of BREEAM's New Industrial Units Version 5/93 and was given a BREEAM rating of 'excellent'.

Presented with a RIBA Award in 2002, the Gateway was designed to set a standard for the rest of the redevelopment of the site. Although built to a tight budget, it incorporates novel environmental features and integrates renewable energy provided by photovoltaic cells.

Services

The 100 m² of photovoltaic cladding is in two forms: thin film amorphous, which provides the entry statements to the reception and production on the south elevation, and crystalline, which inclines at an angle of 45 degrees and provides power and shading to the office. It is calculated that the amount of power produced over a year will pay for external lighting's electricity requirements twice over.

Daylighting scheme

The daylighting scheme was modelled in the artificial sky at Cardiff University, and was estimated to achieve a minimum daylight factor to the production areas of 2%, a large proportion of which is provided through the roof projections that are glazed with U-section cast glass planks.

Ventilation

In the offices, behind the PV awnings, are manually operated windows, cross-ventilation being achieved by buoyancy, as air is drawn out through chain-operated louvres at the roof projections, which act as chimneys for this purpose.

Figure 7.12 Ventilation strategy

Source: Neath Port Talbot County Borough Council (The Welsh School of Architecture Design Research Unit)

An automated version of the same strategy is used to ventilate the factory spaces. Ventilation to the production areas is provided by louvres which are installed to the south elevation of the pop-outs and exiting air is drawn via a roof-mounted louvre, the vents being controlled by a thermostat and rain sensor.

6. Notes

1. Jones, P., 'Low-Energy Factories: 1 Setting Priorities', *Architects' Journal*, 16th May 1990, p. 65.
2. Energy Efficiency Best Practice programme, *Guide 18 Energy Efficiency in Industrial Buildings and Sites*. HMSO, May 2004.
3. See, for example, www.carbon-trust.co.uk, and www.envirowise.gov.uk
4. Op. cit., Energy Efficiency Best Practice programme.
5. *ibid.*, p. 1.
6. BRE, *BREEAM New Industrial Units: Version 5/93*. Watford, BRE,1993.
7. Energy Efficiency Best Practice programme, *Energy Consumption Guide 81 Benchmarking tool for industrial buildings heating and internal lighting*. HMSO, May 1994.
8. Jones, P., 'Low-Energy Factories: 6 Future Trends', *Architects' Journal*, 13th June 1990, p. 63.
9. CIBSE, *Guide F: Energy Efficiency in Buildings* (2004) and *Guide H: Building Control Systems*, (2000), CIBSE, London
10. Jones, P. *Op. cit.*, p. 1.

11. 'Light Industry Passive Solar Factories', *Architects' Journal*, 31st January 1990, p. 59.

12. Energy Efficiency Best Practice programme: *Case Study 106 Barclays Bank plc, Milton Keynes, Buckinghamshire*. HMSO, March 1995.

13. CIBSE, *Guide A: Environmental Design*, Chartered Institute of Building Services Engineers, London, 2006. See Table A4.13, Section A4: Air infiltration and natural ventilation.

14. Energy Efficiency Best Practice programme, *Case Study 144, Reed Southern Print Ltd, Colchester, Essex*. HMSO, March 1995.

15. Anderson, J. and Shiers, D., *The Green Guide to Specification*, Blackwell Publishing, 2002.

16. *ibid.*, p. 13.

Appendix 1
UK-Specific Assessment Tools

Please note: The information in this appendix was gathered in 2002/03. Although we have endeavoured to check its accuracy, organisations are constantly revising and updating their methodologies. Readers who wish to use any of the methodologies described in this Appendix should contact the 'owner' of the methodology to obtain the most up-to-date information.

BREDEM *(Building Research Establishment Domestic Energy Model)*

Indicators	Energy use
Inputs	Building dimensions and construction details, services and appliances details
Outputs	Energy consumption for: • space heating • water heating • cooking • lighting • appliances
Created by	BRE
Assessor	Designer
Methodology	Given in BRE publications
Design Stage	Final/existing buildings
Scope	Whole house energy use
Building type	Houses and housing
Notes	There are two versions: BREDEM-8, which gives monthly data, and BREDEM-12 which gives annual results
Sources of information	**BREDEM-8:** Anderson, B.R., Chapman, P.F., Cutland, N.G. et al, *BREDEM-8: Model description, BRE Report 327*, BRE, Watford, 1997. **BREDEM-12:** Anderson, B.R., Dickson, C.M., Henderson, G., & Shorrock, L.D., *BREDEM-12: Model description, BRE Report 315*, BRE, Watford, 1996. Anderson, B.R., Chapman, P.F., Cutland, N.G., Dickson, C.M., Henderson, G., Henderson, J.H., Iles, P.J., Kosmina, L. & Shorrock, L.D., *BREDEM-12: model description. 2001 update, BRE Report 438*, BRE, Watford, 2002.

BREEAM *(Building Research Establishment Environmental Assessment Method)*

Indicators	• **Management** (overall management policy, commissioning, site management issues, procedural issues) • **Energy use** (operational energy, CO_2) • **Health and well-being** (indoor and external issues affecting health and well-being) • **Pollution** (air and water pollution) • **Transport** (transport-related CO_2 and location-related factors) • **Land use** (greenfield and brownfield sites) • **Ecology** (ecological value conservation and enhancement of the site) • **Materials** (environmental implication of building materials, including life cycle impacts) • **Water** (water consumption and efficiency)
Inputs	–
Outputs	Pass, Good, Very Good, Excellent
Created by	BRE
Assessor	Accredited assessor – but checklists can inform design and give informal prediction of the final rating
Methodology	Full methodology available to assessors
Design stage	Guidance during design, full assessment at final design/construction
Scope	Whole building assessment. New build, major refurbishment and existing buildings
Building types	• Offices, houses (EcoHomes, below), industrial units, retail units, health buildings and schools • BREEAM for schools replaces the self-assessment SEAM (Schools Environmental Assessment Method) tool • A bespoke BREEAM can be used for other building types, such as leisure centres and laboratories
Notes	There are three different BREEAM assessments for offices: • Design & Procurement BREEAM (for new build or refurbishment) • Management & Operation BREEAM (for existing occupied offices) • Core BREEAM (for existing unoccupied offices). There are three different BREEAM assessments for retail units: • Design & Procurement BREEAM (for new build or refurbishment) • Tenant Fit-out BREEAM (retail store fit-out stage) • Operation & Management BREEAM (existing, occupied stores) For health buildings, the NEAT (NHS Environmental Assessment Tool) has two additional categories in addition to the standard BREEAM ones: social issues and operational waste.
Sources of information	Information on all BREEAM assessments, including details of publications and (free) downloadable checklists, can be found on the BRE website at http://products.bre.co.uk/breeam

EcoHomes

Indicators	• Energy (weighting = 21.42%) • Transport (8.65%) • Pollution (14.99%) • Materials (14.98%) • Water (10.00%) • Land use & ecology (15.10%) • Health & well-being (15.05%)
Inputs	• CO_2 emissions (10 credits - C) • Building fabric (5C) • Drying space (1C) • EcoLabelled goods (2C) • External lighting (2C) • Public transport (2C) • Cycle storage (2C) • Local amenities (3C) • Home office (1C) • Insulant ODP and GWP (1C) • NO_x emissions (3C) • Reduction of surface runoff (2C) • Zero-emission energy source (1C) • Timber: basic elements (6C) • Timber: finishing elements (3C) • Recycling facilities (6C) • Environmental impact of materials (16C) • Internal water use (5C) • External water use (1C) • Ecological value of site (1C) • Ecological enhancement (1C) • Protection of ecological features (1C) • Change of ecological value of site (4C) • Building footprint (2C) • Daylighting (3C) • Sound insulation (4C) • Private space (1C)
Outputs	Pass, Good, Very Good, Excellent
Created by	BRE (UK)
Assessor	Accredited assessor – but checklists can inform design and give informal prediction of the final rating
Methodology	Not in public realm: guidelines for design only; requires the completion of a SAP
Design stage	Guidance for all design stages; full assessment at final design/construction
Scope	Whole building assessment; new build, major refurbishment and existing buildings

Building type	Houses and housing
Notes	EcoHomes is the housing version of BREEAM
Sources of information	Rao, S., Yates, A., Brownhill, D. & Howard, N., *EcoHomes – The environmental rating for homes, BR389,* BRE, Watford, 2003.
	Comprehensive guidance for designers can be found in:
	EcoHomes - The Environmental Rating for Homes, The Guidance - 2005, BRE, Watford and http://products.bre.co.uk/breeam

Ecopoints

Indicators	• Climate change • Acid deposition • Ozone depletion • Pollution to air: human toxicity • Pollution to air: low level ozone creation • Fossil fuel depletion and extraction • Pollution to water: human toxicity • Pollution to water: ecotoxicity • Pollution to water: eutrophication • Minerals extraction • Water extraction • Waste disposal • Transport pollution and congestion
Inputs	• Climate change – $kgCO_2$ (eq) • Acid deposition – $kgSO_2$ (eq) • Ozone depletion – kgCFC11 (eq) • Pollution to air: human toxicity – kg.tox • Pollution to air: low level ozone creation – kg.ethene (eq) • Fossil fuel depletion and extraction –tonnes of oil (eq) • Pollution to water: human toxicity – kg.tox • Pollution to water: ecotoxicity – m^3tox • Pollution to water: eutrophication – $kgPO_4$ (eq) • Minerals extraction – tonnes • Water extraction – litres • Waste disposal – tonnes • Transport pollution and congestion: Freight – tonne.km
Outputs	Ecopoints
Created by	BRE (UK)
Assessor	BRE – EcoPoints are then used in designer tools such as Envest 2 and *The Green Guide to Specification*
Methodology	Peer reviewed and ISO14041
Design stage	All
Scope	Components and buildings
Building type	All

Notes	100 EcoPoints represent the impact of one UK citizen per year.
	1 EcoPoint is also equivalent to: 12270 kgCO_2 (eq) (climate change), 58.88 kgSO_2 (eq) (acid deposition), 0.29 kgCFC11 (eq) (ozone depletion), 90.7 kg.tox (pollution to air, human toxicity), 32.23 kg.ethene (eq) (low level ozone creation), 4.085 tonnes of oil (eq) (fossil fuel depletion), 0.02746 kg.tox (pollution to water, human toxicity), 837600 m^{3}tox (pollution to water, ecotoxicity), 8.006 kgPO_4 (eq) (pollution to water, eutrophication), 5.04 tonnes (minerals extraction), 417600 litres (water extraction), 7.194 tonnes (waste disposal), 4140.84 tonne.km (freight transport and congestion)
Sources of information	BRE, *Ecopoints a single score environmental assessment*, BRE, Watford and http://cig.bre.co.uk/envprofiles, May 2004.

Ecotect

Indicators	<ul><li>Embodied energy and capital costs</li><li>Energy use and running costs</li><li>Greenhouse gas emissions</li><li>User well being: lighting, acoustic and thermal environments</li></ul>
Inputs	<ul><li>Building dimensions</li><li>Building orientation</li><li>Building component information – structure and services</li></ul> Ecotect can also import IES (Illuminating Engineering Society) data
Outputs	<ul><li>**Fabric costs**</li><li>**Cumulative resource use:** energy use, water use, rainfall etc.</li><li>**Lighting environment details:** overshadowing, sun-path diagrams, shading tables, interactive sun-path, annual sun-path, shadow profiles, sun penetration, solar rays, projected shading rays, solar projections, solar envelope generation, solar access, PV array sizing and load matching data, solar stress, insolation analysis, surface insolation, daylight factors, artificial lighting levels, lighting vectors (for visual comfort and glare assessment), daylight autonomy and vertical daylight factor</li><li>**Acoustic environmental details:** reverberation times by frequency band, acoustic ray and particle plots, sound levels, linked decay rates and acoustic paths</li><li>**Thermal environment:** internal temperature, heating and cooling loads (and distribution), spatially distributed & mean radiant temperatures and discomfort times</li><li>**Data for Part L submissions**</li></ul> Data can also be exported to: RADIANCE, POV Ray, EnergyPlus, HBT2 Thermal Analysis, OpenGL, VRML …and other programs by application to creators.
Created by	Square One Research (UK and Australia)
Assessor	Designer
Methodology	Software – not open source. Uses: <ul><li>CIBSE Admittance Method to calculate heating and cooling loads</li><li>BRE Daylight Factor and BRE Vertical Daylight Factor methods for daylighting calculation and the Point-to-Point method for electric lighting</li><li>simple statistical reverberation times, particle analysis and ray tracing techniques for acoustic calculations</li><li>A CFD plugin is planned</li></ul>
Design stage	All – as the design progresses more detailed information can be analysed
Scope	Whole buildings
Building type	All
Notes	Produces very beguiling graphics, but is probably only appropriate as a design tool One of Square One's objectives to encourage energy efficient design.
Sources of information	Square One website: www.squ1.com

Envest 2

Indicators	As for Ecopoints
Inputs	• **Main dimensions:** gross floor area (m²), number of storeys, storey height (m), building width (m), plan depth (m)

• **Glazing ratio and doors:** glazing ratio (%), rooflight ratio (%), internal door area (%)

• **Building type:** head office (yes/no), air conditioned (yes/no), catering facilities on site (yes/no), cellular space (%)

• **Other:** operational life (5-100 yrs), discount rate (%), occupancy (m²/person), days in use per year (days), soil type, (rocky, compact sand/gravel, stiff clay, firm clay, loose sand, soft silt, very soft silt)

• **Building shape:** square, linear, offset, courtyard, L-shape, T-shape, cruciform, C-shape

• **Structure.** For example, for an external wall one could choose glass wool insulation

building frame
foundation
external wall
internal wall
floors
external openings
ceilings
roof

{

cladding
outer structural skin
inner structural skin
insulation
inner finishes (1ˢᵗ)
inner finishes (2ⁿᵈ)
internal decoration

{

cork board
cellular glass
expanded polystyrene
extruded polystyrene
glass wool
mineral wool
polyurethane
recycled cellulose
no insulation

• **Services:** types of heating, lighting, water, ventilation, cooling and lifts can be specified. Values for catering, office equipment and humidification are given based on the initial building type data

Outputs	The software can produce reports showing: • building details summary • structural details summary including calculated Ecopoints, whole life cost (WLC) in £ and U-values where appropriate • a life cycle analysis (LCA) breakdown of environmental impact, embodied vs. operational, in Ecopoints as a pie chart • a WLC breakdown of initial cost vs. life cycle replacement cost vs. maintenance cost, in £NPV (net present value) as a pie chart • a breakdown of embodied impact of building elements, in Ecopoints as a bar graph • a breakdown of the total WLC by building element, in £NPV as a bar graph • a breakdown of embodied impact by indicator (i.e. climate change, acid deposition etc.), in Ecopoints as a bar graph • a breakdown of total embodied impact by indicator, in the standard indicator units (see Ecopoints) as a table • a breakdown of operational impact by service type, in Ecopoints as a bar graph • a breakdown of operational impact by indicator, in Ecopoints as a bar graph. • a breakdown of operational impact by indicator, in the standard indicator units as a table • a breakdown of the total building impact by indicator, in Ecopoints as a bar graph • a breakdown of the total building impact by indicator, in standard indicator units as a table Also: • LCA and WLCs for services • breakdown of WLC to initial cost, life cycle replacement cost and maintenance • more than one building can be compared Values of Ecopoints and £NPV can be given as totals or as Ecopoints/m^2 or £NPV/m^2 for comparison
Created by	BRE; financial information is from Boxall Sayer Construction Consultancy (Chichester)
Assessor	The designer can use the software to compare designs
Methodology	Web-based software tool (not open source)
Design stage	Early
Scope	Whole building assessment; new build
Building type	Offices only

Notes	Like the LT Method, Envest 2 is an early design tool to help reduce negative environmental impacts. By changing building parameters the designer can reduce the number of EcoPoints/m² the design will potentially have.
	Two versions of the tools are available: Envest 2 estimator and Envest 2 calculator. The estimator version uses default environmental and financial data. Envest 2 calculator, too, uses default environmental data but allows the user to enter their own financial data.
Sources of information	An online demonstration is available on the Envest website http://envestv2.bre.co.uk A case study (Wessex Water Operations Centre, by Bennetts Associates) is available at http://www.bre.co.uk

Environmental Profiles

Indicators	• Climate change – from CO_2 and other greenhouse gases ($kgCO_2$ (eq)) • Acid deposition ($kgSO_2$ (eq)) • Ozone depletion (kgCFC11 (eq)) • Pollution to air: human toxicity (kg.tox) • Pollution to air: low level ozone creation (kg.ethene (eq)) • Fossil fuel depletion and extraction (tonnes oil (eq)) • Pollution to water: human toxicity (kg.tox) • Pollution to water: ecotoxicity (m^3tox) • Pollution to water: eutrophication ($kgPO_4$ (eq)) • Minerals extraction (tonnes) • Water extraction (litres) • Waste disposal (tonnes) • Transport pollution and congestion: Freight (tonne.km)
Inputs	As indicators for a particular material or construction element
Outputs	As indicators – results in both indicator units and Ecopoints
Created by	BRE
Assessor	BRE in partnership with manufacturers
Methodology	Peer reviewed and ISO14041
Design stage	All - assessments of materials can inform even early design
Scope	Life cycle assessment (LCA) for components and systems
Building type	All
Notes	Environmental Profiles consider the manufacture, use, maintenance, demolition and disposal of materials. The weightings of the indicators in the final assessment are agreed by an industry stakeholder group. • Materials are presented as 'cradle to gate' profiles on a per tonne basis • Installed elements are presented as 'cradle to site' per square metre • Sixty-year elements are presented as 'cradle to grave' per square metre
Sources of information	Environmental Profiles assessments are available on the Environmental Profiles website, http://cig.bre.co.uk/envprofiles, as are .pdf documents: Anderson, J. and Edwards, J., *Addendum to BRE Environmental Profiles Methodology of Construction Materials, Components and Buildings*, BRE, Watford and http://cig.bre.co.uk/envprofiles, July 2000. Howard, N., Edwards, S. and Anderson. J., *BRE Methodology for Environmental Profiles of Construction Materials, Components and Buildings*, BR370, BRE, Watford and http://cig.bre.co.uk/envprofiles, 1999. *Case Studies of Certification of Environmental Profiles*, BRE, Watford and http://cig.bre.co.uk/envprofiles, May 2004. *Environmental profiles life-cycle assessment of construction products*, BRE, Watford and http://cig.bre.co.uk/envprofiles, May 2004.

The Green Guide to Specification and The Green Guide to Housing Specification

Indicators	• Climate change • Fossil fuel and ozone depletion • Freight transport • Human- and eco-toxicity • Waste disposal • Water use • Acid deposition (acid rain) • Eutrophication (emission of nutrients to water which may cause problems such as algal blooms) • Summer smog production • Mineral extraction
Inputs	As for indicators; data given for 1m² of each material/construction element, assuming a 60-year life span; units as for EcoPoints
Outputs	Constructions are ranked from A–C, with A having the least environmental impact and C having the most; breakdown ratings per indicator are also given
Created by	BRE
Assessor	The BRE assesses materials and components – these assessments can then inform design
Methodology	Brief summary looking at procurement, life cycle analysis (LCA) and other environmental issues
Design stage	All
Scope	Construction components and systems
Building type	All
Notes	The *Green Guides* allow the comparison of different construction elements (such as external walls, roofs, landscaping, partitioning and doors) and materials (such as paints, insulation and floor finishes)
Sources of information	Anderson, J., Shiers, D.E. and Sinclair, M., *The Green Guide to Specification*, 3rd Edition, BRE, Watford, 2002. Anderson, J. and Howard, N., *The Green Guide to Housing Specification*, BR390, BRE, Watford, 2000.

LT (Lighting and Thermal) Method

Indicators	• Building energy consumption • CO_2 emissions
Inputs	• Local climatic conditions • Orientation of façade • Area and type of glazing • Obstructions due to adjacent buildings (or parts of the same building) • The inclusion of an atrium (optional) • Occupancy and vacation patterns • Lighting levels • Internal gains
Outputs	• Net annual primary energy consumption, in MWh and kWh/m² • Net annual CO_2 emission, in tonnes and kg/m²
Created by:	The Martin Centre (Cambridge University) and Cambridge Architectural Research (CAR). Validated by the BRE.
Assessor	Designer
Methodology	See Baker and Steemers (2000), below
Design stage	Early
Scope	Whole building
Building type	Schools, colleges, offices and institutional buildings
Notes	The results do not given predicted energy consumption for the finished building, but allows for comparison of early design options The energy consumption of the building is given in terms of primary energy, for example for lighting the energy requirement will include transformation and transmission losses
Sources of information	Baker, N. and Steemers, K., *Energy and Environment in Architecture - A Technical Design Guide*, Spon, London, 2000. See also www.carltd.com

Movement for Innovation
Environmental Performance Indicators for Sustainable Construction

Indicators	• Operational CO_2 emissions ($kgCO_2/m^2$ pa) • Embodied CO_2 ($kgCO_2/m^2$) • Water use (m^3 per person pa) • Waste from construction process (m^3 per $100m^2$ floor area) • Biodiversity • Transport
Inputs	As indicators
Outputs	Six armed 'windrose' representation – arms of different length indicate weightings of indicators relative to each other. For example, for offices: 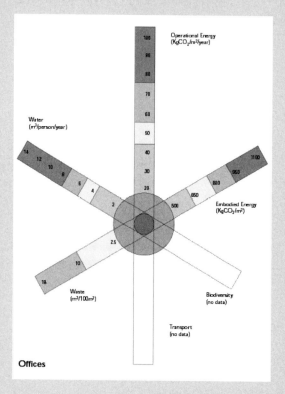 This is similar to Arup's SPeAR in that green (best quartile) is at the centre of the diagram, followed by amber and red (worst quartile)
Created by	Movement for Innovation (which became part of Constructing Excellence in 2004)

Assessor	Designer
Methodology	As in downloadable free report
Design stage	Final design/existing buildings
Scope	Whole building
Building type	Benchmarks for indicators are given for offices, domestic dwellings, retail premises, food retail, hospitals and educational buildings.
Notes	While the assessment does not take into account issues such as indoor air quality (IAQ) it is a relatively quick and easily accessible way of rating a building The benchmarks were developed from data from existing buildings or from government guidelines
Sources of information	Constructing Excellence www.constructingexcellence.org.uk

MFLLP 'traffic lights'

Indicators	Variable
Inputs	Manufacturer's data.
Outputs	• Red (least environmentally attractive option) • Amber • Green (most environmentally attractive option)
Created by	Max Fordham LLP
Assessor	Designer
Methodology	Informal
Design stage	Early
Scope	Largely services components
Building type	All
Notes	MFLLP's Phil Armitage says: "Developed to try to compare options on a quantitative basis (reasonably objectively and simply). There is a dearth of tools available to help make these kinds of decisions. It is especially difficult to analyse the relative benefits of different of options e.g., condensing boilers vs. passive stack ventilation vs. timber structure."
Sources of information	post@maxfordham.com

SAP (Standard Assessment Procedure) 2005

Indicators	• Energy costs for space and water heating • Annual CO_2 emissions associated with space and water heating
Inputs	• Overall dwelling dimensions • Ventilation rate • Heat losses • Water heating requirements • Internal gains • Solar gains • Mean internal temperature • Degree days • Space heating requirement • Fuel costs These all combine to give an Energy Cost Factor (ECF), in £/m² pa, from which the SAP rating is deduced. **N.B. not included are:** • Household size and type (hot water requirements are calculated on a floor area basis, likewise metabolic gains etc.) • Electrical equipment efficiency • Individual heating patterns and temperatures • Geographical location
Outputs	• Energy cost rating – a SAP rating on a scale of 1 (poor energy efficiency) to 100 (zero energy cost). • Dwelling Carbon Emissions Rate (DCER) in kg/m² pa
Created by	BRE
Assessor	Informal: designer Formal certification: accredited assessment method (i.e. approved software)
Methodology	Method devised by BRE; rating can be calculated manually or with an accredited software package
Design stage	Late
Scope	Some question over applicability for multi-residential and mixed-use properties.
Building type	Houses and housing; existing and new
Notes	The SAP rating is based on the BRE's Domestic Energy Model, BREDEM. It has undergone a number of changes, the main and most recent being: **1998 – 2001:** • Maximum SAP rating increases from 100 to 120 • SAP and Carbon Index (CI) become virtually independent from dwelling size • The CI replaces the Carbon Factor (CF)

Sources of information	**SAP 2001:**
	http://projects.bre.co.uk/sap2001
	SAP 2005:
	BRE, *SAP2005*, **http://projects.bre.co.uk/sap2005/** BRE, Watford, Feb 2006.
	BRE, *The Government's Standard Assessment Procedure for Energy Rating of Dwellings*, Draft 2005 edn, BRE, Watford **http://projects.bre.co.uk/sap2005/** Jan 2005.
	BRE, *SAP WORKSHEET (Version - 9.80) draft January 2005*, **http://projects.bre.co.uk/sap2005/** BRE (Jan 2005)
	BRE, *Consultation on SAP 2005 (July - October 2004) - Summary of principal comments received and amendments to the draft*, BRE, Watford, **http://projects.bre.co.uk/sap2005/** Jan 2005.
	A full list of BRE-approved SAP software is available on the SAP website.

SPeAR™ (Sustainable Project Appraisal Routine)

Indicators	**Environment:** • Air quality and microclimate • Land use • Water (reducing flood/storm risk and maintaining quality of resource) • Ecology and cultural heritage • Design and operation • Transport **Natural resources:** • Materials • Water (minimising use of resources) • Energy • Land utilisation • Waste **Societal:** • Health and welfare • User comfort/satisfaction • Form and space • Access • Amenity • Inclusion **Economic:** • Social benefits and costs • Transport (reducing financial implications of travel/transport) • Employment/skills • Competition effects • Viability
Inputs	For example, in the Environment quadrant 'Air quality and microclimate' is assessed using data regarding direct emissions, indirect emissions, background environmental conditions, dust and particulate matter, refrigeration/ODP (ozone depletion potential) and BPEO (Best Practicable Environmental Option) for regulated processes
Outputs	Results are shown graphically with results for each indicator being on a scale of: +3 (best) → 0 (good practice) → -3 (worst case). An example is given in Chapter 1, Box 1.4
Created by	Arup Environmental (UK)
Assessor	Accredited assessor
Methodology	Available to assessors
Design stage	All
Scope	Whole building/development, new build, refurbishment and existing buildings.

Building type	All
Notes	
Sources of information	www.arup.com/environment

Appendix 2
International Assessment Tools

Please note: The information in this appendix was gathered in 2002/03. Although we have endeavoured to check its accuracy, organisations are constantly revising and updating their methodologies. Readers who wish to use any of the methodologies described in this Appendix should contact the 'owner' of the methodology to obtain the most up-to-date information.

Country	Tools	Building type/scope	Sources of information*
Australia	LISA (LCA In Sustainable Architecture)	Houses, offices, warehousing, building materials, civil engineering projects etc.	**www.lisa.au.com**
	NatHERS	Houses and housing	**www.buildingcommission.com.au** and **www.seav.vic.gov.au**
Canada	Athena v.3.0	Industrial, institutional, office, and multi-unit and single family residential designs	**www.athenasmi.ca**
	EnerGuide, R-2000, HOT2000™, HOT3000™ HOT2®XP, HOT2®EC and HOUSTRAD™	Houses	**http://oee.nrcan.gc.ca** and **http://buildingsgroup.nrcan.gc.ca**
	EE4	Commercial buildings	**http://buildingsgroup.nrcan.gc.ca**
	BILDTRAD™	Commercial buildings and housing	**http://buildingsgroup.nrcan.gc.ca**
Denmark	BSim (Building Simulation)	-	**www.dbri.dk**
	Energy Performance Assessment Method for Existing Dwellings (EPA-ED)	Houses	**www.epa-ed.org** and **www.dbri.dk**
	Building Environmental Assessment Tool 2000 (BEAT)	-	**www.dbri.dk**

Finland	BeCost	-	**www.vtt.fi**
	BEE 1.0	-	**www.vtt.fi,** IEA-BCS Annex 31
	EcoPro	Offices, schools, nurseries, housing, shopping centres, etc.	**http://cic.vtt.fi**
	Energy certification for buildings (Finland)	Single family houses, blocks of flats and office buildings.	**www.vtt.fi**, IEA-BCS Annex 31
	LCA-House	Houses	**www.vtt.fi**
France	TEAM	LCA for materials etc.	**www.ecobilan.com**, IEA-BCS Annex 31
	ESCALE	-	**http://international.cstb.fr**, IEA-BCS Annex 31
	PAPOOSE	Housing, schools, offices, etc.	**www.tributribu.com**, IEA-BCS Annex 31
	EQUER	Building LCA	**www-cenerg.ensmp.fr**, IEA-BCS Annex 31
Japan	Green Building Program	-	**www.kankyo.metro.tokyo.jp**
Netherlands	Eco-Quantum	-	**www.ecoquantum.nl**, IEA-BCS Annex 31
Norway	Oekoprofile		IEA-BCS Annex 31
Sweden	EcoEffect		IEA-BCS Annex 31, **www.hig.se**, **www.kth.se**
Switzerland	E2000 Oekobau		IEA-BCS Annex 31
	FIA0123		IEA-BCS Annex 31
	OGIP (Switzerland)		IEA-BCS Annex 31
USA	BEES	Building materials	**www.bfrl.nist.gov**, IEA-BCS Annex 31
	ENERGY 10	Whole buildings	**www.nrel.gov**, IEA-BCS Annex 31
	Green Building Advisor	Whole buildings	**www.buildinggreen.com**, IEA-BCS Annex 31
	LEED™	Whole buildings (houses, commercial, etc.) and developments	**www.usgbc.org**, IEA-BCS Annex 31

* Information on the International Energy Agency Annex 31 (IEA-BCS Annex 31) can be found at **www.uni-weimar.de/scc/PRO/**

Index

volatile organic compounds (VOCs), 20, 116
volume heating *see* space heating

wall finishes
    houses (individual), 56
    housing, 111
    offices, 175
walling
    aluminium curtain walling, 171
    BedZED, 111
    double-skin glazed wall, 172–3
    factories, 279
    houses (individual), 51–2, 54, 56
    housing, 83, 108, 110
    insulation thickness, 92–3
    loadbearing brick and block, 51–2, 56, 108, 211
    precast concrete spandrel panels, 174, 175
    rendered block, 211
    sealed vs breathing, 106
    supermarkets, 243, 246
    timber/steel stud + brick cavity, 108
    U-values, 39, 83
warm air heaters, 265–6
water consumption, housing, 44–5

water heating
    houses (individual), 43
    housing, 120
    offices, 178
    schools, 218–19
water supplies
    BedZED, 87
    houses (individual), 44–5
    housing, 120
weather patterns *see* climate change
White City project, 131–6
windows (*see also* glazing; rooflights)
    BedZED, 112
    composite aluminium-faced and timber frame, 214–15
    houses (individual), 54, 56
    housing, 56, 83, 110
    offices, 158
    u-PVC, 110
    U-values, 39, 83
wood *see* timber
wood-burning stoves and boilers, 27, 28, 65–6

zinc sheet roofing, 212